Topics in Down Syndrome

FINE MOTOR SKILLS in CHILDREN with DOWN SYNDROME

A Guide for Parents and Professionals

Maryanne Bruni, BSc OT(C)

Woodbine House ◆ 2006

All rights reserved under International and Pan-American copyright conventions. Published in the United States of America by Woodbine House, Inc., 6510 Bells Mill Rd., Bethesda, MD 20817. 800-843-7323. *www.woodbinehouse.com*

Library of Congress Cataloging-in-Publication Data

Bruni, Maryanne.
  Fine motor skills in children with Down syndrome : a guide for parents and professionals / by Maryanne Bruni.--2nd ed.
       p.   cm.
  Includes bibliographical references and index.
  ISBN-13: 978-1-890627-67-6
  ISBN-10: 1-890627-67-4
    1. Down syndrome.   2. Motor learning.   3. Motor ability in children.
I. Title.
RJ506.D68B78 2006
618.92'858842—dc22

                                                                    2005034531

Manufactured in the United States of America

10   9   8   7   6   5   4

To Romeo,
Meghan,
Alison, and
Sarah

Table of Contents

Acknowledgements..ix

Introduction: A Parent's Perspective xi

Chapter 1: **A Model of Hand Skill Development** 1
- A Visual Model of the Development of Fine Motor Skills in a Child
- Definitions of the Components of Fine Motor Skill Development:
    The Three Building Blocks
    Dexterity
    Daily Living Skills

Chapter 2: **Building on What Is There: Learning Step by Step** 7
- The Process of Learning New Skills
- Breaking Down Activities into Steps
- Motivation
- Adapting the Environment

Chapter 3: **Fine Motor Development in Children with Down Syndrome** 19
- Physical/Medical Characteristics of Down Syndrome
- Skills to Encourage at Stages of Development:
    Birth–Two Years
    Two–Four Years
    Five–Eight Years
    Nine–Twelve Years
    Thirteen–Adulthood

Chapter 4: **Early Movement in Babies with Down Syndrome** 33
- Early Arm and Hand Control: Relationship to
  Developmental Milestones
- How to Help Your Baby

Chapter 5: **The First Building Block of Hand Skills: Stability** 47
- Stability in Children with Down Syndrome
- Activities for: Body Stability, Ball Skills, Shoulder Stability
- Grandma's and Grandpa's List

Chapter 6: **The Second Building Block: Bilateral Coordination** 57
- How Young Children Coordinate Their Hands Together
- Bilateral Coordination in Children with Down Syndrome
- The Development of Handedness
- Activities for Bilateral Coordination
- Grandma's and Grandpa's List

Chapter 7: **The Third Building Block: Sensation** 67
- The Sensory-Motor Loop: Effects of Down Syndrome
- Activities for Sensation
- Grandma's and Grandpa's List

Chapter 8: **Dexterity**...77
- Components of Dexterity
- Grasp and Release:
    How it Develops
    Grasp and Release in Children with Down Syndrome
    Activity Suggestions
- Pinch and Thumb Control:
    Activity Suggestions
- Finger coordination:
    The Development of Individual Finger Movement
    Hand Stability
    Activity Suggestions
- Wrist Movement:
    Activity Suggestions
- Grandma's and Grandpa's List

Chapter 9: **Daily Living Skills: School-Related Tasks** 105
- Cutting
- Pencil Grasp
- Preprinting Skills
- Drawing and Coloring
- Printing
- Pencil Pressure
- Positioning
- Cursive Writing
- Computers
- Incorporating Fine Motor Goals into Your Child's Education Plan
- Grandma's and Grandpa's List

Chapter 10: Daily Living Skills: Self-Help Skills, Household and Leisure Activities 147
- Self-Help Skills:
   Dressing
   Eating/Drinking
   Grooming
- Household Activities
- Leisure and Recreation
- Grandma's and Grandpa's List

Chapter 11: Sensory Processing 167
- Sensory Processing in Children with Down Syndrome
- Signs of Sensory Processing Difficulties
- Strategies and Activities for Sensory Processing Difficulties
- Grandma's and Grandpa's List

Chapter 12: Hands Up! 193
- Looking Ahead
- Conclusion

Appendix 1: Visual Motor Worksheets 195
- Stage 1: Preprinting Worksheets
- Stage 2: Pencil Control Worksheets
- Stage 3: Letter Groupings (Printing)
- Stage 4: Prewriting Worksheets

Appendix 2: Don't Throw It Out! Household Items to Use for Hand Play 217

Glossary 219

Bibliography 223

Resources 229

Index 237

Acknowledgements

My sincere thanks go out to all those who have helped me personally and professionally in the writing of this book. Thank you to the Canadian Occupational Therapy Foundation for their publication grant for the first edition of this book, which gave me the financial and professional support to continue the project; to all those parents, professional colleagues, and family members who read the manuscript and gave valuable feedback; to Susan Stokes, editor at Woodbine House; to those people at various organizations and agencies who willingly shared their expertise; to Sue Yurkewich for her work on the pencil control worksheet graphics; Cindy (Choy) Leung and Lucy Weston for developing the preprinting program with me at Silver Creek Preschool; to my wonderful colleagues at Silver Creek Preschool; to all the parents who gave me the opportunity to observe and photograph their children, many of whose pictures appear in this book; to the families who answered a Sensory Questionnaire and filled out the Sensory Profile, giving me valuable information for the chapter on Sensory Processing; to all the members of my extended family who are always there for support and encouragement; and finally, to Romeo, Meghan, Alison, and Sarah, who are always there with their love.

Introduction:
A Parent's Perspective

Fifteen years ago, our family began a new journey. At times it has been an emotional path, joyous and sad, demanding and rewarding. We had already embarked on the journey of parenthood, having been blessed with two daughters already. Sarah's birth added a new dimension to our lives as parents. Unexpectedly, we had to learn all we could about the world of parenting a child with Down syndrome.

For eight years prior to Sarah's birth, I had been working as an occupational therapist with children who had a variety of special needs. My experience with children with Down syndrome was limited, however. As parents of a child with Down syndrome, we have had as much to learn as anyone else. We struggle with the same emotions, the same initial grieving, the same uncertainties in raising her as any other family does.

My professional training and experience have given me a framework with which to observe, analyze, and understand the stages of Sarah's development. By her responses, she has helped me learn what is helpful, motivating, and realistic, and has given me ideas that I don't think I ever would have had if I wasn't faced with the day-to-day reality of raising her. I have become more aware of how small changes to an activity or task can make a significant difference between success and failure, motivation and frustration. I have better learned how to provide opportunities for Sarah's development and practice of skills through the many daily activities in our home.

As Sarah developed through childhood, I noticed that she became more self-directed in choosing play activities that were helpful to her own development. She began to respond to some of her own internal messages about what she needs. When Sarah's two older sisters, Meghan and Alison, were infants and toddlers, I was amazed at how much internal drive they had to achieve the next developmental milestone. I didn't need to "program" them; they just did it on their own. Development for our children with Down syndrome unfolds according to each child's own internal schedule, as it does for all children. However, it is usually slower to unfold, and our children benefit from help along the way. The physical and medical characteristics of Down syndrome can interfere with our child's ability to take the next developmental step. For example, our child may be developmentally ready to begin talking, but is hampered by articulation difficulties.

We can help our children move forward in their development, but we need to know how to do it. We need ideas that can be used spontaneously, and are practical, easy to carry out, and, most of all, motivating and fun for our children. None of us needs to feel guilty about not having the time or energy to do the endless programming that is possible for children with Down syndrome. So many aspects of our children's development may need help that it can be totally overwhelming at times for parents. I know; I have felt that way on many occasions over the past fifteen years. I believe that the most important thing for parents is to consistently love, care for, and support their child, recognizing and valuing his or her inherent self in the home and community, no matter what the level of ability or function.

Sometimes, I think it is hard to keep perspective on the big picture. We have so many concerns for our children, and so many books telling us how to do things (and now, another book!). It can be easy for the energetic and ambitious parent to "over-program" their child. Our children also need an opportunity to initiate and carry out their own play. Learning how to initiate play and become absorbed in play activities gives our children self-motivation and self-direction that is essential in adult life. Acknowledging our children's choices of play activities as valid builds their self-esteem. If we spend some "down time" with them, following their lead, we often find spontaneous opportunities to encourage developmental skills.

All children have their own internal strengths and limitations, and sometimes, no matter how dedicated and committed you are as a parent, your child simply may not be able to learn a particular skill. In my experience, many children with Down syndrome are tuned in to the underlying agenda of adults (including their parents) and to the emotional climate of the situation. Rather than always focusing on what our children need to learn and develop, let's also extend our emotional energy on what they can do, and capitalize on it. Sarah can't remember how to spell many words, nor simple math facts. She can, however, remember the dialogue and songs of many, many movies. The challenge for us as parents and educators is to capitalize on the child's strengths in a positive learning environment.

The speech and language difficulties that our children experience usually become obvious very early and demand attention. Although delays in the development of fine motor skills are usually not as obvious as speech and language delays, the impact can also be significant. The ability to use their hands directly determines the amount of assistance our children need to accomplish the many daily activities of home, school, work, and leisure. The more assistance they need, the less independent they can be, and the fewer choices they may have for their futures.

I often have to remind myself to be patient. Nothing I can do as a parent or a therapist will change the fact that my daughter has Down syndrome. However, I remain hopeful that all the small steps, the little achievements, each part of a skill learned, will ultimately give Sarah a feeling of self-worth that will guide her through her life.

All parents want the best for their child. I go through cycles of hope that give me energy, and cycles of grieving that make me feel burnt out. From my work with many parents, I have found these alternating and sometimes conflicting feelings to be typical. It is not my intent to add more pressure to parents who already feel overwhelmed by their child's needs. Rather, I hope parents will use this book throughout their child's developing years for ideas and support.

How to Use This Book

In this book I will share some of my observations and ideas about sensory processing and the development of fine motor skills of children with Down syndrome through daily home and school activities. My intent is that this book will be of use to parents, teachers, and health professionals.

I have developed a visual model of how hand skills develop, represented by the building of a house. This is explained in Chapter 1, and will help you understand how motor development prepares your child to be able to do "fine motor skills" such as holding and using a pencil. Chapter 2 focuses on the steps in learning, how to take things one step at a time, and thoughts on motivating your child. Most of the activities in this book can be done at home or school, without special equipment, using materials that are readily available. Chapter 3 discusses the physical and medical characteristics of Down syndrome that can affect fine motor skill development. An outline of the kinds of skills that will be emerging at different ages is presented. Chapter 4 explains fine motor development in infancy, as it relates to gross motor milestones. Ideas for positioning and play activities to prepare your baby for fine motor skill development are presented.

Chapters 5, 6, and 7 explain the foundation skills for fine motor abilities. These foundations, which I call stability, bilateral coordination, and sensation, are like the building blocks upon which children can develop the precise movements of their hands. The foundation skills develop throughout childhood, and are relevant for all ages. Chapter 8 begins to describe and give ideas for dexterity, which is really what we think of as "fine motor skills." You will read about how your child learns to pick up and let go of things, and develops coordinated hand movements. This chapter is particularly relevant for the toddler and preschooler who is developing patterns of grasping and release during play. Chapter 9 carries the discussion into school-related tasks, such as printing and cutting. The normal development of pencil grasp is described, and activities to promote visual motor skills are suggested. Parents of preschoolers and school-aged children will find this chapter relevant. A special feature called "Grandma's and Grandpa's List" is included at the ends of Chapters 4 through 11. This is a list of suggested toys and activities that will help your child's development in each area. It may help you come up with ideas if interested friends and relatives ask you what gifts to buy for your child for birthdays and holidays.

Chapter 10 covers self-help skills (dressing, eating and drinking, and grooming). Practical suggestions for adaptations and ideas for common dressing problems are outlined. Household chores and leisure activities are also relevant to fine motor development, and they are briefly explored in this chapter. These activities become increasingly important as children with Down syndrome mature into adolescence and adulthood. Young men or women with Down syndrome who have developed and practiced the fine motor abilities needed for self-help as children can spend their energies as adults on organizing their time and taking responsibility for managing their daily living skills as independently as possible.

Chapter 11 provides an overview of sensory processing. Some of the ways that sensory processing can affect behavior, fine motor development, and the development of self-help skills are discussed. Strategies to assist parents in helping their child deal with sensory processing issues are presented. Sensory processing is important, as it can not only affect motor development, but also attention and the emotional state of the child, which, in turn, affects his ability to learn new skills.

In this book, I have made a point of suggesting activities that can be incorporated into daily routines and play time. I know how hard it is as a parent to find the time to sit down and do "therapy" or "teaching" with your child, especially when the child perceives it as such. There is definitely a need and place for doing structured teaching and therapy, and our children benefit from it. However, if we interact with our children mainly in a structured format, and take on the role of a teacher or therapist much of the time, we may end up frustrated, and our child resistant.

When you read through this book, you will probably recognize activities that may interest your child, and others that won't. Choose a few that you think will be of interest; that your child will be able to do without too much difficulty. Then think about how you can incorporate them into your daily routines, so that you do not always have to set aside extra time to do them with your child.

In this book, I have described the *components* of fine motor development rather than *stages* of development. I did this because, at any stage of development, several components of fine motor skills (types of movement and control) are developing at once. To give a sense of the continuity of development of each type of skill, I chose to present each skill individually. Throughout the book, particularly in Chapter 3, there are references to how all the separate skills come together. A child of any age will be developing the various components of fine motor skills simultaneously. Therefore, parents may find it useful to choose activities from more than one chapter at once.

CHAPTER 1

A Model of Hand Skill Development

The development of a child is a wondrous thing, involving a series of seemingly miraculous unfoldings of personality, emotions, relationships, and movements. And it is no less wondrous when the unfoldings occur more slowly, as for our children with Down syndrome. In fact, the achievement of every milestone and development can be the cause for celebration in many families. When Sarah learns to articulate a new sound, or does her buttons up for the first time, or anything at all that is a step forward, she revels in the congratulatory attention we all give her.

Before you became a parent, you may not have heard the terms "developmental milestones," "gross motor," or "fine motor." When a child with Down syndrome joins your family, however, you not only have to nurture and get to know this new little person, you have to start to learn a whole new vocabulary of medical, developmental, and therapy words.

To understand what this book is all about, you need to understand the distinction between the two types of motor (movement) skills that your child will develop. **Gross motor** refers to the development of larger movements, such as those necessary for sitting and walking. **Fine motor** refers to the development of small muscle movements in the hands. When we think of fine motor skills, usually we think of activities such as tying our shoes, printing, or stringing beads. These are all fine motor skills, but they are the end result of a lot of preparation that has been going on in the child's muscles and nervous system.

Development is a continuum, and our hands are not separate from the rest of our body. Therefore, fine motor skills develop in the context of the development of the whole child, including mobility, cognitive, social, and emotional development.

The "House" Model of Fine Motor Skills

The development of fine motor skills is like the construction of a house. The first thing that is laid down is the foundation. This supports all the levels above it. The first floor provides additional support for the second floor, and so on. The foundation for the fine motor skills house consists of Stability, Bilateral Coordination, and Sensation. The next level up is Dexterity. These foundations support the Daily Living Skills, such as dressing and other self-care activities, and school-related skills, such as printing. This is the model of the fine motor skill "house" I will refer to:

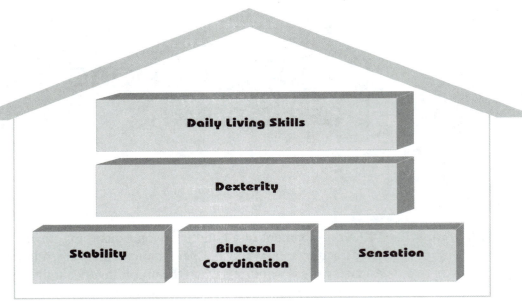

Figure 1

When a building is being constructed, workers never begin with the top floor. They lay the foundation, and then they can build the first floor, second floor, and so on. So it is with fine motor skills. During the early years, the "building blocks" are developing—the foundation upon which children can build the dexterity needed for daily living skills.

What Are the Building Blocks of Fine Motor Skills?

Figure 2

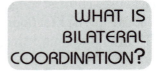

WHAT IS STABILITY?

Stability is being able to push open a heavy door. Stability is being able to put on your shoes without falling over. It is carrying a tray full of drinks. It is holding a camera still while clicking a picture. In short, stability is a combination of strength and balance that enables us to keep one part of our body still while another part moves.

WHAT IS BILATERAL COORDINATION?

Bilateral coordination is holding the bowl with one hand while stirring with the other. It is holding the paper with one hand while cutting with scissors with the other. It is doing up your zipper and shoelaces. Bilateral coordination refers to the efficient use of both hands during an activity. Most daily activities require the coordinated use of both hands, one as the "doer" and the other as the "helper." Bilateral coordination leads eventually to the development of a dominant hand (becoming right or left handed).

Sensation is reaching into your pocket and leaving the Kleenex in while you take out the coins. It is putting a ponytail in your hair. It is knowing where to put your hands to catch a ball. Sensation is knowing where your fingers, hands, and arms are, and how they are moving, without constant conscious attention to them.

We all know the five senses: vision, hearing, smell, taste, and touch. We also have two other senses:

- **Proprioception**—the sense of joint position and movement, perceived by nerves in the joints, tendons, and muscles;
- **Vestibular system**—the sense that tells us the direction and speed of movement and position of our head in relation to gravity.

Chapter 7 focuses on the senses we use to develop coordinated movement, specifically fine motor movement. These are the senses of touch, proprioception, and vision. In Chapter 11, the discussion of the sensory systems includes all the senses, as all sensory information is integrated to enable us to respond to our environment.

The Second Level in the Hand Skills House: Dexterity

Your child begins to develop the building blocks for fine motor skill development at birth, and continues to do so for several years. As soon as he is able to grasp a toy placed in his hand (usually between three and six months), he begins the process of developing dexterity, which also progresses and develops for many years. All the while, the building blocks continue to lay the foundation and support the development of fine hand movements. In other words, the "building blocks" (stability, bilateral coordination, and sensation) continue to be refined while the next level in the house, dexterity, begins to take shape.

Figure 3

Dexterity is picking up a crayon and positioning it in your hand to color. It is opening a jar. Dexterity is opening and closing a safety pin. It is picking up a raisin. It is threading a needle. Dexterity enables us to make small, precise, accurate, and efficient movements with our hands without tremendous effort. When your child has established some of the foundations and is developing dexterity, he is able to use these abilities in his daily living skills.

The Third Level in the Hand Skills House: Daily Living Skills

Figure 4

Getting dressed in the morning is a daily living skill. Participating in classroom learning is a daily living skill. For children, playing is a daily living skill. Our children are expected to participate in different types of functional skills every day:

School tasks related to fine motor development include preprinting, printing, drawing and coloring, cutting, writing, and computer skills. These are sometimes referred to as visual motor skills, because the child coordinates vision with his hand movements to learn these skills. As these skills mature, the movements can become more automatic, relying less on vision to guide the movement, and more on a learned motor movement. For example, someone who has learned to type well doesn't have to look at each finger before pressing the key.

Self-Help skills are all the activities we do on a routine, daily basis to take care of our bodies, and include dressing, eating, and grooming.

Household tasks and leisure activities are hobbies, play activities, sports pastimes, and routine household activities and chores that are part of the everyday life of adults and children.

Putting on the Finishing Touches

The basic structure of the "fine motor skills house" goes up quickly, but all the finishing touches take years to develop and refine. The building blocks provide the foundation, and dexterity provides the specific movements upon which daily living skills can develop. Repeated practice of some of the daily living skills can "feed back" to improve dexterity and reinforce the foundation skills. It is like an electrical current in the wiring of a house; it travels in both directions.

Let us look at an example of how a daily living skill depends on and has impact all the way through the "house model":

Figure 5

    In the construction of any house, the finishing touches seem to take the longest to complete. There are endless details: painting and wallpapering, tiles, light fixtures, kitchen cabinets and fixtures, doors, etc. So it is with the hand skills house. The refinement of all the skills on the "upper floors," all the details of development to make everything work "right," take years to complete. For example, although your child will probably begin to finger feed himself around his first birthday, he will not have refined his eating skills (including cutting and spreading with a knife) until mid- to late childhood.

    The development of fine motor skills begins in early infancy and continues until adulthood. Your awareness of how these skills develop will help you choose activities to do at home. This will help your child continue to improve his fine motor abilities, whether or not he is receiving regular occupational therapy.

Chapter 2

Building on What Is There: Learning Step by Step

When Sarah was about eight years old, I decided to try to teach her our phone number. (I felt it was important for safety and social reasons to know her own phone number.) For several months I tried now and then (not very consistently, I might add), with little success. She just couldn't seem to get it. While she remembered some of the numbers, she would mix them up, forget the rest, skip some, and repeat others. Unfortunately, knowing some of the numbers some of the time doesn't help in an emergency. When we both had more time in the summer, I decided to focus on it a bit more. I made up index cards with the individual numbers of our phone number written on them. We laid them down on the floor in order, numbers showing, and made a hopscotch game out of them. As Sarah jumped from square to square, she called out the numbers. Gradually we were able to turn some, then all, of the cards over. Sarah could now jump and call out the numbers by memory. After a couple of weeks of consistent practice, she could remember her phone number without the cues she first had (visual cues: seeing the numbers on the cards; and motor cues: jumping).

In looking back at my initial attempts to teach Sarah, I can come up with several reasons why I wasn't successful:

1. **She wasn't ready.** Children with Down syndrome need help to learn new skills, but they also need to be "ready." Being "ready" means that their nervous system development, their cognitive abilities, and their motor control have developed sufficiently to allow them to learn that particular skill. Sometimes we won't know that a child isn't "ready" until we try something. If the child cannot seem to grasp the ultimate goal of the activity, then she isn't "ready." For example, you may give her a few small blocks and demonstrate stacking them. After many demonstrations over several days, she continues to toss the blocks over the edge of the table and watch them fall. She is at the stage of understanding object permanence— knowing that the blocks do not disappear, that they fall and land on the floor. She is not quite ready to stack them!

2. **She wasn't able to pay attention long enough to learn.** Children with Down syndrome may be easily distracted and may have dif-

ficulty attending in order to learn. This ties in with being "ready." If the activity is too far beyond her cognitive level, she won't be able to attend well, because it won't have meaning for her.

3. **She learned better with a multi-sensory approach.** Remembering what they hear is very difficult for most children with Down syndrome (this is called auditory memory). Research and the experience of professionals who teach children with Down syndrome have found that they are usually "visual learners"; that is, they learn better when information and skills are taught visually, or with a combination of visual and auditory presentations. Sarah needed to see and hear the numbers over and over. She also needed to be active physically (jumping) to help her remember.

4. **The repetition wasn't consistent and frequent enough.** Children with Down syndrome need much more time and repetition to learn a new skill or ability. Short, frequent exposure to the activity may be more beneficial than longer, less frequent experiences.

If we are trying to help our child learn any new skill, we must start at the level she is at today. We must learn to expect small steps at a time. We must make sure that what we are trying to teach is meaningful to her; that is, she can see the point in doing it. If it is meaningful, it will be motivating. If we keep these things in mind, we learn to recognize every tiny step as a step forward, keeping us and our child motivated to continue trying.

Steps in Learning Skills

Much of your child's learning will take place through her exploration, interaction with her environment and with the primary people in her environment, and through play. Young children with Down syndrome will learn many things through unstructured play experiences. It is not necessary or advisable to have constant adult direction during play. Your child needs many opportunities to be self-directed in her play, which will expand her capabilities to initiate and follow through with planned actions. That being said, most early intervention and infant development programs provide sequential skill guidelines for parents and caregivers to follow, in order to facilitate the acquisition of the next stage of development. Understandably, most parents try to help their child learn the developmental skills that are next on the list.

Here is an example of an infant development activity:

"The child watches the parent place a small toy in a box, and opens the box to retrieve the toy." This activity relates to the child's understanding of the concept of object permanence. That is, she recognizes that even though the toy is temporarily out of sight, it is still there, and she can figure out how to get it. There are many other ways that the child can demonstrate this skill. For example, she can uncover a toy hidden by a blanket in her crib, or she can reach for the keys that you have put in your purse. The point is, it is not always necessary to teach the precise skill as outlined, if you can see that the general concept and understanding is present in your child's spontaneous actions and play.

When there are specific skills that your child needs to learn, it can be helpful to break down the steps in learning. These are the steps we go through with our children when helping them learn how to do things for themselves:

1. Our child is dependent on us to do the whole activity because she is unable to participate yet.
2. Our child watches and shows interest in the activity, but does not yet participate.
3. Our child can start to participate, needing physical assistance to complete the activity. Sometimes, hand-over-hand help gives the child a "feel" for how to do the activity. A lot of children dislike hand-over-hand help, however, and prefer to try on their own. This can be a challenging stage for parents, as your child struggles to attempt the activity but refuses your help.
4. Our child can do part of the activity without hand-over-hand assistance, but still needs us to talk her through it, and to help physically with some of the activity.
5. Our child can complete the activity without any physical help, but needs to be talked through it, with specific verbal instruction.
6. Our child can do the activity herself, without physical or instructional help, but needs the emotional support of your presence. ("You're doing a great job, keep going, you're almost done," etc.)
7. Our child can do the activity completely independently. She then practices the skill over and over until it is consolidated. Until she has had sufficient practice, the skill is not fully learned, and will not be consistent from day to day.
8. Only once the skill is fully consolidated into your child's automatic repertoire of skills will she be able to generalize it to other situations. For example, a young child may learn to drink from one particular cup at home, but seem unable to generalize this skill to a different cup at preschool. The skill is not yet automatic, and the child depends on some of the familiar aspects of drinking (perhaps the color or shape of the cup, or the highchair she sits in, or even how the cup is handed to her) to trigger the appropriate motor response. When she can drink out of any cup in any environment, she has generalized that skill. Sometimes children learn a skill at school, but don't do it at home, and vice versa. The skill has not yet been generalized to the other environment. Generalization of skills may not come automatically for some children with Down syndrome, and the skill may need to be taught in each environment.

Let's apply these steps in learning to a specific skill: tying shoelaces.

1. You tie your child's shoelaces. She is not really interested and her gaze wanders around the room.
2. You tie your child's shoelaces. Now she is interested, watching your movements.
3. Your child is at a developmental age when it is appropriate to begin to learn to do up shoelaces. She will already be untying her laces.

She can hold the laces with both hands, but can't move through the sequence of movements without your help.

4. Your child knows how to do some of the tying, such as doing the initial knot and making the "bunny ears" with your verbal cues, but still needs some physical prompting to cross and tie the bunny ears and pull them tight.

5. Your child can manage the physical aspects of the activity with verbal prompts, such as "cross over, then under."

6. Your child manages the activity, needing your emotional support to set it up and complete, such as "You're doing great; you've done one foot, only one more to go!"

7. Your child can tie her laces without your assistance. She then is expected to tie them consistently, with your understanding that some days she may go back to needing some assistance or support, as the skill will not be totally consistent until she has had sufficient practice. For children with Down syndrome, sufficient practice may be more practice than for the typically developing child.

8. Your child can consistently tie her shoelaces on different pairs of shoes, in a variety of situations, such as at home, before gym class, at a community program, etc. The skill has been consolidated and it is automatic.

Here is another example of the steps involved in learning a specific activity: printing her name.

1. The teacher/parent prints your child's name on her paper.

2. Your child watches as her name is printed, perhaps repeating the names of the letters as they are printed.

3. Your child attempts to print her name, needing some physical guidance to do so. Remember, it is not necessary that the letters be formed perfectly at this stage! In fact, correct letter formation comes with a lot of practice (see Chapter 9).

4. Your child prints part of her name, but needs some physical guidance or physical demonstration, and also verbal cuing.

5. Your child prints most or all of her name, but needs to be talked through it: "What letter comes next?" "Remember how we make an L? Start at the top, make a line down; that's right, now go across. Good!"

6. Your child can print her name, but needs assurance and feedback along the way.

7. Your child prints her name on her own. Hooray!!! Now she practices printing it until it becomes automatic.

8. Once it is automatic, your child will generalize her ability and will be able to print her name with any kind of writing tool, in any kind of situation (e.g., on the top of a worksheet, in a greeting card, etc.).

Bear in mind that it often takes years for a child with Down syndrome to move through the eight steps with some activities, as in the example of learning to print her name. She may begin to learn at age four, and may reach the stage of being able to print her name completely independently at age eight. It's easy to be out of sync with your child with these learning steps. I used to have to remind myself that it was okay that I had to be there to talk Sarah through getting dressed every morning; at least I didn't usually have to guide her through it physically any more. On the other hand, your child might sometimes be ready to move on to the next step, but you are so used to helping her, or helping her more than she needs, that you don't step back and let her try. It's a fine line!

When describing abilities in children with Down syndrome, developmental assessments or checklists with an "able/unable" or "pass/fail" approach will not capture all those stages in between that our children may be in for so long. Assessments that are more descriptive, or that break the skills down into levels of independence, will probably be more useful for parents and teachers in program planning.

ACCEPTING INCONSISTENCY

It's all right to expect your child to do more at certain times than at others. I have learned that "inconsistent" describes Sarah's abilities. For example, when she was first learning to print, some days she could pull it all together and print her name legibly, while on other days she reversed or missed letters and couldn't correct them, even if she recognized her errors. We all have good days and bad days. Our children's abilities on a particular day are related to so many internal and external factors, such as motivation, interest, fatigue, etc. Our child's ability to interpret and respond to sensory information from the environment (sensory processing) can vary from situation to situation and day to day. As parents, the best we can do is to try to be tuned in to our child's "state," so we can judge what to expect of her. This variability in performance within one child has been noted by professionals and researchers working with children with Down syndrome (72).*

It takes longer for children with Down syndrome to learn things, and attention and short-term memory deficits complicate the learning process. Sometimes, even when they seem to have learned a skill, they can't always recall it from their memory. They can't seem to make the connections to enable the skill to come out. Then the next day they have no problem. Although this is sometimes interpreted as "stubborn behavior," I interpret it as a failure of the sensory-motor pathways to make the right neural connections all the time. Most of the time the connection happens, sometimes it doesn't, and as frustrated as we can be with it, imagine how frustrating and demoralizing it can be for the child. She has worked so hard to learn a skill, seems to have learned it, and then can't do it the next day.

Motivation

Your child's approach to learning will relate to her unique personality, health, previous experiences, relationships, abilities, and sensory preferences. Patricia Winders, in her book *Gross Motor Skills in Children with Down Syndrome,* noted that young children with Down syndrome who are learning motor skills tend to be either "motor driven" or "observers." That is, some children want to plunge right in and try a new skill as soon as they can, and other children prefer to watch and wait, and need

---

* Numbers in parentheses refer to references listed at the end of the book.

more encouragement. In addition, research has begun to help us understand the *differences* in learning as experienced by children with Down syndrome as compared to other children. We are starting to understand that it is not always simply a delay in learning (69, 72). Parents, teachers, and educational assistants sometimes struggle with the typical package of parenting and teaching strategies, which may not always be as successful for the child with Down syndrome.

Motivation is critical for engagement of your child in the activity. Any child will show more interest in activities that are "fun" than in those that are presented or perceived as "exercises" or "therapy." A baby's and young child's primary means of learning about the world around her and of developing her abilities are through play and social interaction. "Fun" is, however, a very subjective thing. We have all heard about children who have more fun playing with the cardboard box than with the expensive toy that came in it. What is "fun" depends on a multitude of factors, including personality, age, and culture.

For example, let's consider the child who has learned to pick up a toy with one hand, and to pass it to the other hand (*transferring*). She is now ready to pick up two objects simultaneously with each hand and bring them together in midline (the center of her body). Picking up two wooden cube blocks and banging them together may not be particularly motivating to this child. She may, however, be much more interested in holding a pot lid and banging it with a wooden spoon, or in banging toy cymbals together and making a racket!

When choosing fine motor activities that will be motivating for your child, consider the following points (based on my experience and that of researchers and other professionals):

1. **Have Realistic Expectations:** Know what stage your child is at, and what comes next. This book will help you understand the sequence of fine motor development. You will know if the activity is either too challenging physically or intellectually, or isn't enough of a challenge for your child, by her response. If she is totally unable to participate in the activity, even with your help, the activity is probably too difficult right now. Persisting at skills that are beyond your child's current developmental readiness will result in frustration in both you and your child.

   Bear in mind that your child may not give you signs that she is ready for more challenging activities, or the next stage of an activity. Some children with Down syndrome are quite happy to participate in play and other activities that are at an earlier developmental level than what they are capable of. She may need structure and prompting to move on to the next stage.

2. **Build on Success:** Use activities that you know your child has had success with. Build on that success by adding a bit more difficulty to an already accomplished activity. For example, if your child can pour milk from a very small pitcher into her cereal bowl, and gets enjoyment from that, progress to pouring from gradually larger pitchers into gradually smaller cups. Success and accomplishment

are inherently motivating. The emotional connection to successfully interacting with the environment through a self-initiated activity enhances learning (24,74).

3. **Break Down the Activity into Small Steps:** Remember the stages of learning already discussed in this chapter. Learn to be rewarded by every small step your child is able to make. For example, we don't hand a child a crayon and expect her to color a picture inside the lines the first time! First we expect scribbling all over the page, then scribbling oriented to the space where the picture is, then some awareness of coloring the picture itself, with a gradual refinement and control of the crayon stroke until it can be recognized as "coloring in the lines."

4. **Make It "Fun":** I have certainly found that taking a personal approach with Sarah and the other children I have worked with greatly influences their interest in trying and persisting at an activity. Be very aware of your voice and body language, as they can be powerful tools to help motivate your child. Using a silly voice or building a game out of an activity takes more ingenuity and creativity on your part, but it can pay off. Don't forget to take your turn during any kind of game! Turn-taking is an important social interaction skill, and reinforces your own interest in the activity.

5. **Make It Relevant:** We all know that it is hard to keep at something that is difficult when it doesn't seem important or relevant to our lives. It is the same for our children. Many things that we take for granted will have to be taught to our children with Down syndrome, and will be difficult at first. For example, your child may not see the point of doing up buttons on a button board in the classroom every day for ten minutes. However, she may see the point in doing up buttons on her sweater before recess so she can go outside to play. If your child can practice fine motor skills at times of the day and during routines that make sense and have meaning for her, she will likely be more motivated to try. Also, it doesn't always follow that a child who can do up buttons on a button board will be able to do up her own buttons. She may not be able to generalize her ability with a skill in one setting or with one piece of equipment to other settings or objects. Children with Down syndrome need to learn the skills needed for daily activities by practicing those exact activities.

6. **Be Aware of the Environment:** Learning new skills requires attention and focus. Be aware of distractions that may interfere with your child's attempts at the activity. Other aspects to be aware of in terms of optimal learning are time of day, energy

level, hunger and hydration, physical space, seating, interruptions, background noise, and lighting.

7. **Try it!** If it doesn't work, you can always try something else!

What motivates your child? What is she interested in? What is a meaningful reward for her for trying to learn a new skill? As parents, we often know the answers to these questions intuitively, but we may not always listen to these intuitions, as we try to teach our child what we think, or others think, she "should" be doing. Many children are unenthusiastic about trying activities that they perceive as difficult, in which they expect to fail. It is important to reinforce all the efforts your child makes, and to show her that it's all right to make mistakes, so that she doesn't develop a perception of failure. We all need time and practice to learn new things. Let your child know that.

Adapting the Environment

Making changes and adaptations to the environment can also be important in helping to build your child's success with fine motor skills. This is an important component of occupational therapy practice: ensuring as much of a fit between the person and environment as possible. For example, adapting an infant's seat to promote better positioning for hand play would be considered adapting the environment. Using clothing with a minimum of fastenings to facilitate independent dressing is another example.

The "environment" is the place(s) in which your child spends her day. In broad terms, the environment includes the physical and sensory attributes, and the social aspects, of the places the child spends time in. All contribute to a child's sense of safety, well-being, and readiness to learn. Children with intellectual disabilities are more vulnerable to the state of the environment. Aspects of the environment can have both a positive and negative impact on them. For an infant, the environment includes her home and possibly day care center or babysitter's home. For an older child, the environment is her home, school, day care, camp, community recreation center, etc.

"Adapting the environment" means *changing, eliminating, or adding something* so the child can be more independent or successful. For example, a nine-year-old boy requested drinks from his mother several times a day. His mother made two changes that made it possible for him to get his own drinks. She kept the juice in smaller jugs in the fridge, so they would not be too heavy for him to pour. She also moved the cups to a shelf in a lower cupboard, so he could reach them himself.

In another example, a four-year-old child with Down syndrome continues to hold crayons and markers clenched in her palm when coloring. Instead of markers, she could be given short stubs of crayons or chalk, which promote the use of a three-finger (tripod) grasp. In addition, drawing at an upright easel or paper board would encourage her to use more mature wrist and hand positioning.

"Adapting the environment" can also include making changes to the sensory aspect of the environment. A child who quickly becomes over-stimulated and distracted by a preschool room full of toys and activities may be more successful in a room where she can choose between only a few activities at a time.

For children with Down syndrome, body position can be crucial to success with fine motor skills. Sometimes adding support for the child's body position is all that is needed to adapt the environment so the child can do the activity. For instance, when she was about seven years old, Sarah had a Mickey Mouse watch that talked and told the time when both sides of the watch were pressed simultaneously. It required a fair amount of pressure to activate, and she was unable to do it without taking note of her body position. She learned that she had to place her elbow and forearm down on a firm surface to give her enough stability and strength to make Mickey talk. Due to low muscle tone and joint hypermobility, children with Down syndrome need close attention to body position when they are doing fine motor activities.

Consultation with an Occupational Therapist

This book was designed to give parents, teachers, and others general guidance in encouraging the development of fine motor skills in children with Down syndrome, and in understanding the role of sensory processing on the development of their child. In developing these skills, many infants and children with Down syndrome can benefit from the services of an occupational therapist at some point in their life.

WHAT IS AN OCCUPATIONAL THERAPIST?

Occupational therapists are professionals who promote independence in daily living skills in clients of all ages when a physical, developmental, or psychosocial challenge interferes with the person's abilities. "Occupational" refers to the occupations people perform throughout their daily life, which for children include self-care, leisure, play, and school activities. Promotion of independence occurs within the context of the person's environment and relationships.

An occupational therapist (OT) has at least a four-year college or university degree with courses in sciences, typical development, medical conditions, and the theory and practice of occupational therapy. An occupational therapist can become involved with you and your child either through direct intervention or through consultation, and will focus on your child's ability to interact with her environment in ways that lead to mastery and independence. An occupational therapist can be a resource for both parents and teachers, can provide information about neurological and sensory-motor development, and can assess the physical environment in relation to the child's abilities.

Children with Down syndrome may receive occupational therapy services through an infant development program, a clinic or hospital setting, and in preschools and schools. Some occupational therapists are in private practice. The national associations of occupational therapy listed in the Resources section of this book can provide guidance in finding an occupational therapist for your child.

HOW CAN OCCUPATIONAL THERAPY HELP YOUR CHILD?

For children with Down syndrome, OT involvement may be directed at:
- self-care skills (eating, dressing, grooming, etc.);
- fine and gross motor skills;
- skills related to school performance (e.g., printing, cutting, etc.);
- play and leisure skills.

During infancy, an occupational therapist may become involved with you and your child to assist with:

- Positioning and feeding techniques related to oral motor and feeding difficulties. Sometimes sensory issues around feeding need to be addressed by an OT.
- Gross motor and fine motor milestones, particularly fine motor skills. Physical therapists work to encourage proper movement patterns for mobility and the development of gross motor skills. Occupational therapists promote arm and hand movement patterns and milestones that lay the foundation for refined fine motor skills.

During the toddler and preschool years, an occupational therapist may be involved to:

- Facilitate the development of fine motor skills through play and specific activities to develop control of isolated hand movements (dexterity), such as turning knobs and pushing buttons on toys, and building with construction and stacking toys;
- Observe the child in her environment(s) (e.g., home, day care, or preschool), paying attention to the child-environment "fit" and the sensory needs of the child;
- Help parents and caregivers promote the beginning steps of self-help skills such as eating, drinking, and dressing. An OT can help parents set appropriate expectations, as well as help with positioning and suggestions for specialized equipment and adaptations.

During the school years, an occupational therapist may be involved in:

- Providing direct intervention to your child to help her learn pre-printing and printing skills and/or consultation to the teacher about printing learning methods, adaptations, positioning, appropriate fine motor expectations, etc. Some occupational therapists have expertise in assistive technology, such as computer adaptations, that can be of benefit to the child in the classroom.
- Helping to set realistic expectations for the continued learning of self-help skills.
- Helping your child develop specific fine motor skills that will lead to more success in school and self-help activities.
- Addressing any sensory processing needs that your child may have that may be interfering with her interactions and learning.

As our children grow up and eventually leave school, they will be entering new work and social environments. At this stage, an occupational therapist may be involved in:

- Evaluating the components of a job your child is being considered for and her ability to perform them.
- Helping her master independent living skills.

■ Evaluating physical or sensory challenges to daily living skills, and suggesting strategies and adaptations to minimize the effects of those challenges.

Parents Know Their Child Best

Occupational therapists and other professionals have expertise and can provide guidance and therapeutic intervention, and can help you understand the particular challenges your child faces. They can also point you in the direction of important resources in your community. However, *you* are the expert on your child. You know your child best, her temperament, what helps calm her, what excites and motivates her, etc. The relationship between you and the professionals in your life is ideally as members of a mutually respectful team. Your thoughts and opinions are of utmost importance, and so are your questions. I have learned so much as an occupational therapist by listening to my daughters, the children I work with, and their parents.

Some adaptations, such as the example of the juice jug and cups given above, can be thought up by parents if they ask themselves, "Is there any way I can make this activity easier or more efficient for my child and myself?" Many parents and teachers make these changes automatically, without thinking of it as "adapting the environment." Observing and being aware of your child is the first step to recognizing how a difficult or dependent situation can possibly be changed so your child has more independence.

Depending on the social and cultural environment, adults may think there is only one "right" way of doing things. By keeping an open mind, we can see that there are choices about how to do things, and we can choose the way that is best for our child right now.

CHAPTER 3

Fine Motor Development in Children with Down Syndrome

This chapter describes common aspects of Down syndrome that can affect a child's development of fine motor abilities. Understanding how and why Down syndrome affects your child's fine motor skills can help you determine when to introduce an activity, and when not to push. It can also help you to recognize whether your child needs adaptations to accomplish a skill. In addition, it can help you understand the difficulties your child is having, and whether they are typical for a child with Down syndrome.

Later chapters will discuss how we can try to help our children overcome these difficulties as much as possible in order to learn fine motor skills that are important in their daily lives. In this chapter, the developing fine motor skills are outlined for each age range, using the house model that was introduced in Chapter 1.

How Does Down Syndrome Affect Fine Motor Skill Development?

Each child with Down syndrome develops fine motor skills at his own pace, and has his own individual strengths and needs. In general, however, there are a variety of characteristics associated with Down syndrome that can affect fine motor skill development. These include physical characteristics (such as hypotonia), medical problems, and cognitive delays.

PHYSICAL CHARACTERISTICS

HYPOTONIA

Hypotonia or *low muscle tone* is lower than normal tension in the muscles. Our muscles always have some degree of contraction, even if we are not moving, as they hold our bones upright. Children with Down syndrome have varying degrees of low muscle tone. This makes them appear floppy, and delays the development of head and body control.

Any child with hypotonia has difficulty with the first developmental motor challenge of learning to move into upright positions. Holding up his head, propping up on his arms, lifting his hands and feet into the air, sitting, etc.—all these skills are slower to develop because the infant can't activate enough tone in his muscles to move into a more upright position, and, if he is placed upright, to hold that position.

In children with Down syndrome, hypotonia affects all the muscles of the body. Thus, our children have low muscle tone in their tongue and face, fingers and hands, as well as in their torso, arms, and legs. Just as low muscle tone affects their gross motor development, so too does it affect their fine motor development. A child who is struggling to keep his balance in sitting because of low muscle tone in his body will be less able to reach out and pick up toys. Low muscle tone in the shoulder and upper back area also impair the baby's ability to reach and grasp (66). Likewise, low muscle tone in the lower arm and hand make it difficult for the child to position his finger joints to hold an object such as a pencil without his joints "collapsing." It may be particularly difficult for the child to push with his fingers, such as when pushing a button on a pop-up toy or pushing a thumbtack into a bulletin board. The muscles in the hand may not have enough tone to stabilize the joints.

Generally, the literature suggests that hypotonia in children with Down syndrome decreases with age. The problem is that by then, they may have developed ways of moving that may be detrimental in the stages of motor development that follow. For example, a child with Down syndrome who dislikes being on his stomach may eventually learn to move himself around the room on his back or his bottom by pushing and pulling with his feet. If he never has the experience of leaning, pushing, and pulling himself on the floor with his arms, his arms will be weak and it will likely be harder for him to pull himself up to standing and to eventually learn fine motor skills such as eating soup or printing.

LIGAMENT AND JOINT LAXITY

The ligaments supporting the joints are also looser, allowing more movement at the joints; this is called *"hyperextension,"* or *"ligamentous laxity."* You may think of this as being "double jointed." This increased range of movement in the joints is often very evident in our children's hands, especially when they are young. The thumb in particular may have so much extra movement that it is very difficult for the child to hold and manipulate smaller objects (31). A person without Down syndrome who has some joints that are "double jointed" can usually produce this excessive movement at will, and has control over when it happens. The child with Down syndrome, however, cannot control the excessive joint movement, nor can he prevent it from happening.

Due to laxity around joint capsules, children with Down syndrome could have greater risk of joint subluxation or dislocation. Care must be taken not to pull excessively on your child's limbs. For example, if a young child who can't yet stand up from the floor independently is pulled up by his hands, it may put undue stretch on the shoulders and elbows. If there are any indications that your child may have a subluxed or dislocated joint, such as persistent pain around the joint, awkward positioning of a limb, or a tendency to avoid using a limb, he should be seen by a doctor.

All parents of children with Down syndrome should be aware of a condition called atlanto-axial instability, in which the upper two bones of the spine, in the neck, are unstable. In children who have this instability, extreme movement or force to the head or neck may result in injury to the spinal cord. It is generally recommended that children with Down syndrome have a neck x-ray by the age of three to five to determine their risk for atlanto-axial instability.

SHORTER LIMBS

You may have noticed that your child's arms and legs appear shorter relative to his torso. This is quite common in children with Down syndrome. It will be most noticeable when you are trying to help him learn to sit, and to go into the hands and knees position. (This is discussed in more detail on pages 38-42.) When he is a little older, you may also notice the shorter arm and leg length when you are trying to find a tricycle or bicycle to fit, and when buying clothing. Because your child has a little further to reach, tasks such as putting on and fastening shoes may be more challenging for his balance.

HAND CHARACTERISTICS

Our children's hands may also have some unique physical characteristics:

1. **Single Simean Crease:** Instead of having three creases in their palms, some children with Down syndrome have two. This is one of the signs used in making the diagnosis of Down syndrome at birth. There is no indication in the literature that this has any effect on hand function.

2. **Smaller Hands:** In general, the hand of a child with Down syndrome is smaller than average, and the fingers shorter. This may make it more difficult to grasp and hold larger objects, such as when opening a large jar or when catching a ball with one hand. Activities requiring large finger span, such as using a computer keyboard, or playing guitar or piano, may also be more difficult.

3. **Wrist Bones:** There are seven small wrist bones in the hand. At birth, some children with Down syndrome do not have all of these bones, but they usually develop them by adolescence (8). The absence of one or more wrist bones may make it more difficult for babies and young children to stabilize their hands at the wrist as they are developing grasping patterns. For example, when a child learns to let go of blocks to build a tower, he stabilizes at the wrist to allow his fingers to open and release the block. If all the wrist bones are not present or are undeveloped, the child may lose some wrist stability and control of his hand movements.

4. **Curved Fifth Finger:** The finger (usually the fifth finger in Down syndrome) may be curved inward (called "clinodactyly"), or it may always be slightly bent at the middle (second) joint (called "camptodactyly"). If your child has either of these conditions present in one or both hands, he can't straighten his finger, nor will you be able to straighten it by pulling on it. If you are very concerned about it, your child should be seen by an orthopedic specialist. In the general population, these two conditions of the fingers are sometimes managed by stretching and occasionally splinting (24). In my experience, children with Down syndrome who have this slightly unusual positioning of their fifth finger(s) do not receive stretching or splinting intervention. From a parent's perspective, it seems relatively minor, compared to some of the other challenges their child may face.

Most people place the fifth finger side of their hand down on the table for stability when writing. Try writing with your fifth finger bent up and away from the rest of your hand, and feel the difference. I have seen this pattern of writing without the support of the fifth finger on the paper both in children who have clinodactyly or camptodactyly, and in those who don't. The effect of clinodactyly or camptodactyly on hand function in children with Down syndrome has not been studied, to my knowledge.

MEDICAL CONDITIONS

Most children with Down syndrome who also have a congenital heart condition experience even more difficulty achieving early developmental milestones. *Cardiac problems* impair tolerance and endurance for motor activity. Many children with Down syndrome also have increased susceptibility to, and frequency of, infections due to a weaker immune system and structural differences (such as smaller nasal passages and ear canals). Respiratory and ear infections, in particular, are frequent. We know that when our children are ill, they have much less energy for anything, which affects their development.

Some children with Down syndrome have *visual problems* that may affect eye-hand coordination. For example, difficulties with visual acuity and coordination of the movements of the eyes can make it more difficult for the eyes and hands to move together in fine motor tasks. Since our children have a greater risk for eye and visual problems, their vision should be assessed regularly.

COGNITIVE LEVEL

Fine motor and cognitive skills go hand in hand during the early stages of development, because much of early cognitive learning develops through manipulating objects in the child's environment. Delays in fine motor abilities can affect a child's growing understanding of the world around him if he is unable to manipulate objects in a way that will help him learn. For example, a baby learns by dropping objects that they always fall *down,* or that a toy hidden under a cloth is still there when he lifts up the cloth *(object permanence).*

Young children with Down syndrome need extra guidance, modeling, verbal cuing, and encouragement to learn fine motor skills (32). As a result, fine motor tasks that help the child learn cognitive concepts may have to be taught in a structured, systematic way. It is usually not enough simply to present children with Down syndrome with developmentally age appropriate toys and materials.

As they go through school, children with Down syndrome continue to use fine motor skills to express their developing understanding of materials and concepts through drawing and printing. Fine motor and visual motor difficulties may impede this expression of knowledge and understanding. For example, your school-aged child may understand that plants need sunlight, water, and soil to grow. When asked to draw a picture of what plants need, however, he may not have the visual motor ability to put this down on paper.

Likewise, the development of cognitive ability can affect a child's acquisition of fine motor skills. A child's cognitive level can direct the way he uses his hands. For instance, although a child with Down syndrome may have the physical ability to put Megablocks together to build a structure, he may not initiate this activity on his own. He may not be at the developmental level of combining and taking apart building toys.

He may choose instead to put the blocks in his mouth, bang two blocks together, or poke his finger in the holes. Although he may have the physical potential to develop his fine motor skills further, he may not be responsive to those types of activities. In these situations, the challenge is to find activities that do interest the child, and are cognitively appropriate, to help develop his fine motor skills.

Fine Motor Skills to Look for As Your Child Grows

This section gives an overview of fine motor skills to watch for and encourage at the various stages of development. The material is presented in the house model to show the relationship between the building block foundation skills and the emerging higher level skills. The skills mentioned are based on the average development of children with Down syndrome, and reflect the kinds of activities we can expect many children to participate in by the **end** of each stage. Bear in mind that there is great variability in the age at which children with Down syndrome achieve developmental milestones.

This section will give you an introduction to the developmental sequence of fine motor skills. Subsequent chapters will give more detailed activity suggestions for each building block, dexterity, and the daily living skills.

BIRTH-2 YEARS

Rapid changes take place during these first two years of life. Your child develops enough control of his body so that by the end of the first year, he may be able to sit up alone briefly, and by his second birthday, he may be able to pull up to stand and possibly take a few steps. He also starts to actively explore his world by picking up things, looking at them, and putting them in his mouth. By the end of this stage, he will have developed better sensation in his hands to feel and learn about things, and thus will not need to put them in his mouth as often. The three building blocks—stability, bilateral coordination, and sensation—are the main areas of development of fine motor skills at this stage, but your child will also be starting to develop the skills and movements needed for dexterity, such as picking up small things.

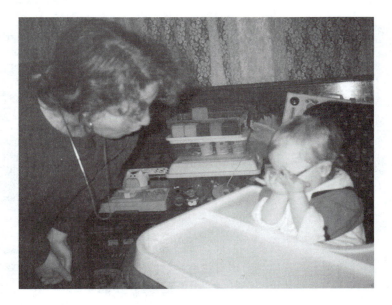

During this stage, many parents choose to introduce signs and gestures to encourage communication. Exact imitation of the sign by your child is not necessary, as some of the standard sign language hand positions may be too difficult for a young child. Rather, adapt the sign so that your child can easily do it. For example, at age two Sarah was unable to verbally indicate toileting needs. The traditional sign (thumb between third and fourth finger in a fisted hand) was too hard for her, so we used a closed fist, moving back and forth.

As parents and caregivers, we usually respond when our child points or picks up a toy by naming it and describing it and what it does, etc. It is important to keep in mind that our child with Down syndrome may not be able to initiate these kinds of fine motor movements without our help at this stage, and thus may not hear as much of the labeling and simple descriptive language from us. Researchers have found that children with Down syndrome who *were* able to engage in more active fine motor play had better language comprehension a year later. They theorized that those babies who could more actively explore and manipulate objects would elicit more specific references to these objects by their parents (25). You can help your baby by assisting him to pick up, hold, and explore toys, and to point to things around him, and by naming and describing these things for him. Listed in the house model below are the kinds of skills to work towards during this first stage. Subsequent chapters give detailed descriptions and suggestions for each area of development.

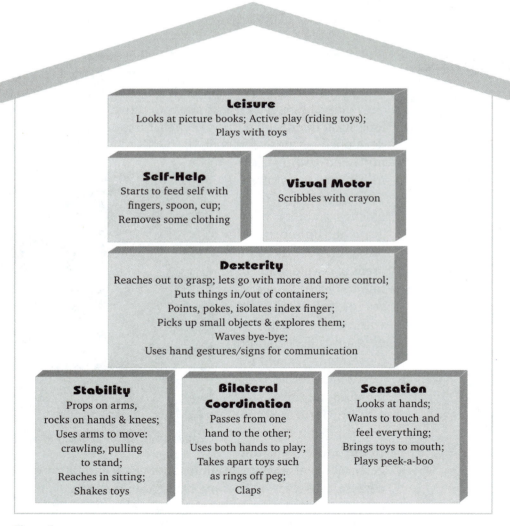

Leisure
Looks at picture books; Active play (riding toys);
Plays with toys

Self-Help
Starts to feed self with
fingers, spoon, cup;
Removes some clothing

Visual Motor
Scribbles with crayon

Dexterity
Reaches out to grasp; lets go with more and more control;
Puts things in/out of containers;
Points, pokes, isolates index finger;
Picks up small objects & explores them;
Waves bye-bye;
Uses hand gestures/signs for communication

Stability
Props on arms,
rocks on hands & knees;
Uses arms to move:
crawling, pulling
to stand;
Reaches in sitting;
Shakes toys

Bilateral Coordination
Passes from one
hand to the other;
Uses both hands to play;
Takes apart toys such
as rings off peg;
Claps

Sensation
Looks at hands;
Wants to touch and
feel everything;
Brings toys to mouth;
Plays peek-a-boo

Figure 6

At this stage, your child will have developed much more control of his body. Although he is continuing to strengthen his "building blocks," he has developed them enough to begin to experiment with and practice many more movements with his hands. Dexterity begins to gradually take over from the building blocks as the primary focus of your child's hand skill development.

Using sign language to augment verbal communication helps your child learn to use his hands for meaningful activity, and improves his dexterity. It is also very important to help your child pick up objects and explore them by turning them around and over in his hands, looking at them, making them work by pushing buttons, etc. Taking apart and putting together insert puzzles (the kind with the little knobs on each piece), manipulative toys such as Duplo, Tinkertoys, train sets, etc., toys with knobs and buttons (like pop-up toys), and toys for stacking, such as rings, pegs and blocks, are all important play experiences at this stage. Your child will begin to participate actively in the routines of daily care, such as dressing, although he usually still needs considerable help.

Leisure
Playgrounds;
Imaginary play;
Rides toys/trike;
Looks at books

Self-Help
Uses a spoon;
Starts using a fork;
Puts cup down; no spilling;
Pulls zipper up and down;
Takes off/puts on
loose clothing

Visual Motor
Draws lines/circles/simple forms;
Holds scissors, snips

Dexterity
Can let go of small objects more accurately;
Develops grasp: from holding in the palm to using fingers;
can pick up small things;
Turns things on/off with switches and dials using thumb
and index finger;
May use signs to augment communication

Stability
Uses arms for climbing
(onto furniture, at
playgrounds);
Plays with push/pull toys
(wagons, carts);
Shovels sand/pours water;
Opens cupboards/closets

Bilateral Coordination
Starts to show hand
dominance;
Uses hands together to
manipulate toys;
Holds toy steady when
necessary while other
hand manipulates

Sensation
Plays with sensory
materials (play dough, sand);
Knows several body parts;
No longer puts things in
mouth—explores with
hands and eyes

Figure 7

EARLY SCHOOL AGE: 5-8 YEARS

At this stage, when your child starts school, he will be using the dexterity skills he has already developed to learn more daily living skills, such as dressing and printing. Practicing daily living skills will serve to further develop his dexterity, so he can try more and more activities successfully. In order to develop dexterity, your child has to be able to move and coordinate the smaller muscles and joints in his hands, fingers, thumbs, and wrists. Your child will begin to handle routine tasks (such as dressing and toileting) more independently. As in previous stages, he will continue to strengthen the foundation skills; this increased strength will help him in new endeavors such as sports and recreation. He will also have better control and timing with his arms and will be able to enjoy ball activities.

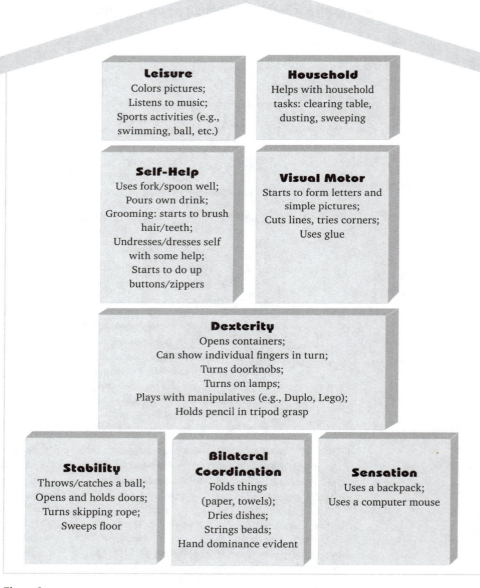

Leisure
Colors pictures;
Listens to music;
Sports activities (e.g., swimming, ball, etc.)

Household
Helps with household tasks: clearing table, dusting, sweeping

Self-Help
Uses fork/spoon well;
Pours own drink;
Grooming: starts to brush hair/teeth;
Undresses/dresses self with some help;
Starts to do up buttons/zippers

Visual Motor
Starts to form letters and simple pictures;
Cuts lines, tries corners;
Uses glue

Dexterity
Opens containers;
Can show individual fingers in turn;
Turns doorknobs;
Turns on lamps;
Plays with manipulatives (e.g., Duplo, Lego);
Holds pencil in tripod grasp

Stability
Throws/catches a ball;
Opens and holds doors;
Turns skipping rope;
Sweeps floor

Bilateral Coordination
Folds things (paper, towels);
Dries dishes;
Strings beads;
Hand dominance evident

Sensation
Uses a backpack;
Uses a computer mouse

Figure 8

At this stage, your child will be continuing to refine the daily living skills that require more dexterity. He probably will also be able to do things faster. Until this stage, the fine motor skills such as printing and doing up fastenings on clothing still required a lot of concentration, and thus were done slowly. By adolescence, hand movements for particular routine activities may have become more automatic, requiring less effort and concentration. Although your child may still have difficulty with tying shoelaces, buttoning his cuffs, and other such tasks, he will probably be able to dress himself with little physical assistance. Fine motor skills may be good enough to enable him to learn to type on a keyboard, to play a musical instrument, and participate in simple arts and crafts activities. Computer use often becomes important to augment verbal, signed, or written communication.

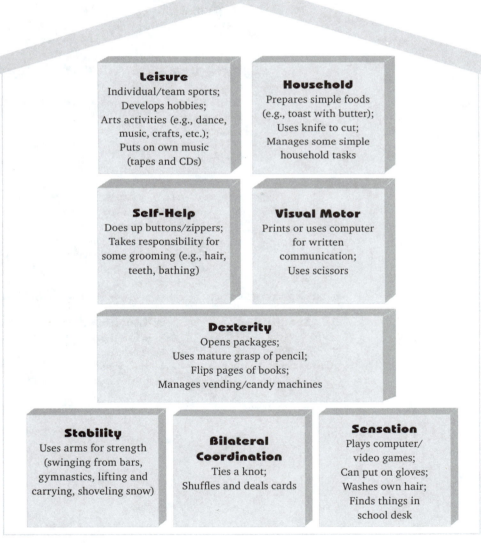

Leisure
Individual/team sports;
Develops hobbies;
Arts activities (e.g., dance, music, crafts, etc.);
Puts on own music
(tapes and CDs)

Household
Prepares simple foods
(e.g., toast with butter);
Uses knife to cut;
Manages some simple household tasks

Self-Help
Does up buttons/zippers;
Takes responsibility for some grooming (e.g., hair, teeth, bathing)

Visual Motor
Prints or uses computer for written communication;
Uses scissors

Dexterity
Opens packages;
Uses mature grasp of pencil;
Flips pages of books;
Manages vending/candy machines

Stability
Uses arms for strength (swinging from bars, gymnastics, lifting and carrying, shoveling snow)

Bilateral Coordination
Ties a knot;
Shuffles and deals cards

Sensation
Plays computer/ video games;
Can put on gloves;
Washes own hair;
Finds things in school desk

Figure 9

TEEN YEARS: 13-ADULTHOOD

During the teen years, fine motor skills learned in childhood expand to broader environments. Your child will generalize his fine motor abilities to all his classes at school, to his social environments, in recreation and leisure activities, and possibly volunteer work and paid employment.

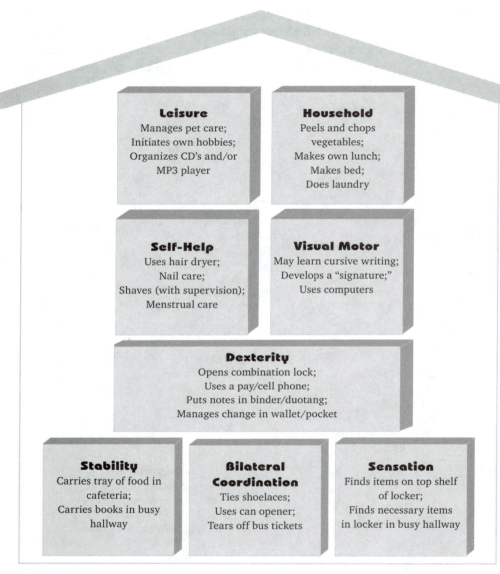

Leisure
Manages pet care;
Initiates own hobbies;
Organizes CD's and/or
MP3 player

Household
Peels and chops
vegetables;
Makes own lunch;
Makes bed;
Does laundry

Self-Help
Uses hair dryer;
Nail care;
Shaves (with supervision);
Menstrual care

Visual Motor
May learn cursive writing;
Develops a "signature;"
Uses computers

Dexterity
Opens combination lock;
Uses a pay/cell phone;
Puts notes in binder/duotang;
Manages change in wallet/pocket

Stability
Carries tray of food in
cafeteria;
Carries books in busy
hallway

**Bilateral
Coordination**
Ties shoelaces;
Uses can opener;
Tears off bus tickets

Sensation
Finds items on top shelf
of locker;
Finds necessary items
in locker in busy hallway

Figure 10

Conclusion

The main points to remember about the overall development of your child's fine motor skills are:

1. **The foundation skills, or "building blocks," are very important for the development of what we think of as "fine motor skills."** Your child needs to hold his body and arms stable when using both hands together and use the "feel" of the movement to guide him when he attempts activities such as stacking blocks, stringing beads, printing, or tying shoelaces.

2. **Children learn "dexterity" through play and daily activities such as eating and dressing.**

3. **All children build on previously learned skills and abilities as they learn to do more complicated fine motor tasks.** That is why a strong foundation (i.e., stability, bilateral coordination, and sensation) helps our children to move on to learn the daily living skills of self-help, school, household, and leisure activities.

4. **Our children will best learn fine motor skills (and other skills) through activities that are meaningful to them.** For example, practicing putting clothespins (clothespegs) on the rim of a container might not be meaningful and motivating for your child, but using clothespins to hang up his bathing suit after swimming may be.

AGES AND STAGES
A Summary of Fine Motor Development

In summary, here are some of the main points to keep in mind for each stage of your child's fine motor development. Some of the things listed will be *emerging* at the end of the stage; they may not be consistent yet. For example, a child just turned two may not be isolating his index finger to point yet, but he may be pointing with his whole hand or thumb.

INFANCY — 2 YEARS

- Encourage your baby to weight bear on his arms and hands (i.e., pushing himself up with his hands when on his tummy).
- Encourage your baby to reach up with his hands when he is on his back.
- Provide supportive sitting positions so your baby can begin to develop accurate reaching and eye-hand coordination.
- Provide toys that your baby can easily grasp with both hands, pass from hand to hand, and put in his mouth.
- Show your child how to take things out and put them into containers.
- Provide activity boxes and cause-effect toys.
- Encourage your child to point at pictures in books and to objects, and to poke his fingers into holes.
- Encourage finger feeding, and introduce a child's spoon and small cup.
- Provide some sensory play experiences.
- When your child is grasping something and banging it, make sure his thumb is around the toy, not tucked into his palm.
- Play simple social games (e.g., peek-a-boo), sing simple songs with actions.

2 — 4 YEARS

- Provide toys that come apart and fit back together.
- Provide toys that have parts that go into holes, slots, and spaces (e.g., puzzles and shape sorters).
- Hold up small items (such as bits of food) for your child to attempt to grasp with his index finger and thumb (pincer grasp).
- Use block and large pegboard activities to encourage the thumb and fingers to pick up in a tripod grasp, and to let go more precisely (e.g., pegs into holes, stacking blocks).
- Provide opportunities for sensory play (water, sand, paint, etc.).
- Introduce markers, crayons, etc. and encourage your child's expression on paper.
- Introduce scissors and let your child experiment with them. Demonstrate the correct grasp, but your child may not be ready to hold them this way yet.

- Use daily activities that encourage your child to hold things in his palm (e.g., pouring soap, shampoo, or vitamins into his palm).
- Provide manipulative toys (e.g., Duplo; Tinkertoys).
- Encourage your child to participate as much as possible in dressing.
- Teach your child how to scoop with a spoon, drink from a cup, and place the cup down after drinking.
- Do pouring activities in the bathtub or sink, or with dry sensory materials.
- Do action songs and rhymes together.
- Provide activities with push-pull actions of the arms (e.g., climbing; push toys).

5 – 8 YEARS

- Sing songs that have individual finger movements and actions (e.g., "Eensy Weensy Spider").
- Encourage your child to position a marker/pencil in a tripod grasp in his hand.
- Do some drawing, preprinting, and when ready, printing activities at various surfaces (easel; table).
- Provide simple matching, dot-to-dot, maze, and coloring activities.
- Do pouring activities with small jugs of liquid or dry ingredients.
- Encourage your child to do most of his dressing and undressing, including attempting fastenings such as zippers and buttons.
- Encourage your child to pick up and release small items into a precise spot (e.g., coins into a piggy bank).
- Encourage your child to hold scissors with his hand in mid-position with his thumb up, and to snip, cut across a strip, etc.
- Provide opportunities for strengthening pincer grasp (e.g., clothespins, play dough activities).
- Provide bilateral hand activities and manipulative toys (e.g., threading beads; building with Duplo and Lego).
- Introduce printing activities on lines and in workbooks as he is ready.
- Encourage your child to begin to participate in household activities, such as folding laundry, setting the table, sweeping, etc.
- Encourage your child to cut his own food, pour his own drink.

9 – 12 YEARS

- Encourage your child to more actively participate in household chores (e.g., sweeping and vacuuming, folding laundry, etc.).
- Provide bilateral hand activities that require small movements of the fingers and wrists (e.g., sticker books; stencils; folding paper, as in making a paper airplane).
- Provide opportunities for individual finger movement, such as with a computer keyboard, a music keyboard, or recorder.

- Encourage your child to hold a fork in a mature grasp, and to cut and spread with a knife.
- Encourage your child to pour drinks.
- Encourage your child to pick up small items one at a time and store them in his palm.
- Encourage strength and control of pincer grasp with activities such as using thumbtacks and large paper clips.
- Help him practice choosing his own clothes to wear, and fastening his own zippers and buttons. Encourage him to dress himself.
- Encourage your child to manage some of his grooming, such as hair care, washing himself, etc.
- Support him in his printing efforts, and perhaps introduce pre-writing activities if it is appropriate.
- Help your child develop rewarding leisure time activities.
- Play games that involve finger movement and control, such as Ker-Plunk, Barrel of Monkeys, Jenga, etc.

13 YEARS — ADULTHOOD

- Encourage your child in regular physical activity and leisure activities.
- Maintain upper body strength through activities such as swimming, basketball, baseball, gardening, etc.
- If the teen has been successful at prewriting and printing and is motivated, introduce a cursive writing program.
- Encourage him to choose his own clothing and to dress independently.
- Encourage him to shower/bathe independently.
- Teach aspects of adolescent self-care (such as shaving, menstrual care) by modeling, gradually reducing assistance as appropriate.
- Encourage continued development of dexterity with speed and control of fine movements in activities he enjoys (e.g., cooking, sewing, building models, etc.).
- Encourage using fine motor skills for learning community living skills, such as using a computer to find a library book, using a bank machine, etc.

CHAPTER 4

Early Movement in Babies with Down Syndrome

In the early months, development of fine and gross motor skills goes hand in hand. With each new gross motor skill learned, your baby is also preparing her arms and hands for the many hand functions she will have to perform as she matures. She is building stability, sensory awareness in her arms and hands, and learning to use both arms to help her move around on the floor. She is building her foundations for fine motor skills: *stability, bilateral coordination,* and *sensation.*

Stability	**Bilateral Coordination**	**Sensation**
Gaining control of her movement; Holding herself upright	Using both hands and both sides of her body for movement and play	Learning to respond to what she feels and to the sensation of changing her body position

Figure 11

This chapter will describe how your baby is preparing for fine motor skills while she is mastering gross motor milestones. For detailed descriptions of how to help your child achieve gross motor skills, refer to *Gross Motor Skills in Children with Down Syndrome* (Patricia C. Winders, Woodbine House, 1997).

How Can I Help My Baby Learn Early Arm Movements?

Every child's development is influenced by the complex interaction of genetics and environment. Personality, family dynamics, early stimulation, genetic ability, birth order, environment, and other factors all affect development to varying degrees. In other words, no two children with or without Down syndrome will develop in exactly the same way, at exactly the same pace. There are, however, specific difficulties that most children with Down syndrome encounter in learning motor skills, so it is possible to generalize about what you might expect.

Here are some of the stages of early movement, with a brief explanation of how these stages relate to later fine motor development. Suggestions are given to help your baby and young child with Down syndrome achieve these movement milestones, while using coordination of muscles to help her progress to the next stage.

LIFTING ARMS WHEN ON BACK

Lifting arms and feet when on her back prepares your baby for accurately placing and holding her arms within her visual field, the beginnings of eye-hand coordination. Early on, this will simply be too difficult for your baby, because of low muscle tone and poor stability in the shoulders. These are the steps in learning to lift her arms up and hold them there:

1. lying in side lying, bringing her hands up in front of her face;
2. sitting in a supportive, semi-reclined infant seat, bringing her hands together in the center;
3. swiping at toys in side lying and in an infant seat;
4. reaching up for faces and to swipe at toys in back lying, with support under the shoulders;
5. reaching out and grasping toys in side lying and in an infant seat;
6. reaching up and grasping suspended toys in back lying;
7. holding and playing with a toy, such as a rattle, in an infant seat;
8. holding and playing with a toy, such as a rattle, in back lying.

Side Lying: In this position your baby will be able to bring her hands together and look at them without having to work against gravity.

Infant Seat: In an infant seat (including a car seat), your baby can begin to develop arm strength against gravity in a semi-reclined position, which is easier than lifting her arms when on her back.

Back Lying with Support: If your baby attempts to lift her arms when she is on her back, but can't lift them up high enough to be able to see them, place small rolls (towels or baby blankets), or a cloth infant car seat insert under her shoulders. At first you may need to place a soft toy right on her chest, as this may be as far as she can reach. This helps her lift her hands up where she can see them. Looking at her hands is very important at this stage. As her shoulders and arms get stronger, you can progress to reaching for overhead toys.

Babies also like to lift their feet up into the air when on their backs, reaching out for their toes with their hands. Often, a baby with Down syndrome will attempt

In side lying, this young baby can easily bring his hands together to hold toys where he can see them and bring them to his mouth.

Soft Velcro wrist toys help an infant become aware of his hands. The toy can also be placed around his ankle.

Your baby will enjoy reaching up to touch your face and hair.

Help your baby to reach up and grasp his toes.

to grasp her feet by bending her knees outward, and bringing her feet together. If she grasps her feet in this way, she isn't using her tummy muscles to pull her legs up. She needs your help initially to hold her knees in line with her hips, so she can learn to use her tummy muscles to lift her legs. Developing strength in her tummy muscles is important for fine motor skills because these muscles help the baby have a stable base from which to move her arms and hands.

Fine Motor Skills in Side, Semi-Reclined, and Back Lying: Side, semi-reclined, and back lying are good positions to begin fine motor skill development in the first few months of life. The baby is comfortable in these positions, and can easily

A car seat head support can help position the baby's head and shoulders to enable him to lift his arms.

hold her head in the center (midline), without having to work hard to hold her head up. In side lying she can easily bring her hands up in front of her face where she can see them. Sitting in an infant seat and back lying are natural positions for face-to-face interaction with parents, siblings, etc. Babies are instinctively interested in faces, and quite early on learn to discriminate features of familiar faces and voices. Playing with your baby in this position will encourage her to reach up to your face and hair. Your positive response will lead her to do this again and again. This is the first step in learning to reach out, touch, and grasp something she wants. It will help her develop early control of her arm and hand movements.

Initially, any reaching out your baby does is with large swiping movements that are not very accurate. At this stage, suspended overhead toys are helpful, as your baby can reach up, swipe at the dangling toy, watch it spin and move, and listen to the noise it makes. Some baby activity gyms have toys along the side bars that are useful when the baby is playing in side lying. Weighted toys that make a noise but don't roll away when the baby moves them, such as the Fisher-Price Roly Poly Chime Ball, or the Happy Apple, can be positioned within reach when your baby is in side lying. She is reinforced for her efforts to reach out by the noise and movement of the toy.

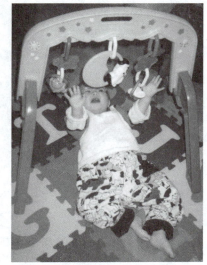

Overhead suspended toys can help motivate a baby to lift his arms.

This baby can reach up and hold both arms up to play. His hands are together in midline where he can easily see them.

Your baby can also be encouraged to lift and move her hands in the air by putting a soft wristband toy with a bell inside on her arm. These soft toys will not hurt her if she drops her arm to her face. They can also be placed around your baby's ankle, if you are at the stage of encouraging her to lift and play with her feet.

As your baby's arm movements become more accurate, she will be able to bring her hand directly to the toy without the large sweeping arm movements of the first few months of life. At this stage, you can progress to toys that can easily be grasped. These include toys that have handles, such as rattles, or rings. Place the toy on the floor, if your baby is in side lying, or hold it above her if she is in an infant seat or lying on her back. Now she will be able to grasp the overhead play gym rather than simply swiping at it; if she has difficulty grasping it because it moves, hold it steady for her.

PROPPING UP ON ARMS WHEN ON TUMMY

Propping up on her arms when on her tummy (prone) helps your baby develop stability and strength in her shoulder, arm, and neck muscles. It also prepares your baby's shoulder muscles for accurate reaching and the stability to hold her arms steady while performing precise hand movements.

This is the progression of fine motor development in the propped position, when your baby is on her stomach:

1. lifting her head with support on elbows;
2. lifting her head and chest with support on elbows;
3. lifting her head and chest with support on hands;
4. reaching forward with one hand, with support on other elbow;
5. reaching forward with one hand, with support on other hand;
6. reaching up with one hand, with support on other hand;
7. pivoting in a circle, using arms to move.

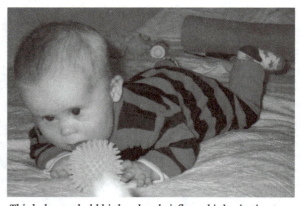

This baby can hold his head up briefly and is beginning to take weight through his forearms. He can move one hand forward on the surface to reach for the toy.

At first (about two or three months of age), your baby will use her neck and shoulder muscles to lift and hold her head up. Help her position her arms with her elbows directly under her shoulders, so that she is taking weight through her shoulders and forearms. This will help her lift her head up. At this stage, activity quilts can be fun. These baby quilts have small mirrors, squeeze toys, animal faces, etc. sewn right into them. Your baby will be motivated to prop herself up on her arms to see in the mirror or to reach for the squeeze toys. Eventually, she will be able to push right up, supporting herself on her hands. This position is excellent for developing strength in the neck, shoulders, arms, wrists, and hands.

A baby with Down syndrome may "hyperextend" her neck when on her stomach. She literally pulls her head back and rests it on her upper back, due to weakness in the neck muscles. If she continues to do this, she will not develop the strength in her neck muscles necessary for holding her head up in other positions, such as sitting. If your baby hyperextends her head, try moving her elbows in closer to her body and lowering anything that she is looking at (including yourself!). Continue to work on head control when holding her upright on your shoulder and when on your lap. (See: *Gross Motor Skills in Children with Down Syndrome,* by Patricia Winders.)

Sometimes therapists use a small roll or rolled-up towel under the baby's chest to help position the arms for propping. This can initially help to give your baby the idea, but should be discontinued as soon as she can hold herself up briefly, as she may lean into the roll and rely on it rather than using her arms.

With a small roll under his chest, he can lift his arm up off the surface to reach. He may roll onto his side, but will get better control of his head position and width shifting as he gets stronger in this position.

The baby then begins to try to push up on his hands.

Reaching and Pivoting When Propping on Arms: When your baby can hold herself in a propped position briefly, either on elbows or hands, she is ready to begin reaching out with one hand. In order to do this, she must shift her body weight over to one arm, while reaching forward for a toy with the other hand. When first learning to do this, your baby might shift her weight too far and consequently roll over. For some babies, this may be the way they learn to roll from stomach to back.

It is important for your baby to learn how to move her weight over to one side in order to learn how to creep and crawl. When she shifts her weight to one side, she increases the stability and strength on that side. She should take turns shifting weight to either

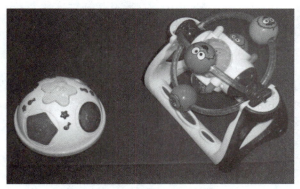

Examples of toys that respond to touch with lights and music; motivating for a baby beginning to reach out when on her stomach.

side and reaching with both hands. First she will reach forward for a toy on the floor. Because she is working so hard to hold herself up while moving her arm forward, she will need a toy that she can swipe at, or a toy that can be easily grasped (such as the Skwish rattle). She may grasp it and pull it in towards her body so she can put it in her mouth. Be sure to use soft toys that will not hurt her as she pulls them in toward her face.

As she gets stronger in the propped position, she will be able to lift one arm right up off the floor to reach a toy you are holding up for her. At first she will immediately drop her arm back down to the floor, but as she develops more strength, she will be able to hold her arm up to shake or bang the toy. If your baby always falls over onto her side when trying to reach in this position, it

This baby can hold himself up on his hands, and has enough stability to reach for a toy with one hand.

may be because she is moving her head too far over to that side as well. She has to learn to shift her weight onto one arm while holding her head steady in the center. This is how you can help her learn to support her weight on one arm while reaching with the other:

1. If you would like her to reach with her right hand, place your hand firmly over her left hip to help her shift her weight over to the left side of her body;
2. With your other hand, support her left shoulder so she holds herself up through her arm without rolling to the left. This will also help her keep her head upright.
3. If necessary, prompt her to reach for the toy with her right hand.

When your baby has learned to reach up with one hand, she will be ready to pivot around on her stomach. To pivot, your baby turns to one side, where a toy is positioned, and uses her arms to move herself around in a circle to reach the toy. To do this, she must shift her weight alternately from one arm to the other, and pull her body around, using mainly the movements of her arms. Pivoting helps to develop strength in your baby's shoulders and arms.

ROLLING OVER

Rolling from stomach to back usually develops before pivoting. Rolling over prepares your baby for using one arm differently from the other by changing her center of gravity from one side to the other. All of these activities that involve shifting weight from one arm to the other are important in helping your baby develop the adjustments in her body and arms necessary for balance later on. Body and shoulder adjustments are also very important during the school years, in visual motor activities such as cutting, as your child guides her hands through complex movements.

Rolling from stomach to back usually develops before rolling from back to stomach, often when the baby leans over while propping on her stomach. When rolling from her back to her stomach, your baby has to be much more active with her movements, lifting her legs to initiate the roll, and lifting her arm up and over to the other side.

SITTING

Babies with Down syndrome usually take a long time to learn to sit independently because of hypotonia and shorter arm length. A delay in independent floor sitting should not hold your baby back from playing and using her hands while sitting, however. At this stage of development, babies are learning how to pick up and let go of toys of various sizes and shapes. If your baby spends part of her day in a well-supported sitting position, she will be able to begin developing more controlled grasp and release patterns for play. Give her opportunities to play while sitting in a highchair or similar supportive seat.

Babies love to look at their hands and play with their fingers.

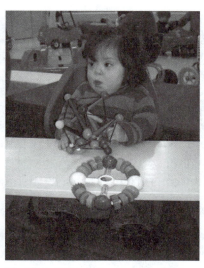

A "Bumbo seat" provides support for the baby who is not yet able to use both hands freely in play when sitting on the floor.

The Flip 'n Sit is another example of a floor seat; it can also be used on a chair. Here, a wooden bench is used as a play surface.

Two examples of supportive seats that provide good positioning for floor sitting once your baby has developed head control are the "Bumbo Babysitter" seat and the "Flip 'n Sit" seat. (See Resources section for availability.)

Floor Sitting: Most babies use their hands on the floor to prop themselves up when they are first learning to sit. This is a difficult position for babies with Down syndrome, because their arms are shorter, and they have to lean too far forward to prop themselves. If your baby tries to sit propping on her arms, she may rest her head back on her upper back, which is not a position you want to encourage. Give her some support in front to rest her arms on, so she can sit up straight while propping herself. I like to use a cardboard box (with a cutout for the baby's legs), upon which toys can be placed. A cushion or firm stuffed animal could also be used. She may also need some support behind her, so she doesn't fall backwards. A firm sofa cushion, mother's nursing cushion, or similar support behind the hips can be used.

Your baby will need the support of your hands, or supportive cushions, pillows, or rolls around her hips and lower back when sitting on the floor until she develops enough control of her tummy and back muscles to sit up on her own. With help and practice, your baby will gradually develop the strength in these muscles to be able to sit independently. These are the steps in fine motor development in floor sitting:

1. with arms supported on a box or cushion, looking at a toy;
2. one arm props on a box or cushion for support in sitting, while the other hand holds a toy;

An infant seat offers a symmetrical, supported position for the infant to play with toys and develop a variety of movements in his hands. These pictures give some examples of good infant toys: Skwish rattle; Slinky; suspended toys that are easy to grasp.

3. the toy is still supported on a box or cushion, but the baby can now use both hands to play;
4. the baby can play with a toy using both hands without front support;
5. the baby can reach out and take a toy from you;
6. the baby can reach forward to pick up a toy from the floor and sit back up;
7. the baby can reach to the side to pick up a toy and sit back up;
8. the baby can shake, bang, and throw toys in sitting and maintain balance;
9. the baby can turn to reach a toy behind her, leaning on one hand and reaching with the other, then sitting back up.

As your baby gains better control of her back and tummy muscles to maintain her balance in sitting, her arms become freer to move.

Once they have learned to sit independently, babies with Down syndrome often prefer to sit on the floor with their legs in a "frog-legged" or "ring" position: spread wide at the hips, knees out, feet together. It is important that your baby also experience sitting with her knees in line with her hips and her feet flat on the floor. A booster seat on the floor provides some back and side support, while encouraging weight bearing through the feet. Similarly, a small stool encourages her to sit with her feet flat on the floor. This helps her develop better use of all her leg muscles, and allows her to learn to balance using her tummy and back muscles. Practicing balance, reaching, and turning in different sitting positions will help your child develop body and arm stability and control for fine motor skills. The muscles of the back, tummy, and neck provide the base that the arms need in order to move and direct the hands into position. When she is ready, challenge your child to reach in different directions for toys, both in floor sitting and on a bench or stool. By doing this she learns to control the movement of her body while accurately reaching out with her arms.

Sitting on a stool or booster seat helps the child learn to take weight through his or her legs and feet, in preparation for standing. The little girl on the right is reaching to one side to practice sitting balance and rotation.

Young children with Down syndrome often move their whole body rather than turning (rotating) part of their body. For example, rather than turning to one side to lower down to the floor or to begin crawling from floor sitting, your baby may do the "splits," lower her upper body down to the floor, and then swing her legs back behind her. Although effective (she gets down!), she is avoiding challenging her balance and isn't turning her body. It is better to help her place one arm down to the side while turning herself to that side. Again, this helps strengthen the shoulder muscles.

This little boy is beginning to be able to rotate (turn) to the side in sitting to reach for a toy. He is reaching for a Swish rattle, which is a wonderful toy for babies: it is easy to grasp, colorful, and has bells on it.

Reaching while sitting helps the child develop body and arm stability, a building block for hand skills.

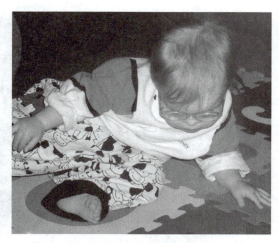

Pushing up into sitting from lying helps develop arm and body strength and balance reactions.

Sitting in a Highchair: Today highchairs are usually designed with good support, safety straps, and a tray. Sitting in a highchair for some play activities gives your baby a chance to move her arms, hands, and fingers more freely than she can on the floor. Because she has good support from the highchair, she can focus on using her hands to learn and discover things, and doesn't have to worry about falling over. This positioning helps with sitting balance and keeping hands in the center (midline), so your child can play using both hands.

Provide side and/or back supports (such as a rolled-up towel or piece of firm foam) if your child needs a little more support than the highchair offers. If your baby slides forward out of the seat, try putting a piece of non-slip matting on the seat, such as

A rolled towel can help the baby sit in the highchair without falling to one side.

If the highchair seat is too deep, a piece of sturdy foam helps the baby sit up straight.

the kind you buy to use as a grip to open jars or Dycem. (See the Resources section for sources.)

You will be able to offer your baby more challenging fine motor toys when she is sitting in the highchair than when she is on the floor. For example, she will likely be better able to grasp and move the knobs and buttons on a busy box when she is sitting in the highchair than when she is sitting on the floor.

This baby uses one hand for balance in floor sitting. He can manage a one-handed activity, but would have more success with two-handed activities like this puzzle seated in a highchair or at a table.

PUSHING UP INTO A CREEPING POSITION (HANDS & KNEES)

On hands and knees, the baby prepares her hands for fine movements by rocking backwards and forwards, and side to side. Leaning on her hands and rocking helps the baby develop the different muscles in her hands, and strengthens her shoulders and arms.

Again, low muscle tone and shorter arms will make it harder for your baby to assume and hold this position at first. A firm cushion under her hands will help initially. Once she is able to hold herself in this position, you may be able to encourage rocking back and forth by singing or playing music. Her hands should be open; her fists shouldn't be clenched.

These are the steps in fine motor development in the hands and knees position:

1. the baby supports herself on hands and knees, with someone supporting her at her hips;
2. the baby holds herself on hands and knees, with a cushion under her hands;
3. the baby holds herself on hands and knees without a cushion;

A little support at the hips helps this child hold herself in the hands and knees position. She will progress to holding this position independently, and then to lifting one hand to reach for a toy, in preparation for standing.

This child has developed enough stability to lift his hands to crawl.

4. the baby rocks forward and backward, side to side on her hands and knees;
5. the baby reaches out with one hand for a toy, holding the hands and knees position;
6. the baby moves into hands and knees from sitting, then moves back into sitting by turning to one side.

Leaning on the hands while playing (weight bearing through the hands) helps develop shoulder and arm stability and control, and develops the small hand muscles. This is preparation for the positioning and holding the child will need for precise hand movements as she gets older.

The progression of use of the hands is essentially the same as in the propped position. First the baby must learn to hold the position, then assume and hold the position, and then she learns to shift her weight to one side so she can reach with the other hand for a toy. This weight shifting will eventually help her learn to creep forward on hands and knees.

PULLING TO STAND AND STANDING

Your baby develops stability and strength in her shoulder muscles as she uses her arms to pull herself up to standing. To help her:

1. Start by having her sit on a stool or in a booster seat, with her feet firmly on the floor.
2. Give her a firm surface to pull up on, such as the edge of a coffee table, a chair, or stair banister.
3. When she can pull herself up from a stool, progress to having her start in the kneeling position, bringing one foot forward first, then the other, as she rises.

Fine Motor Development in Standing: Your child can practice fine motor skills in standing with either front or back support. Standing with her back in a corner or against a wall allows her to use her arms more freely. Be aware that the level of fine motor play that she will be capable of when learning to stand will be lower than the level she can accomplish in supported sitting. For example, if she can fill and empty containers with blocks when she is in her highchair, she may be able to watch a music box or bang a xylophone when learning to stand. When she is learning to stand, she will primarily be using her hands for balance, not for fine motor skill development.

With front support, she will need to hold on to the table edge or rail with both hands initially, and thus her hands will not be free for play. As she gets stronger and develops better control in standing, she will be able to lift one hand to play while supporting herself with her other hand. Still holding herself with one hand on the surface, she will next be able to reach to the side, and squat down to reach a toy on the floor. Gradually she will be able to use her hands more and more while standing, shifting her supporting hand from one side to the other, then letting go very briefly with both hands.

It is better not to let your child lean into the supporting surface (e.g., coffee table) with her chest in order to play in standing. If she has to lean in for chest support,

Standing against a wall in a corner or pushing against it for support helps children learn to use their arms while balancing their body in standing.

the activity is probably still too difficult for her. Practice standing with both hands supporting, then one hand supporting, until your child has good standing balance in these positions, before giving her toys that require two hands to play with. From the coffee table or rail she can progress to placing one hand on the wall or fridge for support, while reaching and playing with her other hand.

When standing with back support, your child can progress from standing in the corner or against the wall to standing with support behind her legs, as with a small chair or stool. In these positions, you can give her progressively more challenging reaching and play opportunities, as her balance in standing improves.

Conclusion

In the first stages of development, the focus is on the achievement of gross motor skills. This chapter has described how your baby will use her arms and hands during gross motor development, and how these early fine motor skills relate to the more precise hand movements she will develop in the next stages. While your baby is working on gross motor milestones, she will also be ready to develop aspects of dexterity, such as picking objects up and letting them go, pointing, and passing things from hand to hand. Whatever your child's stage of gross motor development, you would therefore benefit from reading the following chapters.

Many of us are fortunate enough to have parents who ask for suggestions of what to buy our children for their birthdays and other special occasions. Here are a few suggestions of toys and equipment that help fine motor development in approximately the first two years of your baby's life. Bear in mind that although I may give an example of the type of toy, there are often several other brands of the same type of toy that would work just as well.

Grandma's and Grandpa's List

- Baby play activity gym (sometimes called infant development systems, or play zones)
- Activity center/board/table
- Activity quilt
- Infant seat
- Chair support (tie-around support to use in a regular chair, if a highchair is not available)
- Head hugger (support for head in car or infant seat)
- Sleep time support pillow (to support neck in car seat)
- Highchair (with wrap-around tray and contoured sides)
- Soft wristband toys
- Rattles and squeeze toys
- Chewing toys/teething rings
- Touch and feel books; board books
- Skwish rattle
- Baby mirror
- Soft stuffed animals
- Suction toys (for standing up on the highchair tray)

CHAPTER 5

The First Building Block of Hand Skills: Stability

At seven and a half, Sarah could pull a toboggan up a hill. She could push another child on a swing and swing from her arms across a row of monkey bars. She had developed reasonably good stability in her body and shoulders to do these things. But, when she was printing, the letters were usually so light you could hardly see them. She had not yet developed enough consistent stability and strength in her hands. I say consistent, because she could briefly use enough strength to print darker, but couldn't maintain it when she was concentrating so hard on the formation of the letters.

Consistent stability is difficult for many children with Down syndrome. By "consistent stability," I mean the ability to maintain the muscular contraction around a joint to hold it in a certain position. Low muscle tone makes it more difficult to hold a consistent degree of muscle contraction over a period of time. You may find that your child can seem very strong when he wants to be. Perhaps when he gets hold of a candy bar in the grocery store, you may find it almost impossible to release his tightly clenched fingers. This, however, is different from the contraction needed by the same child to hold his arms and wrist steady while building a block tower. It is also different from the contraction needed by a baby to prop himself up on his arms

Figure 12

and play in that position for several minutes. The stability that is often challenging for our children is not to intermittently tighten the muscles briefly and then release, but to hold and position themselves most efficiently for the activity.

There are three main types of stability our children need to develop:

1. **Body stability:** Body stability allows the child to move his arms freely without fear of losing his balance.

2. **Shoulder stability:** Shoulder stability allows the child to move his lower arms and hands freely while his shoulders position his arms (such as when cutting). It also enables the arms to support the weight of the body (as when doing a push-up).

3. **Hand stability:** When the child is developing the ability to perform more difficult fine motor skills, such as printing, he needs to learn to use one part of his hand for stability and the other part for movement. Usually the outer edge of the hand (the baby finger side) is steady while the thumb, index, and middle fingers manipulate the object. This type of stability will be discussed in Chapter 8.

How Can I Help My Child Develop Stability?

When your child is still at the pre-walking stage, using the positions and adaptations described in Chapter 4 will help develop the early stability in the body and shoulders that he needs. Even after your child has learned to stand and walk alone, he continues to improve his stability for many years. This section includes some activities that will help your child practice the stability that will provide him with a good "building block" for fine motor skills. The activities are divided into "Early Activities," for children who are at a younger developmental level (usually up to approximately three or four years), and "Later Activities," for children who are developmentally ready to attempt more challenging activities. Many activities, however, can be begun during your child's early development, and can continue to be used to build skills for several years. These activities can gradually be made more challenging as your child masters the early steps.

1. Body Stability

EARLY ACTIVITIES

PUSH TOYS

Your child can use push toys both to help him maintain balance while walking and to help him develop body stability. Most toddlers and young children love to play with a variety of push toys. The progression will be as follows:

Two examples of push toys.

1. A push toy of suitable height and weight can assist your child in learning to walk. The handle should be approximately at elbow height, or slightly higher. The toy should be stable enough not to topple if your child leans on it. There are many commercially available early walking/push toys; an example is the Fisher-Price Activity Walker. Try the toy with your child before purchasing it, if possible, to check the height and weight.

2. Pushing a light wheeled toy, such as the Fisher-Price Popper, while standing or walking helps your child learn to balance while moving his arms freely. These long-handled toys are usually pushed with one hand while the child stands or walks. An example of a lightweight push toy that needs to be pushed with both hands is a toy lawn mower. As these toys are lightweight, they can be used once your child can stand and walk independently, without needing support.

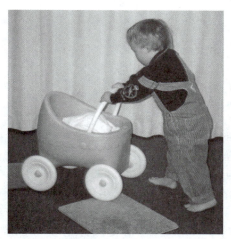

Walking while pushing toys develops body and shoulder stability, as well as hand strength.

3. Initially, your child will push the toy in a straight line. Next he will learn how to back up and pull the toy when he gets stuck.

4. As your child's balance in walking improves, he will be able to steer the walk toy to change direction and go around corners. He will learn to initiate this movement from his shoulders and to make adjustments with his arms and body as he refines his steering. This ability to make fine adjustments is important later when he is learning visual motor skills, such as tracing.

PUSHING/PULLING OPEN DOORS

1. Most children go through a stage when they love to open and close cupboard doors and drawers (usually emptying the contents in the process!). This is a normal and important developmental stage, and rather than restricting all cupboards and drawers with child safety latches, assign one that is safe for your child to experiment with.

2. Doors at home and in the community provide opportunities for opening and for holding open the door, which improves strength and stability. Let your child do the door opening and holding when you are going into grocery stores, etc.

3. When your child is old enough (approximately seven years and up), and you feel it is safe to do so, encourage him to open and close the car door when he gets in and out of the car.

SHOVELING ACTIVITIES

While sitting or standing, the arms lift, adjusting to the weight on the shovel, while maintaining balance. These activities also develop strength in the hands. Examples of shoveling materials are sand, snow, or dry materials in a bin or container, such as dried beans, macaroni, or cornmeal.

Shoveling develops stability and movement control in the upper arm and shoulders, while also developing hand strength and wrist control.

1. Laundry detergent scoops are good to try when learning to scoop sand.
2. Begin with small shovels in sitting.
3. Progress to larger shovels that have long handles, so your child can shovel while standing.

HAMMERING

Trying to hit a target with a toy hammer or mallet helps children develop accuracy in their arm movements, while stabilizing with their body and shoulder. Examples of this type of toy are the Tap 'n Turn Bench (with pegs and plastic mallet), Activity Hit a Ball (tapping a ball with the mallet causes it to roll down a ramp), and toy workbench or carpentry sets.

Hammering develops motor accuracy, as the child targets the pegs with the mallet.

POURING

Whether it be in the bathtub, at a water table at school, or while watering plants at home, the body provides the stability while the arms develop the controlled movement for pouring, eventually without spilling. Here is the progression of steps in learning to pour, beginning with activities appropriate for a toddler, and progressing to those appropriate for the school-aged child:

Pouring helps the child develop body and shoulder stability while learning to control movements of the arm and hand. Do pouring activities with a young child at a sink, tub, or water table where spills don't matter.

1. In the bathtub, hand your child a container or cup with some water in it and show him how to turn his wrist to pour it out.
2. Standing at a water table or sink, your preschooler can scoop and pour water back into the basin.
3. Your child can pour water from one container into another, or into a toy such as a water wheel. Continue to do the pouring at a sink, water table, or in the bathtub, so it doesn't matter if there is spilling.
4. The beach or sandbox is another fun place to practice pouring without worrying about spilling. If a bucket of water is handy beside the sandbox, your child can scoop water into a smaller pail or watering can to do his pouring.

BALL SKILLS

When bouncing, throwing, and catching a ball, your child uses the stability in his body as a base upon which to move his arms and hands. Ball skills are more challenging than some of the other activities described so far because they involve a moving object, the ball. Learning to catch a ball can be very challenging for the young child with Down syndrome. He must learn to plan his arm and hand movements to both the placement and the timing of the ball. The following progression is recommended to build success, beginning with activities for toddlers and preschoolers, and progressing to activities for the older child:

1. With your toddler, roll a large ball back and forth while sitting on the floor. A soft ball that will not hurt him should he miss it is best. Try a Nerf ball, "Gertie" ball, beach ball, or soft plastic ball.

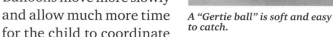

2. Many children find it easier to begin with balloons rather than balls when learning to catch and throw. Balloons move more slowly and allow much more time for the child to coordinate

A "Gertie ball" is soft and easy to catch.

his movements. Try to find sturdy balloons that do not break easily (e.g., punching balloons with the elastic removed). Begin gently tossing the balloon back and forth in either sitting or standing, depending on your child's balance. You can also experiment with the best size for your child by blowing the balloon up to various sizes. Be careful not to leave your child alone with the balloon, if there is a possibility he might put it in his mouth.

Early ball skills: sitting and rolling a ball back and forth.

3. When your child can catch balloons easily, progress to a mid-sized soft ball that does not have a slippery surface. Gertie balls are good for this. Some balls actually have grooves to make it easier for the child to grasp. Stand a few feet away and gently toss it back and forth. Your child will not have good aim initially, so be prepared to chase down a few balls!

4. Some children find it easier to catch a beanbag than a ball. It has a different shape and more weight, and some children may be more successful with it. To make a beanbag, sew together three sides of two squares of durable fabric, fill with dried beans or peas, then sew up the fourth side.

5. When your child is able to catch and toss a ball or beanbag two or three feet with some consistency, stand further apart. Bounce the ball on the ground to your child. This gives him more time to prepare for the catch.

6. When your child can catch a bounced ball with some consistency, try tossing it from the same distance.

When helping your child learn to catch and throw, begin with balloons, which are slow moving and give the child time to react; then beanbags; then a large, non-slippery ball; progressing to smaller balls.

He should now be ready to bounce the ball at his own feet and catch it. Again, his aim may not be good at first, and he may bounce the ball on an angle, so that it bounces away from him. If this is the case, show him how to drop the ball, without trying to catch it, until he can bounce it straight down.

7. Progress to smaller balls, such as a tennis ball.

8. Your child may enjoy a variety of ball activities, such as basketball (a child-sized set will be more successful), or Velcro ball.

POURING

1. Let your child help you pour ingredients into the bowl when cooking or baking. Dry ingredients pour more slowly than water, and thus are easier to control. Let your child practice pouring dry things like rice, cornmeal, etc. into a cup in preparation for pouring liquids into cups.

2. Put some liquid into a small jug with a sturdy handle when practicing pouring into a cup. Make sure your child is sitting or standing in a sturdy position. The table height should be at elbow level or lower, to give him room to lift his arms up to pour. The jug from a child's tea party set may be the right size, although the cups will probably be too small!

3. Eventually your child will be ready to attempt pouring from a regular-sized jug or container into a glass.

SWEEPING THE FLOOR, VACUUMING, RAKING

The body and legs remain stable while the arms work together in a sideways or forward/back motion. As your child gains skill, sweeping out from under furniture, requiring bending of the body, offers more of a challenge. A child-sized broom or rake will be more manageable when your child is young. Vacuuming offers similar opportunities to develop stability. Sweeping, vacuuming, and raking are also good bilateral coordination activities, as both arms move and apply force together. A Dust Buster offers an additional challenge of pressing and holding the button down while moving the arm back and forth, which strengthens the finger muscles.

STREAMERS

Waving a streamer through the air develops movement and strength in the shoulders, and it is fun! You can make a streamer out of crepe paper or a strip of light material, about 3 to 8 feet long, depending on the height of your child. He should be able to lift the streamer off the floor and keep it up when waving it. If it is too long, it will drag on the floor and won't be as much fun! Secure the end of the strip to a 6- to 10-inch length of dowel. Hold the dowel to wave the streamer to music, or outside in the wind. Streamers are used in rhythmic gymnastics and are also commercially available.

BUBBLE WANDS

Dip a wand of any size (now there are some very large bubble wands), hold it up in the air, and either wave the arm or hold the arm up steady and run around to push the air through to create the bubbles.

PUSHING A SWING

Here, the force of a moving object is added, which is more challenging for balance than some of the other activities above. The arms must absorb the force and push against it.

1. Initially, place a doll or stuffed animal in a baby swing for your child to push.
2. Progress to pushing another person. Your child must be careful not to stand too close to the swing to avoid being hit.

TURNING A SKIPPING ROPE

Even if your child cannot skip yet, he can turn the rope for other children. His body provides stability while the arm moves

When pushing a swing, the older child keeps her body stable while moving her arms to push.

through a full circular movement at the shoulder. This can be quickly tiring (try it yourself!), and frequent changing of arms is a good idea. Also, change from an inward to an outward movement.

In all these activities listed above, the child is developing balance while learning to move his arms and hands with more accuracy and control. In order to be able to freely move the arms and hands through space with precision, his body has to provide a stable base. While his arms are moving, the muscles of his back, tummy, chest, and neck are holding and adjusting to the slight changes of body position.

2. Shoulder Stability

The muscles of the upper back and shoulders provide the base for the child to perform accurate movements with his lower arm and hands. A pianist positions and holds his arms from the shoulders and elbows, while performing intricate movements with his fingers and wrists. This is the same kind of stability needed by the young child building a tower of blocks, who needs to position from the shoulder, elbow, and wrist while accurately placing one block on top of the other with his hands. Also, shoulder stability helps to keep the arms steady while the body is moving. When you carry a bowl of soup to the table, your shoulder muscles help you to hold the bowl steady while you walk. Doing activities to help your child develop shoulder stability lays the foundation for fine grasping skills.

EARLY ACTIVITIES

PICKING UP/PLACING DOWN OBJECTS AT DIFFERENT HEIGHTS

Some activities that involve these movements are:

1. Pick up large blocks, such as those pictured here, and stack them in a tower or structure, or place them down on the floor in a row.
2. Place large stuffed animals on the floor; up on a bed, etc.
3. Reach up to get something off a high shelf.

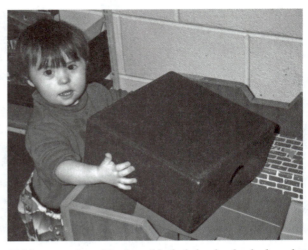

Picking up and stacking large blocks helps develop body and shoulder stability, and is a good bilateral activity. Shoeboxes can be used instead of blocks.

CLIMBING

When climbing, your child uses his arms to pull his body up to a higher level.

1. Climbing on furniture: You can encourage this by removing sofa cushions to make the height of the sofa more accessible to your child. Your child can be encouraged to climb on furniture even before he can walk. You must supervise him closely at this stage, as young children need help to discriminate what is safe to climb up on and what isn't! Appropriate climbing experiences include climbing up onto sofa cushions placed on the floor; climbing onto the sofa with cushions removed; climbing into small child-sized chairs; climbing onto a low bed; climbing onto a sofa with the cushions on.
2. Climbing stairs: When your child knows how to climb onto cushions and low furniture, he can begin to learn to crawl up stairs. He will have to do this with close supervision to ensure safety.
3. Climbing onto regular furniture: Climbing up onto a regular-sized chair, bed, or couch will challenge your child to use more arm strength to pull himself up.
4. Playground equipment with platforms is the next step. Once your child is safe climbing onto furniture at home, he can begin to try to climb up onto platforms at playgrounds.

Using arms to help go up stairs and climb improves shoulder stability.

LATER ACTIVITIES

CARRYING A SMALL TRAY

When carrying a tray or plate of food, children need to hold their arms steady to keep the tray level and steady while walking.

1. Begin with the tray or plate alone, without anything on it. Next place something small on the tray while your child carries it.
2. Next, your child can carry plastic plates, cups, or other objects on a tray, or a sandwich on a plate.
3. Next, your child will be able to carry a tray with non-liquid food on it. When he is able to carry this tray and keep it level

Profile: David

(Throughout the book, examples of how some of the suggested activities can be incorporated into daily routines will be given through brief profiles of children.)

Six-year-old David goes to the grocery store with his mother. When they park, she gives him the coins to put in the parking meter. (This lets David practice dexterity.) In the store, David pushes the cart around the aisles if it isn't too busy. (He is developing stability in his shoulders and strength in his arms as he pushes and maneuvers around corners.) His mother lets him lift some of the boxed items off the store shelves and put them in the cart. When they get home, David carries some of the lighter bags into the house, and helps to unload and put away the groceries. (Lifting and carrying also develop stability and strength.)

while walking, he will be ready to attempt carrying a tray with liquid, and later may begin to be able to carry a tray with food and drink up a flight of stairs.

SWINGING FROM A BAR

Your child can begin by swinging from railings, as these are usually lower to the ground and thus safer. As his strength and overall coordination improves, he will be able to swing from a monkey bar, which is at a higher height, and later to move from one bar to another across a row of bars. You can help your child by hugging his hips and legs as he holds the bars and moves across, so that you are supporting most of his body weight. Gradually reduce the amount of support you give as he develops better strength in his arms to hold himself. Do not let your child swing from a bar high off the ground if he has very low muscle tone and is not able to lift his feet off the ground while holding a low railing, as it may overstretch the shoulder muscles.

Swinging along a set of monkey bars is a very challenging activity for children with Down syndrome, as it requires a lot of shoulder stability, strength, overall coordination, and confidence.

HAMMERING GAMES

Games such as Don't Break the Ice promote stability and control of shoulder movement by directed hammering.

Grandma's and Grandpa's List

- Inflatable roll: for baby to roll over, pushing off with arms and legs
- Walking toys, sometimes called activity walkers
- Push and ride toys
- Pull/push toys, e.g., toy doll stroller; grocery cart; lawn mower
- Hammering toys and games
- Activity Hit a Ball
- Spinning top (spins when button on top is pushed down)
- Wagon for pushing and pulling (also handy for longer walks with the child who tires, but is too big for a stroller)
- Pails and shovels of various sizes
- Child-sized broom, rake, snow shovel
- Water play toys for pouring
- Child's tea set with tray
- Trapeze bar
- Balloons
- Beanbags
- Beach ball
- Easy to grasp ball (e.g., Ball Jellies; Gertie ball)
- An assortment of regular balls of various sizes
- Child's basketball set and other ball activities
- Large blocks (shoeboxes are an alternative)
- Skipping rope
- Streamers
- Twister game
- Butterfly net
- Bubble wands

CHAPTER 6

The Second Building Block: Bilateral Coordination

Young children naturally explore and play with toys using both hands. This allows them to develop variety in how they manipulate and explore the toys. The way your child uses her hands together during play is important because it leads to the natural development of handedness (being right or left handed). This is also called "dominance." Most people use one hand as the dominant hand, and have better skill and more speed with that hand compared to the other hand.

How Do Children Develop Bilateral Coordination?

An infant begins to move objects back and forth from hand to hand in the first year. This is called *transferring.* Practicing transferring helps the infant to develop these important skills:

- grasping and releasing patterns as the object is passed from one hand to the other;
- eye tracking as the eyes follow the path of the object;
- coordination between the two sides of the body.

Figure 13

During a baby's first year, you see a lot of passing of toys back and forth from hand to hand as the baby carefully looks at the toy during play. At this stage she likes to shake, bang, and throw the toys. During the second year, the baby is ready to pick up two identical or similar objects, one in each hand, and to bring them together in midline. Midline is the center of the body, where your hands meet when you bring them together in front of yourself. In the toddler years, children play with toys using both hands in a more coordinated fashion: lifting and dumping out containers, building simple structures with Duplo blocks, etc.

Toddlers begin to engage in cause-effect play, in which they do something specific to make something happen. For example, your child pushes the button and Big Bird pops up. In these types of activities, you notice that both hands are usually involved, but are doing different things. One hand is more actively doing; the other is holding or helping.

The most difficult bilateral activities are those involving different actions with both hands at the same time. Cutting out shapes with scissors is an example of this type of bilateral coordination. While one hand holds and manipulates the scissors, the other hand holds and turns the paper to allow the shapes to be cut out accurately. Many self-care activities, such as getting dressed, involve the coordination of different movements in each hand.

Even when a preschooler seems to be right handed, it is quite common to see switching to the left hand, particularly in new activities. During these preschool years of explorative play, the child gradually develops one hand as a consistent "doer" and the other as a consistent "helper." In other words, she develops handedness, or a dominant hand.

How Do Children with Down Syndrome Develop Bilateral Coordination?

Sometimes young children with Down syndrome have difficulty coordinating both hands together during play. This may be due to poor body stability or developmental immaturity.

POOR BODY STABILITY

Poor body stability is probably the most common reason for children with Down syndrome to have difficulty with bilateral coordination. If your child needs to use one hand for balance, due to low muscle tone and poor body stability, she will have only one hand free for play. In this situation, your child cannot use both hands to hold and manipulate a toy in midline, which is a very important step in the development of bilateral hand skills.

Even if your child doesn't need to put one hand down for balance, poor body and shoulder stability may prevent her from reaching out. She may lock her upper arms at her sides in an attempt to stabilize, so that she has a very limited range for hand play. Poor balance and stability may also prevent a child from crossing the midline (center) of her body when reaching. This may affect the child's ability to develop hand dominance (28).

DEVELOPMENTAL IMMATURITY

Your child may not have reached the developmental stage of bringing the hands together in midline and passing a toy from hand to hand. As with many developmental skills, children with Down syndrome may have to be shown how to do this. In the toddler years, your child may not seem to gradually develop one hand as more dominant, due to developmental immaturity.

There is tremendous variation in the general population as to when a parent can tell if their child is right or left handed (hand dominance). There is also great variation in the age of development of hand dominance in children with Down syndrome, with anywhere from twenty-four months to six or seven years being possible. It is normal for children to switch hands during activities in the preschool years, especially when they are learning a new skill, such as coloring or cutting. These activities are very challenging at first and it is both normal and appropriate for your child to experiment by switching hands, even if you think that she is really "right handed" or "left handed."

There is no detriment to being left handed, other than needing some left-handed utensils, such as scissors and can openers. There is a slightly increased incidence of left handedness in children with Down syndrome (69).

DELAYS IN HAND DOMINANCE

In my experience, children with Down syndrome do tend to develop a hand dominance concurrent with the rest of their development. There are a number of possible reasons why some children are delayed *beyond the normal range in the acquisition of hand dominance,* or do not seem to develop dominance at all. Observation of your child during play and activity may help you rule out some possible factors:

1. **Body Stability:** Does she attempt to use only one hand (when it is a two-handed activity) because she is using her other hand for balance? Or, is she limited in her reach because of balance concerns, and can't reach across her body to pick something up? If so, try a more stable position for the activity, and see if that helps her to use both hands more freely.

While pushing the train around the track, this child crosses the midline with her hand. This type of activity can help children who have trouble establishing hand dominance and avoid crossing the midline.

2. **Difficulty Crossing the Midline:** Some children have difficulty crossing the midline of their body, and thus will switch the pencil from one hand to the other when they get to a point at the midline of their body. For example, a child who has difficulty crossing the midline may pick up a pencil if it is on her left side and will begin to print with the left hand, but will switch to her right hand when she gets to the middle of the paper. This is really only a notable observation if your child does this in all activities when they are familiar to her.

3. **Ambidextrous:** Some people are ambidextrous, using one hand for some activities, and the other for different tasks. Development of consistent hand dominance is only a concern if the child is having difficulty developing skills with either hand to be able to function in her everyday life.

4. **Vision:** A visual problem, such as a "lazy eye," myopia (nearsightedness), or strabismus, may affect the development of eye-hand coordination. It is probably unrelated to the development of hand dominance.

Helping Your Child Develop Bilateral Coordination

POSITIONING

In infancy, make sure your baby is positioned so she can bring both hands together in the midline, where she can see them. For example, the extra support of small rolls or towels behind her shoulders when lying on her back may enable her to lift both arms up to grasp toys. Semi-reclined infant seats, again with support behind the shoulders, may enable your baby to reach out with both hands for a suspended toy. (See page 39.)

It is crucial that your child have the opportunity to play in a supported sitting position from a young age. A child with Down syndrome may not have the balance to sit unsupported on the floor until she is twelve to eighteen months old. This should never prevent her from sitting and developing important bilateral hand skills through play. Make good use of your infant seat and highchair!

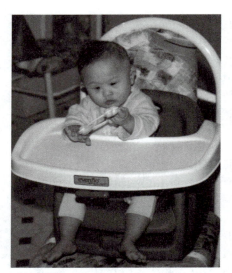

This child is transferring the toy from one hand to the other.

TRANSFERRING TOYS

At approximately six to twelve months of age, your child should begin to pass toys from one hand to the other ("*transferring*"). Help her do this if she doesn't do it on her own, by bringing the toy in her hand to the center in front of her, and guiding her other hand to grasp and take the toy. The release from one hand to the other should take place in the midline, with your baby watching her hands.

HOLDING A BOTTLE

Babies usually start to hold their own bottle in their first year. Help your baby do this, holding hand over hand. You may find that your baby doesn't have the strength to hold the bottle up herself (I found this with Sarah for the longest time), but placing her hands on the bottle helps her develop bilateral coordination. Eventually, although I didn't think it would ever happen with Sarah, your baby will be able to hold her bottle! A plastic bottle is lighter than glass. It may help to use a small (4 oz) bottle, or the kind with the space in the middle, with two more easily grasped sides. There are also angled bottles (e.g., Playtex angled bottle), which the baby can hold closer to her chest, rather than holding it up straight, which takes more strength. For the older baby, there are now bottles with straws rather than nipples, which are non-spill, and also don't have to be held straight up.

BANGING TOYS TOGETHER

By about eight to fifteen months of age, your baby will be ready to pick up two small toys at the same time. Toys that she can bang together help her develop early skills in coordinating both hands together (for example, toy musical instruments and blocks).

CLAPPING GAMES

Clapping games such as pat-a-cake are early bilateral coordination activities that bring the hands together

Banging two objects together is an early skill in coordinating the two hands.

in midline. There are many songs that encourage clapping (such as "If You're Happy and You Know It, Clap Your Hands"), and of course we can clap to any rhythmic music.

APART/TOGETHER ACTIVITIES

Simple toys that involve taking apart and putting together help children begin to coordinate the movements of both hands in the midline. Some examples are:

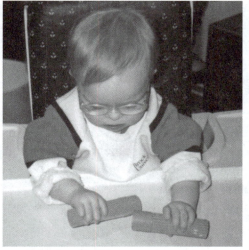

A toothbrush holder is a handy item to practice holding with both hands, taking apart, and trying to fit together.

1. Taking tops off markers.
2. Pulling apart and putting together travel toothbrush holders. These are plastic containers that hold a toothbrush; interesting objects can also be placed inside to spark your child's motivation to open one up!
3. Pop apart beads. These are large plastic beads that fit together with a little knob in a hole. They require some strength to take apart and to push together, and I have found that they can be frustrating for children with low muscle tone until they have enough strength to manage them.
4. Bristle blocks. These are blocks with plastic "bristles" all over them that easily fit together. Begin by simply pushing together and pulling apart two blocks. Later your child can attempt to put more blocks together.

SENSORY ACTIVITIES

The term "sensory activities" is used here to describe activities that focus on a variety of touch experiences. Playing with play dough, water, sand, bins of dried beans or cotton balls, and shaving cream are all examples of sensory activities. These activities encourage children to use both hands in play. You cannot use play dough or other inedible materials until your child stops putting things in her mouth. However, food offers wonderful opportunities for sensory exploration! Recognize that a baby's natural desire to put her hands in her food and muck about is actually helping her develop her sensory abilities in her hands and need not always be discouraged. Pudding, Jello, baby cereals, and pureed fruits and vegetables are examples of foods with a variety of textures and tastes that can provide fun sensory experiences.

LARGE TOYS

Building with large building blocks, catching a balloon, and rolling a large ball are examples of activities in which children have to coordinate both hands to play.

BOOKS

Holding a book with one hand while turning pages with the other hand encourages bilateral coordination. Board books for young children are easiest for page turning. Don't worry if initially your child turns several pages at once. She will not have the finger dexterity yet to isolate individual pages, even with a board book. As your child gets older and uses regular books, she may have difficulty turning the individual pages. You can add tabs to the edge of the page, or glue a bit of sponge between the pages to separate them so they can be more easily turned.

SELF-HELP ACTIVITIES

Most self-help skills require the coordination of both hands. Holding the dish while eating, holding a sandwich or hot dog, and putting on socks and mittens are examples of self-help activities in which the child coordinates both hands.

HOUSEHOLD ACTIVITIES

There are many household activities that help develop components of fine motor development, including bilateral coordination. Some examples that are appropriate for children with Down syndrome aged five and older are:

1. Sweeping the floor. Observe your child when she is sweeping and notice how she holds the broom handle. Try it yourself and compare. If your child was holding the handle with her hands in a different position than yours, try to reposition her hands so her movements can be more effective. Many children with Down syndrome persist with holding objects with a long handle (such as a broom or hockey stick) with both palms facing down. If you try this yourself you will find that it is not as effective as holding with the upper hand palm down, and the lower hand palm up.
2. Vacuuming; raking;
3. Folding towels and laundry;
4. Opening jars;
5. Using salad tongs to dish out salad;
6. Using a salad spinner;
7. Holding a bowl while stirring;
8. Spreading jam on bread;
9. Opening Velcro straps (e.g., on running shoes).

RECREATION ACTIVITIES

Sports activities in which both hands are used together, such as swinging a baseball bat or using a hockey stick or golf club, help develop bilateral coordination and stability.

APART/TOGETHER ACTIVITIES

Toys that fit together help your child practice coordinating the movements of her hands, and learn about size discrimination. Some examples are:

- Barrels;
- Stacking cups;
- Russian dolls;
- Megablocks;
- Duplo; Lego;
- Velcro toy food (food items that are cut in half and joined with Velcro: good for apart/together, and also for matching the two halves together);
- Bubble tumblers with a slot for the wand to fit inside.

TOYS WITH MOVING PARTS

If you browse the shelves of your local toy store, you will probably find a variety of toys that require two-handed operation. Some examples include:

- Wind-up toys: Toys that are wound up, such as a jack-in-the-box or a music box, require one hand to wind it up and the other hand to hold it steady.
- Kaleidoscope: One hand holds the kaleidoscope up to the eye; the other turns the end to change the colorful display.

Toys with moving parts: The child holds the kaleidoscope with one hand and turns with the other. The open, encircling hand position helps develop thumb positioning and control.

- See 'n Say: This popular toy has to be held firmly with one hand while the other hand pulls down the lever to start the turning dial and tape identifying animal sounds, letters of the alphabet, etc.

LACING ACTIVITIES

Simple lacing and stringing activities give children the opportunity to experiment with hand dominance. Usually the dominant hand does the lacing, while the other hand holds the bead or lacing shape. If your child switches hands back and forth when she begins doing these types of activities, it isn't anything to be concerned about; it is a normal developmental process. As she develops better control, she will probably be more consistent with which hand she uses to hold the bead and which to string with. The developmental progression of lacing/stringing activities is:

1. Stringing beads with a large hole onto a straw or pipe cleaner;
2. Stringing beads onto a stiff shoelace (wrap masking tape around the end to lengthen the stiff end);
3. Stringing small beads onto gimp or a shoelace;
4. Lacing activities; e.g., plastic or cardboard animal shapes with holes for lacing.

Lacing activities: Stringing beads requires good coordination of both hands and is a common activity for developing dexterity. Begin with stringing large beads onto a pipe cleaner, and progress to a stiff shoelace and smaller beads, as shown here. Notice how the child uses her thumb and index finger to do the activity and stabilizes with the rest of the hand.

PAPER AND PENCIL ACTIVITIES

Opportunities to draw and paint give children the chance to experiment with handedness. For quite a while (sometimes a few years), a child may switch back and forth between hands with markers, brushes, and crayons. Gradually she will begin to more consistently choose one hand to hold the utensil.

Removing the perforated stickers in a sticker book requires good coordination between the two hands, and good dexterity. This activity is appropriate for a child aged about seven and up, but may be frustrating for a younger child.

Separating perforated paper helps the child learn to control the movements of the hands together.

Tracing stencils is another activity for the older child who likes paper and pencil activities. The child traces around the stencil with her dominant hand holding the pencil, while her other hand holds the stencil steady. You can make simple stencils by cutting shapes out of plastic margarine container lids. There are also commercially available stencil sets (e.g., Magna Doodle letter stencils) or books with stencils. Magna Doodle can be a motivating activity for the child who has difficulty exerting enough pressure with a pencil or crayon, as very little pressure is needed to make a dark line. Tracing around your child's own hand is another fun activity.

Stencils can help the older child, who has established hand dominance and pencil control, to coordinate the stabilizing of the stencil with one hand and the tracing with the dominant hand.

SALAD SPINNER ART

Use an old salad spinner that you won't be using to wash salad anymore. Place a circle of colored paper into the spinner, then drizzle poster paint of various colors and sprinkle sparkles. Put the lid on the spinner. The child holds the spinner steady with one hand (she may need some help with this), and turns the knob with the other hand. Remove the paper to dry. The result is a beautiful kaleidoscope of color on the paper.

Profile: Amanda

Twenty-two-month-old Amanda is not yet walking independently, but can push herself up to standing from her booster seat, and can maintain her balance in standing while reaching. One day when her dad was unloading the dishwasher, he decided to bring Amanda over to where he was working so he could talk to her about what he was doing. He put her booster seat on the floor beside the open dishwasher and sat Amanda down in it. Amanda immediately pushed herself into standing using the sides of the booster seat and began reaching for her plastic cup. Her dad handed it to her, and she placed it down on the open dishwasher door. She reached out again, and her dad handed her another plastic cup, suggesting that she put it in the other cup.

This continued, with Amanda stacking the plastic cups, using one hand to hold the stack and the other to put the cups into each other. When there were no more cups, her dad suggested that she take them apart and make another tower, this time with the red cup on the bottom. It took her dad longer than usual to unload the dishwasher, but this spontaneous activity gave Amanda an opportunity to develop her standing balance, bilateral coordination skills, and dexterity, and to hear her dad label colors.

Grandma's and Grandpa's List

- Infant toys with easy-to-grasp handles
- Baby bottles: small, light, easy-to-grasp shapes; angled bottles; bottle straw
- Small building block set
- Magnetic blocks
- Toy musical instruments that require two hands to play
- Travel toothbrush holder
- Play dough accessories: rolling pin, shape cutouts, plastic molding tools, etc.
- Large building blocks (shoeboxes will substitute)
- Bristle blocks
- See 'n Say
- "Star" shaped rings

CHAPTER 7

The Third Building Block: Sensation

How Does Sensation Affect Fine Motor Skill Development?

Our hands are one of the most sensitive parts of our body. There are many nerve endings in our hands and fingers that all send information to our brain about what we are feeling so we can move our hands accurately. We have many more nerve endings in closer proximity in our hands than in our arms, legs, or feet, for example. This ability to perceive sensations helps our hands develop the coordination and variety of movements unique to humans.

The senses of touch, position, and movement, perceived by the sensory receptors in our skin, joints, and muscles in our arms and hands, all influence the development of fine motor skills. Sensation enables us to feel things, and to understand what we feel. It enables us to feel the difference between a coin and a paper clip without seeing them. It also lets us know the position of our joints and muscles, without always watching ourselves move. We don't constantly bump into things because our sensory systems are telling us where we are.

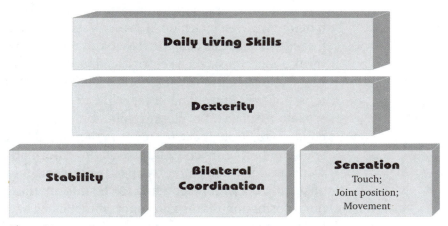

Figure 14

Sensory awareness and discrimination are important in the development of fine motor skills because:

1. They help the child learn awareness of his body for skills such as dressing and grooming.
2. They help the child learn to guide his finger movements so that skills such as printing, using utensils, and tying his shoes can become automatic.

Movement and sensation form a continuous loop. We receive sensory information to tell us to move, and once we begin to move, there is constant feedback from the sensors in our muscles and joints, enabling us to adjust and refine our movement accurately. Many of us have had the experience of walking downstairs when our vision was obscured, and have had the sensation of either expecting one more step than was there, or thinking that the flight of stairs was finished when in fact it wasn't. In both cases, our brain had prepared our muscles for a situation that did not occur. We had to make quick adjustments based on what did occur, and after a second of feeling disoriented, our muscles adapted. We don't experience this sensation when we can see the stairs, because we anticipate and our muscles prepare for what we see ahead.

Similarly, if we pick something up with our hands, we immediately adjust the muscles in our hands and arms to the size and weight of the object. When we can see the object, we anticipate its size and weight and our muscles are already prepared for it before we even pick it up. If we can't see what we are picking up, we can't anticipate it, and our muscles can only react and adjust as we actually touch and lift it. If you think about times when sensory feedback from your hands was limited, as when you were wearing gloves or your hands were very cold and you were trying to do up buttons, you will know what it feels like to have decreased coordination due to limited sensory feedback. Developing good sensory discrimination is very important for our children to be able to learn to move their hands and fingers accurately.

Our brains are constantly receiving information from all of our senses about the world around us. An important part of development of the nervous system is the process of sorting out and responding to the information from our senses, while screening out information that is not important (such as background noise). This process will be covered in detail in Chapter 11, Sensory Processing.

How Do Children with Down Syndrome Develop Sensory Skills?

Young babies have better sensation in their mouths than in their hands. That is why they bring everything to their mouths. They are exploring things with their mouths because they have a need to "feel" them, but the sensory abilities in their hands aren't yet as acute as in their lips, tongue, and gums. Late in the first year of life, babies begin to spend more time looking at and feeling things with their eyes and hands, and less time exploring things in their mouths. Their nervous system is developing, giving them better sensory perception in their hands. Because the sensory perception in the hands is becoming more precise, it gives the child more information about the world.

Nervous system development is slowed down in most children with Down syndrome. Thus, the sensory development in the hands will also be slower. Your child may continue to put toys in his mouth for longer than usual. Sometimes a child with Down syndrome will continue to mouth things for an inappropriately long time. He can't seem to move on to using his hands for more sensory exploration. This may become more difficult to manage as the child gets older, and there are toys at day care or school that are unsafe for him to put in his mouth. If he is prevented from putting anything in his mouth, he may resort to putting in his hands, which can result in red, sore hands and skin breakdown.

I have sometimes found it helpful to designate one or two appropriate small mouthing toys that are readily available to the child, even attaching them with a clip to his clothing (the way that a pacifier can be clipped onto a baby's clothing). The child can be taught that this particular toy is okay to put in his mouth, but other things are not. This child may need particular attention to helping him learn how to explore with his hands rather than his mouth. For the child who continues to need to put things in his mouth well past the expected age, emphasis on sensory experiences to his hands may help improve sensory awareness and discrimination, thereby decreasing the need for mouthing. Children who seem to crave chewing on toys may be seeking the deep pressure through the jaw that is achieved during chewing. Discussion of this sensory need is included in Chapter 11.

Some studies point out that there may be dermatological differences in children with Down syndrome (differences in the structure of the skin) that may affect how sensation is perceived. Some researchers have found that children with Down syndrome use excessive force when grasping objects, and don't adjust as readily to changes in the object's characteristics, such as a change in the weight of the object. The researchers felt this was due to a sensory deficit in the sensory-motor loop (8). In my experience, I think this use of excessive force could be due to these possibilities:

1. Children who have hypotonia have more difficulty "grading" the movements of their muscles. That is, because their joints are less stable and their muscles are floppier, they have to contract their muscles more than we would to be able to activate the muscles to move, reach, and grasp.

2. Processing of sensory information may be slower in children with Down syndrome. Therefore, when they are going to pick

something up, their muscles may not have had time to anticipate the size and weight of the object from the information they get by looking at it.

Children with Down syndrome will develop sensory discrimination abilities as all children do, through the experiences of their daily life. If they have opportunities to experience variety in what they feel and do with their hands, they will develop better abilities to anticipate, discriminate, and adjust their hand and arm muscles in response to sensory input.

AVERSION TO SENSORY PLAY

Some children do not like many of the types of sensory activities described in this chapter. They dislike getting their hands wet or sticky. This may be due to environmental expectations (they are told not to get their hands dirty), or to a dislike of the feeling. If your child doesn't like "wet" sensory play (e.g., water, finger paint, play dough), he may tolerate "dry" sensory activities (such as sand, dried beans, or macaroni). If your child likes to put everything to his mouth, you may want to choose sensory play activities that are edible, such as using chocolate pudding as finger paint, scooping and pouring with partially set Jello, or squeezing cornstarch and water instead of play dough.

It is normal for many children to dislike a new sensory experience at first, particularly if it is a cold sensation. The tactile part of the nervous system has to "figure out" every new sensory experience and determine whether it is harmful or safe. Also, be aware that the look and smell of a tactile activity can affect the way we respond to the feel of it, just as the smell and appearance of food seems to influence how good it tastes. However, when a child perceives *every* kind of tactile experience, even familiar experiences, such as a touch on the arm by another child, as threatening, his nervous system may be over-responding to the touch sensation. This may be referred to as "tactile defensiveness," or "tactile over-responsiveness." If your child seems to feel threatened by even familiar tactile experiences, you may wish to consult with an occupational therapist, who can help assess your child's sensory and motor development, and suggest a program to help. Tactile defensiveness and other sensory processing disorders will be discussed in more detail in Chapter 11.

Helping Your Child Develop Sensory Awareness and Discrimination Skills in His Hands

EARLY ACTIVITIES

MOUTHING

Infants bring everything to their mouths. This is because in the beginning, the sensory receptors in the mouth are more developed than in the hands. Make sure your child has a variety of safe, clean toys to put in his mouth at this early age. Follow the suggestions in Chapter 4 to ensure that your baby is positioned to encourage hands-to-mouth activity. As your baby's hands develop better sensation, he will stop putting things in his mouth and use his hands and eyes to explore.

Appropriate toys for your baby to put in his mouth are those that are designed for infants, and:

- have no removable parts, or parts that can break off;
- are made of a durable material that will not break down over time;
- will stand up to being bitten and chewed, as many children continue to put things in their mouths after they have teeth;
- offer a variety of textures (e.g., bumpy; smooth);
- are bright and colorful and offer other sensory information, such as visual and auditory (e.g., has a bell inside and different colors or shapes).

MASSAGE

Massaging your child's hands and arms helps alert the sensory receptors and muscles. You may find that massaging your child's hands for a few minutes using firm pressure before a fine motor activity helps prepare his hands for the coordination required. Lotion may make the experience of the massage more pleasant, but it is not necessary.

RHYMES AND SONGS

Many rhymes and songs for young children help them learn about their bodies and hands. See Chapter 8 (page 93) for words and movements to some rhymes that infants and young children often enjoy.

This little boy reaches into a tissue box to pull out frozen juice can lids.

FEELING GAMES

Games that involve guiding the hand without vision and feeling for an object can be an enjoyable way to develop sensory awareness in the hands. When Sarah was about 18 months old, we kept her small toys in a cloth bag. She would "choose" which toy to play with first by reaching in and taking one out without looking. For more of a challenge, the "Feely Bag Game" can be fun: Place a few familiar objects in a cloth or plastic bag, then either you or your child states which object he is going to find, and does so just by feeling. Another activity that is very motivating is opening and reaching into a bag of cookies, to take one out and enjoy!

Likewise, place little toys in the pockets of your child's clothing. Have him use sensation to reach in and pull them out.

SENSORY PLAY

Sensory play refers to playing with any common substances and materials that stimulate many sensory receptors on a large surface of the hand. Keep a container, such as a dishpan, alternately filled with various sensory materials such as sand, flour, corn-

Giving the child toys in a bag rather than handing the toy to him helps him develop sensory awareness as she reaches in to pull it out.

meal, dry macaroni, dry beans, play dough, ribbons, wool, cotton balls, etc. Examples of fun activities with these materials are:

1. Let your child push small toys, such as cars and trucks, through the sand, etc.
2. Scooping, pouring, filling, and emptying are entertaining activities for busy preschoolers who get their hands into various sensory materials. Your child can also scoop sand into his palm, then pour it out slowly into a dump truck, or let it run through his fingers.
3. You can wrap ribbon or yarn loosely around your toddler's individual fingers, then let him work at getting it off.
4. Playing with play dough or plasticine, as well as being a sensory activity, helps to strengthen hands and fingers, and encourages imaginative play and creativity. Some examples of what can be done with play dough to develop sensory awareness and strength in the hands are:

   - squeeze the play dough into a big ball;
   - break off little pieces and roll into small balls;
   - roll out with both hands into a snake;
   - flatten a big ball of play dough using open hands.

Play dough tools, such as plastic mallets, shape cutters, play dough knives, and other available play dough products, also help develop hand strength and coordination. See below for a recipe for homemade play dough.

PLAY DOUGH RECIPE

Walk into any daycare and you will find play dough. It offers a child many opportunities for sensory play and developing finger movements, as well as creativity and imagination.

2 cups all-purpose flour
1 cup salt
2 teaspoons alum (available at drug stores)
1 tablespoon oil
2 cups of boiling water, with food coloring for color

Mix dry ingredients well. Add boiling water and oil. Mix well. Once cooled enough, knead by hand until dough is no longer sticky. Keep in a plastic bag or air-tight container.

Sensory play helps develop sensory awareness in the hands.

SHAVING CREAM/FINGER PAINT

Many preschoolers love to create masterpieces with finger paint. Another alternative is to squirt some shaving cream or bath foam (e.g., Funny Foam) on a mirror and have your child use his fingers to trace designs. If you are concerned about your child licking his fingers, use Cool Whip, pudding, or jam instead!

WATER PLAY; BUBBLE BATH

Finding floating toys amongst the bubbles is fun, and helps your child discriminate between the different sensations: water, bubbles, toys. Washing dishes is a similar activity for the older child.

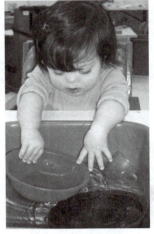

Toddlers and preschoolers love water play. Bubbles can be added for even more sensory fun.

STICKERS

To help a young child learn to be aware of the different parts of his hand or body, place small stickers on his fingers, thumb, palm, cheek, forehead, etc. that he can peel off. The sticker helps him focus in on the sensation of that part of his body; you can work on body part names at the same time.

LATER ACTIVITIES

PURSES/BACKPACKS

Many children love to have their own little purses and backpacks to carry their treasures in. These offer great opportunities for opening and closing buckles and zippers, as well as the experience of taking things in and out.

HIDE THE SCARF GAME

This is a game that Sarah enjoyed when she was three and four years old. We took turns scrunching up a small scarf and hiding it under our clothing (inside a pant leg, inside the back of the neck, inside a sleeve, etc.) When I guessed where she had it hidden, she would have to pull it out again. It helped develop body awareness, and sensory awareness in her hands.

PUSHING AND PULLING ACTIVITIES

Activities in which the arms are pushing and pulling (as described in Chapter 5: Stability) give extra sensory input to the muscles and joints, helping your child be more aware of their position and prompting his muscles to respond. In other words, these activities give input to the proprioceptive system, which enables us to detect the position and movement of parts of our body. Climbing, swinging from the arms, pushing open doors, pulling a wagon, pushing a doll stroller, toy lawn mower, and vacuum, and carrying a pail full of sand are all examples of activities that will increase the input to the proprioceptive system.

GROCERIES

Helping to put away groceries is another activity that children often enjoy. Picking up and carrying objects of different sizes and weights gives sensory information that helps them learn how to adjust their movement, balance, etc. to the needs of the task. We handle a case of eggs differently from a sack of potatoes. Offering your child experiences like this will improve his ability to make the small muscular and postural adjustments to perform everyday tasks more effectively.

GARDENING

The sensation of dirt, grass, leaves, seeds, etc. provides wonderful sensory experiences for the hands. Also, digging, raking, and shoveling are excellent for proprioceptive input into all the joints of the body, and for stability and bilateral coordination. Child-sized rakes and shovels are available for younger children.

USING A COMPUTER

When using a computer mouse, your child is relying on the sensory feedback from his hand position and movement to help guide the mouse while his eyes are focused on the screen. A variety of skill levels are required, depending on the type of computer, mouse, and program. (See page 135 for more details on computer use.)

Using a computer mouse requires good sensory awareness of hand and arm position ("proprioception"). The child's ability to use a computer also depends on cognitive development, attention, and comprehension.

Profile: Daniel

Daniel, who is four, sits at the kitchen table every morning and watches the flurry of activity around him as his parents and older siblings hurry to get their lunches packed. Today he reaches out to help, and his eight-year-old brother hands him the bag of cookies and asks him to take out two for his lunch. He then gives Daniel a piece of foil to wrap the cookies in. His mom picks up on the fact that Daniel is interested in helping, and asks him to take out two cookies for each family member, and wrap them in pieces of foil. She then gives Daniel a sandwich to put into a sandwich bag. Daniel is pleased to be able to contribute to this daily flurry of activity. Taking cookies out of the bag and putting the sandwich into a bag helps him develop his sensory and dexterity skills. Counting the cookies helps him reinforce counting skills, and the difference between one and two. Most importantly, Daniel is learning that he can contribute to the routine, and about some of the things that go into making a lunch.

Grandma's and Grandpa's List

- Suitable toys for an infant to put in his mouth; e.g., soft teething rings, infant rattles, and squeeze toys
- Cloth tunnel for crawling through
- Stickers
- Play dough, plasticine, modeling clay
- Play dough shape cutters, rolling pins, etc.
- Bubble bath or bath foam
- Backpack or purse
- Finger paint and finger paint paper
- Rocking horse or similar rocking toy
- Backyard swing, slide
- Sand art
- Stuffed toys that vibrate when pressed
- Fuzzy puzzles
- Touch and feel books
- Ball pool
- Play tent; Adventure play zones
- Tactile mats
- Touchabubbles (thicker bubbles that float more slowly and last longer)
- Labyrinth mazes that you guide a ball through by tipping the board slightly

CHAPTER 8

Dexterity

The building blocks described in the previous chapters provide the foundation upon which your child can develop more precise hand and finger movements. We call this ability to make skillful, precise, and efficient hand movements "dexterity."

As you can see from the activities suggested for helping to develop stability, bilateral coordination, and sensation, children continue to develop these foundations well into their school years. The smaller, more precise movements in the hands develop simultaneously, with the foundations permitting the control, precision, and speed to improve.

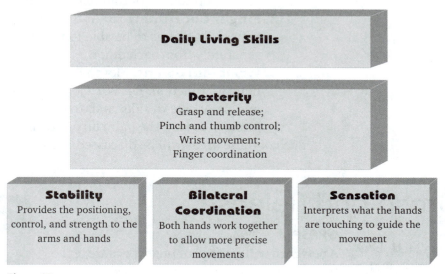

Daily Living Skills

Dexterity
Grasp and release;
Pinch and thumb control;
Wrist movement;
Finger coordination

Stability
Provides the positioning, control, and strength to the arms and hands

Bilateral Coordination
Both hands work together to allow more precise movements

Sensation
Interprets what the hands are touching to guide the movement

Figure 15

What Is Dexterity?

Dexterity is skill and ease in using the hands. Figure 16 shows the types of movement and control that children gradually develop that contribute to dexterity.

1. **Grasp and Release:** Grasping is reaching for, picking up, and holding an object. Release is letting it go purposefully.

Figure 16

2. **Pinch and Thumb Control:** "Pinch" refers to the ability to oppose the tips of the thumb and index finger in order to pick up very small objects. It is the final stage in the development of grasp, and is called "pincer grasp." To reach this stage, your child needs to develop control of thumb movement.

3. **Finger Coordination:** As fine motor development progresses, your child begins to be able to move and coordinate her fingers separately from each other.

4. **Wrist Movement:** Movements at the wrist help to position the hand for function. The wrist joint can move up and down (extend and flex); side to side; and, together with the elbow, rotate the forearm to turn the palm up or down.

Each of these areas will be discussed in turn.

1. Grasp and Release

HOW DO GRASP AND RELEASE DEVELOP?

GRASP

A newborn will grasp your finger because of the "grasp reflex." Between three and six months of age, the reflex is weakening and the baby can grasp things because she wants to. This is called "voluntary grasp." For the first several months, the baby uses her whole hand to pick things up and hold them (this is called "palmar grasp"). As she begins to move the toy around, passing it back and forth between both hands (called "transferring"), and bringing it to her

Palmar grasp.

mouth ("mouthing"), she gets sensory information about her hands and fingers. Her first attempts to pick up small items involve using all her fingers to "rake" the item into her palm ("raking grasp"). Gradually she learns to use her thumb and first two fingers to pick up objects ("tripod grasp" or "radial-digital grasp"); next, to use her thumb and index finger to pick up objects ("inferior pincer grasp"); and finally to use the tip of her thumb and index finger to pick up even the tiniest crumb ("superior pincer grasp" or "pinch").

Tripod grasp of a toy: the thumb, second, and third fingers are used to grasp and release.

RELEASE

An infant initially lets go of something in her hand accidentally, without control. Usually, this is the process: your baby is holding a toy, putting it to her mouth, until her gaze focuses on something else, when she immediately drops the first toy. As infants, babies have to be looking at something to be able to pick it up and hold it. Gradually, babies develop the ability to pick up and hold things without always having to be looking directly at them.

Inferior pincer grasp: the thumb approaches the index finger, but can't yet touch tip to tip.

Next in the development of release, she lets go with one hand while passing the object (transferring it) to her other hand. This is the beginning of bilateral coordination (Chapter 7). Then an infant begins dropping things purposefully; at this stage,

Superior pincer grasp: the thumb is rounded, allowing it to touch the tip of the index finger when grasping small things.

food often ends up on the floor as it is dropped over the side of the highchair! Dropping and throwing continue while the baby begins to let go with more control. Now she is happy to hand you something, or to release into a hole or onto a firm surface. At first, a baby needs to support the toy or her wrist on the surface as she lets go. Most babies go through this stage so quickly it is hardly noticed. Once the baby can let go of something where she wants to, she practices putting things into containers and stacking things on top of each other. By doing this, she develops more and more precision.

Building a two block tower.

Researchers have found that children with Down syndrome are delayed in their acquisition of grasping patterns, and that there is also a difference in the quality of movements they use (8).

GRASP

Your baby with Down syndrome will probably lose her reflexive (involuntary) grasp between approximately four and ten months, when her grasp becomes voluntary. Babies with very low muscle tone may take longer to develop the strength to hold onto things. It will also be more difficult for your baby to lift and move her arms to reach for things. This is because of low muscle tone and decreased stability, as described in Chapters 4 and 5.

Before developing pincer grasp, the baby approaches the Cheerio with the index finger, then scoops it into her palm.

Often, young children with Down syndrome continue to pick up objects by scooping them into their palm with all their fingers (the raking grasp) for a longer time than other children. They also use a palmar grasp to hold objects for a long time (until approximately age one and a half to three and a half years) before beginning to isolate their thumb and first two fingers. They often find it hard to pick up very small objects because their thumb can't curve to touch the tip of their index finger. Sometimes they use their thumb and third finger together, because it is easier for them to touch tip to tip with the third finger. Usually, pinch using the index finger and thumb does eventually develop, when the thumb control and positioning has improved (sometime between one and a half and four years).

Using the thumb and third finger for pincer grasp is not unusual in young children with Down syndrome, as it is often more difficult to position the thumb to touch the tip of the index finger.

Sometimes a young child with Down syndrome tucks her thumb into her palm when trying to pick up small things. This is a normal developmental stage that will change as she develops better control of her thumb, and can position it to touch her finger tips. If your child persists with this thumb position beyond the age of about two and a half, gently position her thumb when you are handing her something, so that she doesn't tuck it in.

The literature suggests that there is great variability in the age at which children with Down syndrome acquire the various grasping patterns. For example, while one child with Down syndrome may be able to pick up a raisin with a pincer grasp at 15 months, it is also within the normal range for another child to demonstrate the same skill at 42 months. Don't worry if your child takes many months to progress from one grasping pattern to another, but do continue to give her opportunities to attempt the next step.

THROWING

During the toddler years, some parents of children with Down syndrome become frustrated by their child's tendency to throw anything she picks up. In fact, this is often a real exercise in frustration tolerance for the parents! Usually this is described in a behavioral context: it is a stage that the child with Down syndrome might get "stuck" in for a prolonged

Sometimes young children with Down syndrome tuck their thumbs into their palms when grasping. This baby has one of his thumbs tucked under, and the other out straight. Try to encourage your baby to grasp with his thumb out, rather than tucked under.

This child is beginning to orient the puzzle knob towards his thumb and index finger, but still uses a raking motion to grasp it.

Low muscle tone and joint hypermobility in the thumb make it difficult for many children with Down syndrome to develop a superior pincer grasp with a rounded thumb.

period of time. If she is flinging everything, she is not able to learn some of the cognitive skills, such as taking rings on and off a peg, doing puzzles, etc., that are recommended at this stage.

This behavior pattern of throwing everything may initially develop because your child lacks the motor control to let go of things in a controlled way. She may have learned that flinging her arm causes her wrist to drop, which automatically opens her fingers and releases the toy. This can then become a behavior pattern as your child reacts to all the attention she gets when she throws things, and to the sheer fun of throwing. She also may not be able to discriminate between "throwable" items and "nonthrowable" items.

Some young children with Down syndrome take a long time to move on from the dropping and throwing stage. They need to have some opportunities to fling and throw with appropriate items, as this is a normal stage of development. Be clear and consistent about what is okay to throw, and what is not. Continue to model for your child other ways to play with the toys, and reinforce turn taking. Some baby toys have suction cups on the bottom to keep them still on the table top; using these as well as toys that are hard to throw because they are large may help reduce your child's inclination to throw everything.

Your child also may need to be taught better control of releasing things (letting go), so she won't become frustrated in her fine motor attempts, such as putting rings on the peg or blocks in the container. The throwing stage can be very discouraging for parents, but remember that it *is* a stage, and it will eventually pass. The next few pages will describe specific activities to help your child develop the skills to grasp and release.

How Can I Help My Child Develop Grasp and Release?

EARLY ACTIVITIES

GRASPING TOYS

The best toys for an infant are those that are easy to grasp and to pass from hand to hand, such as soft rattles with handles, or rings (the Skwish rattle is one example).

BANGING

When your baby has developed a firm grasp, she can strengthen it while learning to control her arm movements by banging a toy. She can do this while sitting in a high-chair, banging on the tray, or sitting in an adult's lap, banging on the tabletop. Suitable items are a spoon or rattle. Toy hammering benches (as described in Chapter 4), in which the child hammers pegs or balls with a plastic mallet through the holes, are also suitable banging toys.

DROPPING

Around the same age that she learns to give you a toy (see below), your baby will also learn to drop things. Demonstrate dropping a toy, then hand her the same toy and encourage her to let go. If she has difficulty letting go at first, hold her wrist and gently bend it down a little bit. This will release the grasp and she will drop the toy. Praise her, then encourage her to do it again on her own. Some activity examples are:

Banging toys is a normal developmental stage that helps the child strengthen his grasp and develop wrist movement.

1. Dropping a toy into the bathtub: This can be a motivating and fun bathtime activity. Using a rubber duck or similar bath toy or sponge, drop it into the water so it makes a splash, then encourage your child to do the same.
2. Dropping rubber toys onto a highchair tray, or over the edge of a highchair: It can be fun for a baby to drop something over the side of her chair, then to look for where it has gone (she is also learning about object permanence).
3. Dropping a toy to make a noise, such as into a metal bowl, or a toy that squeaks when it is dropped.

"GIVE IT TO MOMMY/DADDY"

This activity helps your baby learn how to put something down with control. Infants naturally go through the "give it to mommy/daddy" stage. They take great delight in releasing their toy into their parent's hand on request. Because they need the stability, they first place the toy down into their parent's hand, then they let go. When your child with Down syndrome is at this developmental stage, practice this skill with her, letting her see how pleased you are when she does give it to you. Immediately give it back to her, and repeat the process.

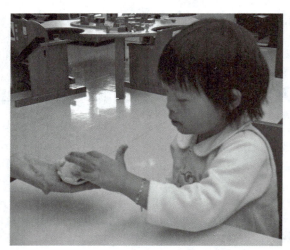

This child has just placed a toy in an adult's hand.

Once this routine is well established, you can ask your child to "put it down for mommy/daddy" on the tabletop. Have your hand ready to grasp the toy as she releases it onto the table. Gradually, the table will become the transition between your child and you, and she will learn that you will give it back to her by placing it back down on the table. Initially, your child may need to rest her wrist on the table edge before releasing the toy, giving her the support she needs.

TAKING ITEMS OUT OF CONTAINERS

Children usually take things out before they put them back in! We all know that we are more likely to find a drawer, cupboard, or our purse emptied, with the contents scattered over the floor, than to find things around the house put back where they belong! This "emptying" stage can help your child develop grasp patterns for items of different sizes and shapes. I keep all my plastic containers in a low kitchen cupboard. As a toddler, Sarah used to love to remove them all, and carefully separate the stacks. I could see that separating one from the other was helping her thumb and finger dexterity, so I put up with the disordered kitchen floor! Sometimes I would put smaller items, such as small boxes of raisins, inside the containers for her to remove. There are countless activities at home in which your child

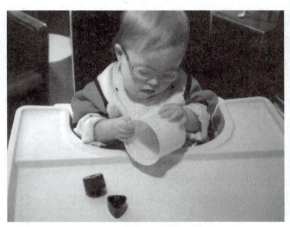
Initially, a baby will attempt to empty a container by dumping out the contents. He will then learn to reach in and take things out one at a time.

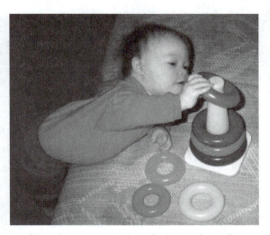
Stacking rings are a good toy for beginning to learn to put on and take off.

can practice removing things. Babies usually begin by taking parts out of their container, such as blocks out of the bin, little people out of the school bus, etc. Here are a few more ideas, progressing to activities for the preschooler:

1. Take shapes out of a shape-sorter bin.
2. Remove blocks from the bucket.
3. Take toy people out of dollhouses, Fisher-Price bus, etc.
4. Take a peg out of a pegboard.
5. Take knobbed puzzle pieces out of the puzzle board.
6. Take spools of thread out of a sewing caddy.
7. Take shoes out of a cupboard and match the pairs (don't forget to try on the shoes—that's the fun part!).
8. Take things out of a "knick-knack" drawer and reorganize into categories (for the older child).

RELEASING INTO CONTAINERS OR HOLES

When your child has learned to hand you a toy and to drop a toy, she is ready to release into containers. Picking up and putting things into containers is a normal developmental stage that helps children learn to release accurately. It can be built into your routine by tidying up toys when finished with them.

1. Using the same toys that she has learned to drop, demonstrate dropping them into a box, bag, bowl, or container. For example, drop blocks into a box where they are usually kept. Dropping things into a metal bowl will make a noise that may be motivating.

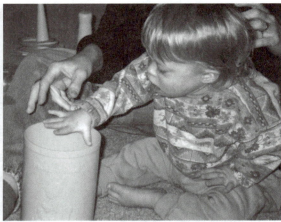

This little girl prepares to let go of the block by supporting her wrist on the rim of the container. This is a normal developmental stage in learning to let go accurately.

2. Cut a round hole in the top of a plastic yogurt or margarine container and drop in ping pong or small plastic balls. It makes an interesting noise when you shake it! Make the hole larger than the ball, so it is easy to get the ball in.

3. Some children's toys provide opportunities to practice letting go. For example, we had a Fisher-Price house with a chimney; the people figures could be dropped down the chimney and came out the other end, much to the delight of Sarah!

4. Releasing a large peg into a hole on a pegboard is another appropriate activity at this stage. You can make a "home-made" pegboard by cutting holes in a Styrofoam block and using film containers or marker lids as pegs (see Appendix 2).

5. Shape sorters, including those that make a noise as the shape moves down, are usually too difficult when the child is just learning to let go into a hole. With shape sorters, the child has to match and orient the shapes as well, so they are good activities when the child is a little bit older and is ready to learn the concept of matching shapes. The sound shape sorters can be very motivating!

Releasing into a defined hole is the next stage in learning to release with control.

Circle shapes are usually the first that children are able to match, as they are the easiest. Next are the square and triangle, and later on, the more complex shapes. Your child will probably be able to match the shape before she can orient it properly to put it in the hole. She will know that the triangle block fits the triangle hole, but may need help turning the piece until it goes in. Help her if necessary, so she won't become frustrated.

PLACING ITEMS DOWN

As your child is developing the ability to let go with enough control to put things into containers, she will soon be ready to begin placing things down in an upright position on a flat surface. You have been preparing her for this by asking her to hand you things into your hand.

Placing objects down in an upright position helps the child develop better control.

For many children, these stages of handing, dropping, releasing into containers, and placing down all seem to happen almost simultaneously, and you may find that you don't need to plan specific activities for each of the stages. Other children need specific guidance through the stages, as they do represent small increments in control of letting go. This may be especially true for children who have very low muscle tone and have difficulty controlling the movements of their arms due to poor stability. Again, I could suggest pages of possible activities for learning to control release when placing down. In general, I recommend using toys or household items that your child is interested in. Here are a few specific suggestions:

1. Placing a cup down on the table after drinking. To make this more successful, pour only a small amount of liquid into the cup, and if necessary, use a weighted cup, so that even if your child doesn't place it down flat, it rights itself (such as a "Tommee-Tippee" cup).
2. After dropping toys into the bathtub, show your child how to pick them up and place them on the side of the tub. The toy is then ready for another "dive"!
3. Release a toy car at the top of an incline (such as on a toy garage set) and watch it roll down.
4. Place Fisher-Price people figures standing up on the table or floor.
5. Place salt and pepper shakers upright.
6. Set toy bowling pins down on the floor in an upright position to play a game of bowling.

POWER "PALMAR GRASP"

Your child is already banging toys together, and on a surface. Look for toys that encourage your child to encircle the handle with her fingers and thumb. This will help her strengthen the joints in her thumb, in preparation for isolating her thumb and fingers to pick up smaller items. Make sure that the object fits between the thumb and index finger as it is held in the palm. Some children with Down syndrome tuck their thumb up beside their index finger as they hold an object in their palm. This can lead to delays in developing control of their

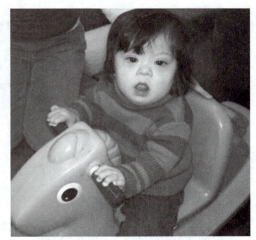

Grasping handles (known as the "power grasp") helps shape and strengthen the child's hands.

thumb joints and the ability to touch the tips of their thumb and index finger together (superior pincer grasp).

Some examples of objects appropriate for encircling with the thumb and fingers are:

1. A cup without a handle, placing the thumb around the cup;
2. Toy plastic hammer and other toy tools;
3. Plastic travel toothbrush holder;
4. Small balls;
5. Balls of play dough/plasticine;
6. Any toy with a handle.
7. Push toys, such as a doll carriage, lawn mower, and early walking push toys.

POINTING

Your child will now also be pointing, an important stage in isolating the index finger (see page 92). Sometimes young children with Down syndrome point and poke with their thumb. When they do this, they are pushing back on their already loose thumb joint. It is better for their thumb to encircle the other fingers while the index finger points. Guide your child into this position if she needs help. Pointing to body parts, to pictures in books, and to familiar items and people (e.g., "where's daddy?"; "where's the dog?") can encourage this skill.

PUZZLES

Puzzles challenge your child to release accurately. She also gains concepts of matching and visual perception when doing puzzles. Here is a guideline to the types of puzzles available, in a developmental sequence:

1. Wooden or foam insert puzzles of only three or four large pieces. The wooden ones have large knobs to hold onto when removing and putting the pieces back in. Teach her to remove a single piece, then place it right back in. Next, remove two pieces, and place them back in, and so on. Name the puzzle shape and describe what she is doing; e.g., "You're putting the banana *in*."

2. Foam or wooden puzzles with a few pieces that fit together to make one picture;

3. Wooden insert puzzles with more pieces and smaller knobs (such as those made by Simplex). This is often the first type of puzzle a child experiences, but it may be too difficult to begin with. Try the first two types of puzzles first, until your child gets the idea of each shape fitting in only one space, and understands that she may have to move it around a little bit so it will

Puzzles: (L-R top row) large knobs insert puzzle, large knob fit together puzzle, small knob insert puzzle; (L-R bottom row) foam insert puzzle, small knob fit together puzzle, large piece fit together puzzle, interlocking piece puzzle with frame, interlocking piece puzzle without frame.

fit in. Then move on to the puzzles with the small knobs, which also provide the opportunity to practice pincer grasp.

4. Wooden, cardboard, or foam puzzles with interlocking pieces, in which the puzzle piece matches the picture underneath, and there is a border or frame for structure.

5. Puzzles with interlocking pieces without a frame or border. Whether they be foam, wood, or cardboard, this type of puzzle also comes in all levels of difficulty.

TOYS THAT PROMOTE TRIPOD (RADIAL-DIGITAL) GRASP

Through all of the above activities, your child has been gradually refining the movements in her hands. She is beginning to isolate her thumb and first two fingers to pick up and release things. At this stage, she benefits from having opportunities to play with toys that promote this "tripod grasp." If your child seems to need help learning how to approach an object without raking it into her palm, begin by holding the object up for her to grasp. I have seen many children who will rake an item into their palm when it is on the table, but who will use a tripod grasp when the item is held up for them to grasp.

Some toy and activity suggestions to promote a tripod grasp are:

1. square blocks;
2. large pegs;
3. puzzles with large knobs;
4. putting marker lids back on (usually young children with Down syndrome use their whole hand to remove marker lids, because they are on too tightly for a tripod grasp to work);
5. spice bottles or film canisters (these can be filled with something that will make an interesting noise, such as rice);
6. lat discs, such as frozen juice can lids, which encourage tripod grasp and are a good preparation for pincer grasp. You can paste fabric onto them so they have different textures. Your child can practice releasing them into a slot cut in the top of a plastic container.

(left) Toys such as these rings that promote opening and rounding between the thumb and index finger are appropriate for the toddler who is developing tripod grasp. (middle) Pegs and blocks promote tripod grasp (using the thumb in opposition to the first two fingers), in preparation for developing the more precise pincer grasp. Placing the blocks into the holes and onto the table helps the child refine his control of letting go. (right) Pegboards help her direct her hand to a specific target.

Profile: Emily

Emily is an active three-year-old who loves bubble baths (and since she is into everything, she seems to need one every night!). She loves to pour the bubble bath liquid into the running water in the bath, but pours too much in, so her mom replaced the bubble bath bottle lid with one from a shampoo bottle that has a flip top and a small hole. Every time she has a bath, Emily flips up the lid (developing finger strength) and squeezes a bit into the tub (hand and finger strength). She then stirs the water with her hand to make more bubbles (wrist movement, and moving the wrist and hand while keeping the shoulder and body stable). While in the tub, she enjoys "cleaning" the sides and rim with colorful sponge shapes. She can squeeze the water out of the sponges to make a rain shower (also strengthening hand muscles). Also in the bath she has squirt and squeeze bottles (hand and finger strength) and some cups and containers for pouring (wrist movement and stability).

2. Pinch (Pincer Grasp) and Thumb Control

A baby initially uses her whole hand to grasp and release things. As she develops, she begins to use her thumb, index, and middle fingers for most activities requiring accuracy and control. The most challenging grasp is the pincer grasp, the ability to pick up very small items using the thumb and index finger in opposition. Children first learn to bring the sides or pads of their thumb and index finger together for grasp (this is referred to as an *inferior pincer grasp*). Picking up fingertip to fingertip, such as when picking a straight pin up off a table, is called the *superior pincer grasp.* This grasp is particularly difficult for children with Down syndrome due to hypermobility of the thumb joint. The thumb joint often hyperextends (bends backward) in this position, making it more difficult for the grasp to be precise. Developing correct positioning and control in the thumb joints using the activities on pages 86 and 87 will help build the strength in the thumb to begin to attempt activities using a pincer grasp.

EARLY ACTIVITIES

FINGER FEEDING

For Sarah, the most motivating activity to develop pincer grasp was picking up little pieces of food. Blueberries and Cheerios were her favorites! Other examples of food that can be used are little pieces of bread, mini marshmallows, and raisins. If your child can't pick up food from the table top, hold the piece out for her, and, if necessary, guide her thumb and index finger to take it from you.

Holding up small pieces of food for your child to take from you helps him in his attempt to use a pincer grasp.

Initially, I had to actually break Cheerios in half and soften the pieces with a little bit of milk for Sarah. She was ready to develop her fine motor skills of picking up small pieces, but didn't have the oral motor skills to manage a whole dry Cheerio. Some small foods pose a choking hazard and should not be used. These include peanuts, other nuts, whole grapes (can be cut into small pieces and pits removed), and hot dog slices. Use your judgment; if your child coughs, or in any way has difficulty with small pieces of food, do not use this activity.

STACKING CUPS

Encourage your child to separate stacking cups or plastic containers without dumping them. She need not stack them on top of each other, if this is still too difficult, but can just practice taking them in and out of each other and learning about size differences. You can make your own stacking cups with different sizes of plastic containers or plastic cups nested together.

Separating stacking cups encourages the child to use his thumb and fingers in a tripod grasp.

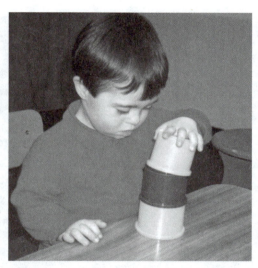

Stacking cups offer opportunities for size discrimination, accuracy of release, thumb control, and fun!

RELEASING INTO SLOTS

To release into a slot, your child must hold the object between her thumb and fingers, and hold her wrist stable. As mentioned above, give your child juice can lids to put into slots you have cut into the lid of a plastic container. It will be easier at first for your child to put the lid into a horizontal slot, rather than a vertical slot. This is because with a vertical slot she also must turn her wrist. Adding another movement always makes the activity harder!

LATER ACTIVITIES

RELEASING INTO SLOTS

As your child gets older, she can try these activities:
1. releasing poker chips or coins into a piggy bank;
2. putting the coins into the parking meter, pay phone, newspaper dispensing box, or other coin-operated machines in the community.
3. playing the game Connect Four.

STACKING ACTIVITIES

The final stage of learning accuracy with release is to be able to stack things on top of one another. How high a child is able to build a block tower is a standard item that is evaluated on many developmental tests. In typical development, a child can stack one block on top of another by about 14 months, 6 blocks by 2 years, and 10 blocks by 3 years. Your child's ability to stack blocks indicates the degree of control she has achieved in shoulder, arm, wrist, and hand movements, as well as cognitive understanding of the task. You can help your child prepare for being able to stack blocks by doing some of the following activities:

1. Stack rings on a peg. A toy such as the Fisher-Price Stacking Rings can be used, or a home-made alternative (see Appendix 2).
2. Stack large blocks, tissue boxes, or shoeboxes on the floor, and be sure to give your child the pleasure of knocking down the tower!
3. Stack paperback books on top of each other.
4. Stack full rolls of toilet paper.
5. Stack magnetic blocks. The magnets hold the blocks together, so it is not as frustrating for the child.
6. Stack stacking cups, such as the Battat Sort and Stack set. You may have to hand your child the cups one at a time, until she learns to discriminate size and can do them in order.

TOYS WITH MOVEABLE PARTS

When your child no longer puts things into her mouth, she can play with toys that have smaller parts. This is *not* recommended until your child is at the developmental age of three years, and no longer puts toys in her mouth. Toys that have small parts that can be manipulated or moved encourage children to use tripod and pincer grasps. Here are examples of but a few types of toys:

Toys such as these people figures promote individual finger movement during play.

- construction toys (such as Tinkertoys, Lego, Mechano Junior, K'nex, or Construx);
- people/animal figures that have limbs that move (such as Playmobil, Little Tykes);
- small pegboards (Lite Brite is an example, but I have found that it can be difficult to push the pegs in and this can be frustrating for the child);
- Mr. Potato Head;
- trucks and cars that have levers to move parts (such as a dump truck).

STRENGTHENING ACTIVITIES

When your child can use the pincer grasp to pick up and release small objects, she can continue to develop strength in this position, which will help her later with activities such as printing. Activities that can help:

- breaking off little pieces of crusty bread or bagel;
- pinching off bits of play dough or plasticine;
- popping plastic "bubble" packaging material (don't leave children alone with this!)

Clothespins help strengthen pincer grasp in the older child.

Pushing thumb tacks into a cork bulletin board strengthens pincer grasp.

- pulling apart Lego pieces;
- squeezing clothespins (helping to hang up or take down clothes on the clothesline);
- pulling caps off/on pens and markers;
- poking toothpicks into a firm substance, such as pieces of cheese, or play dough
- games with "pop-a-dice" (plastic dome that you press on to "shake" dice), such as Frustration or Trouble
- peeling the backing off bandaids and putting it on a doll (or themselves!)
- grasping a zipper and zipping it up and down.

3. Finger Coordination

One way a baby learns about her hands is by moving her fingers separately. She pokes and points, and gazes attentively as she plays with her fingers. Sensory play, as described in Chapter 7, helps develop separate movements of the fingers. Toddlers and preschoolers also enjoy songs and rhymes, many of which have actions and finger plays. I have listed some finger rhymes below. This is a wonderful stage for helping your child develop individual finger movements.

The ability to move the fingers separately from each other becomes important for activities such as using a computer keyboard, and many self-help skills, such as tying shoelaces and using a can opener.

In Chapter 5, body and shoulder *stability* were discussed. When the child reaches this level in fine motor development, *dexterity,* she begins to develop the third type of stability: hand stability. For many daily activities requiring dexterity and finger coordination, we stabilize the little finger side of our hand while the thumb side of our hand coordinates the movement. Think of turning a key in a lock, of writing, and of using a can opener. When doing these activities, we usually keep our fourth and fifth fingers still (stable) while moving the thumb, index, and middle fingers. As mentioned in Chapter 3, some children with Down syndrome who have clinodactyly or camptodactyly keep their fifth finger lifted away from the surface during fine motor activities. By doing so, they may be losing some stability and control in their hand.

EARLY ACTIVITIES

POINTING

This early developmental activity is the beginning of developing finger coordination for more complicated functions. The index finger points while the rest of the hand is stabilized. If your child points with all her fingers extended, or uses her thumb, gently guide the rest of her hand to close, leaving just the index finger to point.

POKING

When your child can isolate her index finger for pointing, she begins to poke her finger into holes and openings. Sometimes children with Down syndrome will poke with their thumb or middle finger. Help your child to position her hand to poke with the index finger. Children are quite interested in poking their finger into holes, and usually don't need much encouragement. Some safe opportunities for poking are:

- Fisher-Price toy people, which have little holes in the bottom, perfect for little poking fingers;
- holes in Duplo blocks;
- preschool books with finger holes;
- finger puppets;
- toy dial phones;
- button holes in clothing;
- plastic pop bottle tops.

(left) When pointing, the child begins to isolate his index finger. It is not uncommon for children with Down syndrome to use both the thumb and index finger to point, as seen here, or to use just the thumb. Encouraging him to close his thumb will help him develop hand arching instead of the flattening palm so frequently seen in children with Down syndrome. Turning pages of a books helps develop control of thumb and finger movements. (right) These stacking cubes have little holes that are perfect for inserting little fingers.

SENSORY ACTIVITIES

The activities described in Chapter 7 help your child establish sensory awareness and discrimination that help her learn to recognize sensory information from the different parts of her hand. This then forms the foundation for being able to move the different parts of her hand separately, rather than as one unit.

1. When she is playing with a sensory material, such as shaving cream, encourage her to spread her fingers apart and then bring them together.
2. Weave a piece of ribbon or yarn in and out of her fingers to give her a sensory and visual awareness of her individual fingers.
3. Scoop a handful of sand or cornmeal and let it slowly run down through the fingers.

The child uses thumb and finger movement to push and turn knobs on the pop-up toy.

BUTTONS AND SWITCHES

Most children love turning things on and off. Having opportunities to do this at home helps your child develop individual finger movement and thumb-finger control. Some examples of daily home activities are:

Using a phone develops thumb control.

- turning light switches on/off (you may have to lift your child up to reach);
- letting her ring the door-bell when you go into your house, just for fun;
- pop-up toys;
- pushing the elevator button;
- switching on the stereo;
- pushing buttons on a child's tape player;
- pushing the buttons on a phone.

ACTION SONGS AND FINGER RHYMES

Preschoolers love action songs and finger rhymes! They are fun and they help children imitate actions and develop finger coordination.

Begin with action songs that are familiar and are sung in preschool programs, such as "Wheels on the Bus," "If You're Happy and You Know It," "Eensy Weensy Spider," etc. Through these songs your child learns to imitate actions. When she understands imitation, and knows many of the actions on her own, you can recite finger rhymes, which use imitation to reinforce separate movement of fingers. Here are some examples of finger rhymes, in approximate developmental order:

1.
Round and round the garden
Like a teddy bear (circling your finger around your child's upheld palm)
One step, two steps ("walking" your fingers up child's arm)
Tickle you under there! (tickling under child's arm)
(Your child can take a turn doing it for you.)

2.
I have ten little fingers
And they all belong to me (wiggling all fingers)
I can make them do things
Would you like to see?
I can shut them up tight (squeezing into a fist)
I can open them wide (stretching them apart)
I can put them together (interlocking them)
And I can make them hide (putting them behind your back)
I can make them jump high (reaching up)
I can make them jump low (reaching down)
I can roll them around (rotating hands around each other)
And fold them just so (put them together in your lap).

3.
Two little blackbirds
Sitting on a wall (lifting index fingers of both hands)
One named Peter
The other named Paul (wiggling each finger in turn)
Fly away Peter (move one hand behind your back)
Fly away Paul (move other hand behind your back)
Come back Peter (bring back first hand, finger wiggling)
Come back Paul (bring back other hand) (23).

4.
Where is Thumbkin, where is Thumbkin? (hiding both fists behind back)
Here I am, here I am! (lifting both thumbs in front)
How are you this morning?
Very well I thank you (wiggling one thumb, then the other)
Run and hide, run and hide (tuck thumbs into fists again)
(Continue for each finger, trying to lift each individually and wiggle. Often they are named Pointer, Middle Man or Tall Man, Ring Man, and Baby or Pinkie.)

5.
Here is the beehive (holding up fist)
Where are the bees?
Hiding inside where nobody sees
Here they come, out of the hive
One, two, three, four, five! (lifting fingers one at a time)
Bzzzzz! (wiggling fingers and tickling)

6.
One, two, three, four, five (lift fingers from fist one at a time)
Once I caught a fish alive
Six, seven, eight, nine, ten (lift fingers from other hand one at a time)
Then I let it go again
Why did I let it go?
Because it bit my finger so
Which little finger did it bite?
This little finger on my right (wiggling baby finger)

BOOKS

The many benefits of books for all children are well known. An early introduction to books helps develop language skills, cognitive concepts, and an understanding of the world. Books can also be useful in helping your child develop fine motor skills.

1. Board books are best for infants and toddlers, as the pages can't rip and are easier for children to hold and turn.
2. Holding a book open with both hands is a good bilateral activity.
3. Pointing to pictures develops pointing and picture recognition.
4. Preschoolers enjoy lift-the-flap books, such as the Spot the dog books. These help the child anticipate what is to come next. I have found that

the flaps may be tricky for young children with Down syndrome to grasp and lift. Rather than lifting the flap for your child, either fold a corner of the flap, or add a divider tab (used to indicate sections of a school binder) to the flap to make it easier to grasp.

5. Picture books with tabs to push, pull, and turn are also readily available. It is easy to pull too hard and rip the tab. Try reinforcing the tab with scotch tape.

6. As your child gets older, she will look at books with paper pages. When holding the book open with the left hand she gets good thumb control practice, as she lifts her thumb to "catch" the next page being turned.

LATER ACTIVITIES

CARD GAMES

Picking up and holding cards can help develop hand stability and finger coordination. Some activities to do with cards are:

1. Pick up and put away cards one by one into the box.
2. Pick up cards one at a time and add them to the cards being held in the other hand.
3. Deal cards: Even though your child is slow at dealing (goodness knows Sarah is!), try to be patient! Dealing cards not only is a good fine motor activity for the school-aged child, but it is good for sequencing and counting.
4. Fan the cards to hold while playing a game. If this is too difficult, use a plastic card holder (often used by seniors), which you can probably find at a toy store.

A card holder may make things easier for the child who has difficulty holding, releasing, and adding cards during a game.

GAMES

Many commercially available games use finger movements, particularly of the index finger, to play the game. Some examples are: Don't Wake Daddy; Ants in the Pants; Rebound; Kerplunk; Hungry Hungry Hippos; and games that have spinners.

HOUSEHOLD ACTIVITIES

There are many opportunities throughout the day to let your child try things that you would normally do. When Sarah was about eight, she was keen to try unlocking the door with the key and opening the door latch, both of which helped her dexterity. When we weren't too rushed, she buttered her own bread or toast. Spreading helped develop hand stability, which helped her later when she learned to tie shoelaces and use a can opener. A small-sized knife with a blunt end should be used by a child.

Pushing buttons on a microwave helps finger coordination as well as developing food preparation skills, number recognition, and a sense of time. Likewise, using a TV remote control and entering the numbers on a phone helps finger control, while teaching number skills. Video games (used in moderation) can help your child develop better control and speed of finger movements.

DRESSING

Putting on gloves can be a dress-up game, with your child trying on adult-sized gloves. This helps her move each finger separately into the finger openings. Doing up zippers and buttons requires the ability to move fingers separately, and stabilize the rest of the hand. Specific strategies for dressing and other self-help activities are in Chapter 10.

SPRAY BOTTLES AND SQUIRT GUNS

To operate a squirt gun, your child must stabilize it in the hand while the thumb and index finger pull and release the trigger. Trying to pop bubbles with water from a squirt gun is a good eye-hand coordination activity. Your child can also help you clean your windows and mirrors or water your plants using a spray bottle.

"COLLECTING" IN THE HAND

Picking up several small objects one by one and tucking them into the palm is challenging because you are doing two things with your hand at once. These activities are appropriate for the older child who has good pincer grasp. If your child needs to help with her other hand initially, that is fine. Some activity examples are:

This picture demonstrates thumb rounding for pincer grasp, and collecting in the hand. Releasing into a vertical slot, as shown here, is usually more difficult than releasing into a horizontal slot, because of the wrist positioning required. Once the first coin is released, the child uses hand movement to bring the coin forward to her fingertips to release it as well.

1. When tidying up small pieces of a game or toy, make a game out of it by challenging your child to see how many pieces she can pick up one at a time and hold in her hand before it "overflows."
2. Let your child help you count your change by picking up the coins one at a time and keeping them in her hand.
3. Have her pick up raisins one at a time to collect a handful for a "flavor burst!"
4. After your child can pick up and hold several small items, she can try bringing them out, one at a time, without helping with the other hand, such as we do when putting a handful of change into a parking meter or vending machine one at a time.
5. Some games, such as Don't Spill the Beans, involve holding small pieces in the palm while placing them down one by one.

Profile: Alexander

Nine-year-old Alexander is the official "toast maker" in his family. Each morning he is responsible for making toast. First he undoes the twist tie on the bread bag (developing finger coordination). Then he puts the bread into the toaster, pushing down the lever (developing finger strength). When the toast pops up, he butters it using soft butter or margarine (hand stability). If somebody wants honey on their toast, he dips the knife into the honey jar and turns the knife in his fingers until the honey stops dripping (individual finger movement). Although this was a little bit messy at first, with the daily practice Alexander has developed a lot more finger control, which seems to be carrying over into some school tasks, such as cutting and gluing.

4. Wrist Movement

Our wrist positions and stabilizes our hand for function and precision. Whereas our elbow only moves in and out, our wrist moves from side to side, up and down, and helps to turn the palm up and down. If you turn your own hand palm up and pretend you are catching some sand being poured into it, you will notice that your hand arches in several directions, enabling your hand to form a little "cup."

Sometimes rotating the forearm to turn the palm up and "cup" the hand is difficult for young children with Down syndrome. Often the hand appears flattened, without the development of the "arches" in the hand. This is not unusual when there is low muscle tone in the hands.

Placing the back of the hand down on the table can help your child hold something in her palm.

When we hold a pen and write, we usually bend our wrist up (in extension) to position our hand most efficiently. Positioning our wrist in this way is a developmental progression and will not be seen in the very young child, who keeps her wrist straight. Some children with Down syndrome may not automatically progress to using an extended wrist position for fine motor activities. Because our hands work more efficiently in this position, your child's speed and control will be more likely to improve if you help her learn to position her hand in wrist extension.

EARLY ACTIVITIES

PLAY AND EATING

Wrist movement starts to develop for toddlers during play and eating. Your child will turn her wrist and forearm while holding something in order to see it better, or to bring it to her mouth. As she grows, she will rotate her wrist to help position toys and parts, especially toys that have interlocking pieces.

"GIVE ME FIVE"

This familiar, fun greeting encourages your child to rotate her wrist to offer her palm to get "five." You can also promote accuracy of arm movements by doing the "up high, down low, to the side" version.

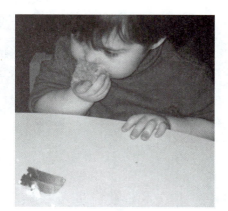

Wrist rotation usually occurs spontaneously during play and eating.

SENSORY PLAY

Pouring sand, dry beans, or macaroni into your child's palm encourages her to rotate her wrist and "cup" her palm. This will be easier if she cups both hands and holds them together.

PLAY DOUGH/PLASTICINE

Flattening a ball of play dough with the palms of the hands promotes wrist extension, as does rolling out play dough with a rolling pin.

DRAWING AT AN EASEL

Using an upright surface such as an easel or blackboard helps promote wrist extension when painting or drawing. Ideally, the surface is at the child's eye level. The same wrist motion is used when painting walls (you may or may not want to attempt this!)

SELF-HELP ACTIVITIES

You can request the cupped hand position, palm up, from your child in many daily activities:

1. If your child takes daily vitamins, pour the vitamin (or have her pour her own) into her palm.
2. When washing her hair, squeeze the shampoo into her palm.
3. Squeeze liquid soap or lotion into her palms.
4. If she is helping you in the kitchen, she can pour the salt into her palm to put into the pot.
5. What better motivation than another child who wants to share their Smarties or M & M's!

Some younger children may not be able to hold things in their palm. For a routine activity, such as the vitamins, have your child hold the bottle cap in her palm, as it places her hand in the correct position, and enables her to "catch" the vitamin. Reinforcing this position day after day will eventually help her develop the ability to arch her hand on her own to hold things in her palm.

CANTEEN

There are many colorful drinking cups with lids for children. The type that has the straw inside the lid, which must be turned to expose the straw, promotes wrist movement from side to side.

HOUSEHOLD ACTIVITIES

Some activities that encourage wrist movement are:

- opening jars and lids;
- turning a key in a lock; e.g., Chicco toy with keys;
- turning doorknobs;
- turning knobs; e.g., on the dishwasher or washing machine;
- stirring; e.g., mixing a glass of chocolate milk;
- shaking; e.g., shaking a bottle of salad dressing, fruit juice, or anything else that says "shake before opening";
- sprinkling; e.g., sprinkling parmesan cheese on spaghetti;
- pouring a little bit of fish food into the hand to sprinkle into the fish bowl;
- rolling out dough or pie crust;
- moving a computer mouse;
- using a hand-held pencil sharpener.

TOYS AND GAMES

- shaking dice during a game and holding cards, which encourages wrist rotation;
- throwing a Frisbee (your child must flick her wrist down, then up);
- tossing a small beanbag from one hand to the other (to catch it, she'll turn her palm up, and to toss it, she'll turn her palm and wrist downward);
- playing with a Slinky, palms up and holding the Slinky in both hands while it "slides" from one side to the other;
- winding and unwinding kite string from the spindle;
- playing racquet games (ping pong, badminton, tennis);
- playing Foosball;
- playing with a magnetic dart game, where the wrist is cocked back to release the dart.

MUSICAL INSTRUMENTS

Shakers, maracas, bells, and tambourines all use wrist movement. It can be a lot of fun to join in with your favorite CD with your own instrument!

Dexterity: Summary

There are four main developmental patterns that occur as our children develop dexterity:

1. More control is gained at the wrist, leading to the ability to rotate the wrist to turn the palm up, and to performing precise hand skills with the wrist bent up (extended).
2. Grasp and release patterns progress from grasping in the palm to using the tips of the thumb and fingers.
3. More control is gained in the thumb, leading to the ability to position the thumb to oppose the index finger.
4. Movement control in the fingers progresses so that the fingers are able to move separately from each other, and your child can perform a variety of movements with different parts of the hand.

Grandma's and Grandpa's List

GRASP & RELEASE
- Bath toys
- Activity center/floor gym
- Building blocks
- Stacking rings/stacking cups and other stacking toys
- Shape sorters
- Workbench/tool play set
- Puzzles: with large knobs; sponge puzzles; small knobs; interlocking pieces, depending on the developmental level of the child
- Toy diggers
- Baby Discovery toys (Fisher-Price)
- Fisher-Price Little People (e.g., school bus)
- Ball mazes (larger balls for younger children, marbles for older children)

PINCH & THUMB CONTROL
- Peg boards (large pegs or small, depending on the developmental age of the child)
- Piggy bank
- Etch-a-Sketch
- Bead stringing set
- Modeling clay, plasticine
- Stamp pad
- Duplo, Lego, other construction toys
- Wire bead frames (colorful beads can be moved along the interwoven colored wire)
- Tweezer games (such as tweezer marble games; Operation)

FINGER COORDINATION
- Spray bottles
- Squirt guns
- Simple card games
- Musical instruments (toy or real): piano, recorder, sax, guitar, or banjo
- Puppets and finger puppets
- Books: board books, flap books, pop-up and tab books, picture books, etc.
- Toy dial phone
- Child's tape player
- Games such as Connect 4, Ants in the Pants, Ker-Plunk, Mr. Potato Head
- String art
- Construction toys, such as blocks, Duplo, Lego, Tinkertoys, Mechano (junior), K'nex
- Moveable people/animal figures or dolls such as Little Tykes, Playmobil, Fisher-Price
- Gloves
- Toy cash register
- Dressing puzzles

WRIST MOVEMENT
- Frisbee
- Slinky
- Beanbags
- Drink Canteen
- Barrel of monkeys
- Racquet games
- Musical instruments (bells, shakers, maracas, tambourines)
- Magnetic dart game
- Toy football
- Bubble wands

Handy Basket: Toys and Activities to Keep Handy

Over the years I have found it helpful to keep a number of activies handy in a plastic basket. They are ready to be pulled out whenever there is an opportunity for Sarah to play with "her basket." These pages can be copied and posted for quick reference, to give parents a general idea of the type of activities that can be kept handy to help their child develop dexterity skills.

HANDY BASKET: BIRTH–2 YEARS	HAND DEVELOPMENT GOALS	ITEM/ACTIVITY	SKILLS DEVELOPED
	watching hands	hanging toys to reach for and grab onto	swatting; moving hands in visual field
	reaching	rattles, toys with handles to grasp and shake	grasping and holding; moving whole arm; stability
	grasping in palm	toys safe to put in mouth	sensory exploration
	passing from hand to hand	easy to grasp with both hands	hands working together
	grasping on thumb side of hand	blocks/container; large pegboard	thumb control; using fingers for grasp
	placing toys down	pegs and rings	accuracy of placing and letting go
	uses both hands for play	simple manipulative toys (e.g., pop apart beads, Duplo, activity boxes)	coordinating both hands to pull apart/put together

Toys for birth to two years.

Toys for two to four years.

isolated finger movement	ribbon/wool; board books; toys with holes for poking	sensory awareness of fingers; pointing; poking
moving/rotating objects with hands	insert puzzles; shape sorters	finger coordination; wrist movement

HANDY BASKET: 2-4 YEARS	**HAND DEVELOPMENT GOALS**	**ITEM/ACTIVITY**	**SKILLS DEVELOPED**
	accurate placing and letting go (release)	blocks; stacking rings; pegs in pegboard	accurately aligning objects; positioning and releasing
	using thumb and index finger for pincer grasp	picking up and letting go of small objects, e.g., raisins, Cheerios; removing insert puzzle pieces with knobs	pincer grasp and release; thumb strength
	wrist rotation	pouring activities/water play; pouring objects into palm	turning forearm and wrist to position the hand
	palmar grasp of crayon	preprinting activities with markers and crayons	initial developmental grasp of crayon
	digital-pronate grasp of crayon	drawing, coloring, painting	next stage in progression of pencil grasp
	more use of one hand as preferred (but still switches often)	activities requiring both hands, but the hands have different movements, e.g., Tinkertoys; stringing large beads on pipe cleaner	bilateral coordination; development of preferred hand
	isolated finger movement to manipulate objects	play dough: rolling into snake, balls; breaking off little pieces; picture books; finger puppets; scissors	movement of small joints in hand; sensation in hand
	tripod grasp of crayon	preprinting activities	prepares hand to learn visual-motor skills such as printing; control of pencil; movement

Activities for five to eight years.

Activities for nine to twelve years.

HANDY BASKET: 5-8 YEARS	HAND DEVELOPMENT GOALS	ITEM/ACTIVITY	SKILLS DEVELOPED
	tripod grasp	chalk, marker, crayons, paint brushes; coloring and activity books	holding writing utensils in tripod grasp; directing strokes and coloring
	wrist rotation	wallet: emptying coins to palm; small bottles and jars; turning key toy	forming "cup" with palm to hold items; control of amount of wrist rotation and speed
	accurate pincer grasp and release, with more speed	stringing small beads; coins into piggy bank; clothespegs; small Lego pieces	strength of thumb and index finger; faster, more automatic movements
	uses a preferred hand, other hand assists	lacing activities; stringing beads; tracing stencils; sticker books; kaleidoscope; construction toys (e.g., Lego)	hand dominance; coordination of the two hands working together; assistant hand learns how to make fine adjustments
	control of small joint movement	rolling small balls out of play dough; sharpening a pencil; manipulating small moveable toys (e.g., Playmobil people); doing up snaps, buttoning; doing up zippers; drawing tiny circles; scissors: cutting corners, curves	sensory awareness of movements of small joint of the hand; strength of fingers; using different fingers for different movements; ability to turn an object around in the hand without holding it against the body

HANDY BASKET: 9-12 YEARS	HAND DEVELOPMENT GOALS	ITEM/ACTIVITY	SKILLS DEVELOPED
	automatic, quick movement of individual fingers	putting bobby pins on card; opening and closing large safety pins; tying knot in scarf or stiff shoelaces; twisting pipe cleaners together; opening and closing twist ties; breaking off pieces of tape; doubling elastic bands around a deck of cards; putting paper clips on card	precise control of small movements for functional activities
	in-hand manipulation	put coins in piggy bank, taking one at a time from the palm with same hand; shuffling cards; braiding stiff laces or pipe cleaners; turning pencil around in hand to erase (without using other hand to help)	development of all the muscles in the hand
	automatic visual-motor skills	dot-to-dot books; printing, drawing, or coloring; scissors: cutting small shapes; craft activities	refinement of visual-motor abilities will help develop written communication skills

CHAPTER 9

Daily Living Skills: School-Related Tasks

If you look at the fine motor skills "house model," you will see that your child uses the building blocks and dexterity abilities to take on new challenges when he gets to school. School-related activities challenge children not only to use their developing dexterity, but also to coordinate this with visual and perceptual skills.

At this stage in your child's development, you may hear the phrase "visual motor skills." Visual motor development includes all the skills that require the coordination of the eyes guiding the hands, and are usually in reference to paper-related activities. Visual motor activities discussed in this chapter include preprinting, drawing, coloring, printing, handwriting, computer use, and cutting.

School Tasks: Visual Motor Skills
Cutting;
Preprinting;
Printing;
Drawing and coloring;
Writing;
Computer use

Dexterity
Pencil grasp;
Holding scissors; coordinating movement;
Moving small joints of the hand;
Finger coordination;
Wrist movement

Stability
Upright body;
Head positioned to
see hands;
Shoulder, elbow, and wrist
hold hand steady

Bilateral Coordination
One hand has become domi-
nant over the other;
Other hand assists

Sensation
Sensory memory of how
to move hands to form
shapes, letters

Figure 17

Let us look at how the model of fine motor skills can be applied to visual motor skills. These are the building blocks and the dexterity abilities that contribute to visual motor development.

CUTTING

Cutting is a higher level fine motor skill because it uses many lower level skills:

- **Bilateral Coordination:** The assistant hand positions and adjusts the paper so that the dominant hand can align the scissors with the paper to cut out the shape.
- **Stability:** Body and shoulder stability enable the child to make accurate movements with both hands.
- **Sensation:** Sensory feedback from the joint and muscle proprioceptors help make the small adjustments necessary to cut accurately.
- **Dexterity:** Wrist rotation helps the child position the cutting hand in the thumb-up, midline position. Thumb control allows him to move the thumb joint to open the scissor blades, without moving the whole hand. Hand stability allows him to open and close the scissor blades with the thumb against the index finger, while the rest of the hand is stable and provides the control.

Children begin to experiment with scissors at a young age. As they develop the building block and dexterity skills over the next few years, they gradually learn how to hold and use the scissors in an effective, efficient way.

How Do Cutting Skills Develop in Children with Down Syndrome?

Children with Down syndrome usually go through the same steps in learning to cut as all children do. They will, however, have more difficulty learning to control the scissors because of hypotonia and difficulty with thumb movements.

When first experimenting with scissors, children often hold them in both hands. This is a normal exploratory stage. When they begin to hold the scissors in one hand, children usually use a pronated grasp; that is, with the palm of the hand and the thumb facing down and away from the body. Often the fingers are splayed open. In this position it is difficult even to snip. If your child is at this stage developmentally, do not expect him to be able to cut out corners and curves or even a straight line. It is simply too hard.

Your child will gradually learn to rotate his wrist to position his arm in the midline position, thumb up and palm facing the other hand. In this position, the thumb can move more effectively against the index finger, and more control is achieved. It will probably take your child awhile to progress to holding the scissors in the midline position, and even with his hand in the proper position, he may have difficulty opening and closing the scissor blades because he hasn't yet developed control of thumb movements. A child with Down syndrome may use opening and closing movements of the whole hand until he develops more strength and control in his thumb. Some children

Scissor grasp commonly seen in children with Down syndrome when learning to cut. Lacking control of thumb movement, he uses opening and closing movements of all the fingers to operate the scissors. His arm is turned in (pronated) so that he starts cutting on the side of the paper rather than at the bottom.

prefer to put both their index and middle fingers together in the loop, which is fine, as it gives them more stability.

Initially, the movement directing the scissors comes from the shoulder and elbow. This movement gradually refines until these larger joints are kept stable while the wrist and small joints of the hand direct the scissor movement.

The role of the assistant hand in cutting is important, but often overlooked. Cut out a complex pattern and notice how much you turn and position the paper with your assistant hand. Without all the adjustment and positioning of the paper by the assistant hand, it is much more difficult to cut. Holding and adjusting the paper with the other hand is difficult initially for children with Down syndrome. To prevent frustration, help your child hold the paper.

Helping Your Child Develop Cutting Skills

The activities suggested in the chapters on the "building blocks" of fine motor skill development (stability, bilateral coordination, and sensation) will help prepare your child for learning to cut. In order to cut effectively, your child needs to have body and shoulder stability, and needs to be able to coordinate the movements of both of his hands. In addition, the activities suggested in Chapter 8, Dexterity, will help your child develop the movements necessary for cutting, particularly wrist rotation, thumb control, and hand stability.

EARLY ACTIVITIES

PUPPETS

Hand puppets can introduce your child to the hand movement of opening and closing the fingers and thumb (to move the puppet mouth) that is used when he begins to learn to cut. You can use cloth puppets or puppets made from paper bags.

SQUEEZING ACTIVITIES

Playing games that involve using tweezers and tongs to pick up objects can help develop the thumb movement and control for cutting. Some activity examples are:

1. Pick up small pieces of cut-up sponge with tongs or tweezers, then drop the pieces into a bowl of water or in the bath.
2. Some commercially available games, such as "Giggle Wiggle" involve using tweezers (in this game, the child picks up and releases marbles onto a wiggly caterpillar).
3. Use tweezers to pick up finger foods, such as raisins or marshmallows.
4. Squeezing a baster or puff blower also helps develop thumb movement and strength, e.g.,
   - make bubbles in water with a baster;
   - have ping-pong ball races, using the air from squeezing the baster or puff blower to move the ball.

RIPPING ACTIVITIES

Cut strips of paper that your child can rip into small pieces. Many children find this motivating in itself. After all, usually they are scolded if they rip paper! Some types of paper (such as crepe or tissue paper) have a grain, and are easier to rip in one direction. Grasping the top of the paper strip with both hands and moving the hands in opposite directions to rip it helps your child with the midline hand position and wrist movements used in cutting.

CHOICE OF SCISSORS AND PAPER

SCISSORS

Choosing scissors may require some trial and error until you find a pair that works for your child. Here are some points to keep in mind when choosing scissors:

This girl is using Therapro squeeze scissors (see Resources) as she begins to learn how to coordinate scissors and paper.

1. Your child's hand is probably quite small, so look for scissors that don't require a lot of movement to open the blades.
2. Squeeze or loop (self-opening) scissors, available at educational stores and medical and therapy equipment retailers, are often a good first step to cutting for children with Down syndrome. These scissors help the child position his hand in the thumb-up (midline) position, and he needs only to squeeze them to cut. They then automatically reopen. Self-opening scissors come in small sizes suitable for small hands. Fiskars makes a small pair of "squeezers" and preschool scissors that work well for some children. Therapro (see Resources) distributes a red loop scissor that is perfect for little hands, and is a little easier to squeeze than the Fiskars.
3. Scissors with double finger loops allow an adult to place his hand over the child's to assist him to cut.
4. Metal blades work better than plastic blades, but the tips should be rounded for safety when your child is young.
5. I have found that small sewing scissors sometimes work better than children's scissors, but be careful of sharp points.
6. Self-opening (loop) scissors should work if your child is right or left handed. Once he has progressed to regular scissors, you should look for left-handed scissors if he is left handed, as right-handed scissors won't work as well and may be frustrating.

(left) Loop (self-opening) scissors are often easier when beginning to learn cutting, as they help the child position her hand with her thumb pointing upward and they open automatically. (right) Fiskars scissors.

PAPER

Paper with a slightly heavier weight and stiffness will be easier to manage initially than regular writing paper (which is too flimsy), or bristle board (which is too stiff). Construction paper is often a good choice. I like to use paper the thickness of paint samples or playing cards.

LEARN STEP BY STEP

If your child is just beginning to learn to hold scissors and the paper, don't expect him to actually be able to cut anything out yet! As in all skill development, he needs to learn step by step the developmental progression of cutting:

1. **Snipping: short, individual snips.** Give your child small bits of paper that can be cut into smaller pieces with just a snip. This may be motivating enough in itself, or he may want to collect a pile of tiny bits, and glue them onto a pre-drawn picture, with a mosaic-like result. Picking up the little bits of paper is also good for pincer grasp. Another activity example is to cut a fringe with individual snips, such as to make a lion's mane, or a placemat fringe. A fringe is harder to cut than small bits, as the scissors must be placed quite accurately.

2. **Cutting across a thin strip of paper (e.g., one inch), then wider strips.** Here your child makes two or three cuts in the same direction. He ends up with small squares of paper, which can be glued into a design or onto a picture. Paint samples (you can pick them up at hardware stores) are a good size for beginning cutters.

3. **Cutting a piece of paper in half.** Sarah and I used to cut pieces of scrap paper in half and staple them together for message pads. This was a good opportunity for Sarah to practice cutting across a piece of paper.

4. **Cutting along a straight line.** Pretend the scissors are a race car that tries to stay on the track. Staying on the track is more important than going fast!

5. **Changing direction; for example, cutting an angle or corner, as when cutting out shapes.** You can also use a "driving" analogy here. The scissors are like a car driving on the road; when you get to a corner you stop, turn the scissors and readjust the paper, then carry on.

6. **Cutting a curved line.** Here your child has to gradually adjust the position of the scissors and paper to cut the curve. For example, cut a semicircle off the corner of a paper to make a "piece of pie." Your child can then decorate the pie or can glue several together to make a whole pie.

7. **Cutting a complete circle.** While cutting, your child has to continuously move the paper with the other hand, to keep the cutting going in a curved pattern. When children start learning how to cut curves and circles, they usually cut a couple of straight strokes, then turn the paper slightly and carry on in this manner. They end up with more of an

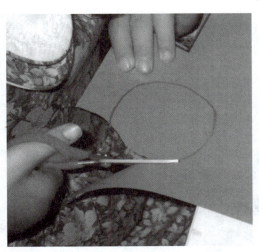

Cutting out a circle is usually more difficult than cutting out lines and corners.

octagon shape than a true circle. Gradually they learn how to continuously adjust the position of the scissors and paper to stay on the curved line. In preparation for cutting a complete circle, you can fold a paper in half and draw a half circle from the fold. Keeping the paper folded, your child can cut the half circle out, which will be a complete circle when opened up.

8. **Cutting combinations of corners, lines, curves, and circles with increasing complexity.** Intricate cutting patterns are difficult for many children, including children with Down syndrome. If this kind of cutting is being done in a school art class or project, pre-cut some or most of the pattern, so that your child can complete the cutting pattern with a few cutting strokes. This will allow him to contribute to the cutting aspect of the activity, without getting frustrated. You can show him how to cut off excess paper as he cuts out a shape. This will make it easier to hold and position the paper with his non-dominant hand.

Preprinting Skills

Pencil Grasp

In this book, the term "pencil grasp" is used to refer to the grasp of all writing utensils, including crayons, markers, pens, paintbrushes, etc. Children learn to hold a pencil in much the same way that they learn to pick up objects. As explained in Chapter 8, your child gradually refines his grasp and release from using his palm and all of his fingers as a unit, to eventually using very fine movements of his thumb and fingers, primarily the index finger. Your child makes the same type of progression in learning how to hold something to write.

Initially, the child holds the pencil in his palm and makes marks. This is called the "palmar grasp." Some children hold the marking end of the pencil close to the thumb

(above) Palmar grasp is the first developmental stage in learning to use a pencil.

(right) When using a radial-palmar (or palmar-digital) grasp, the marker is still held in the palm, but the thumb and fingers begin to position it.

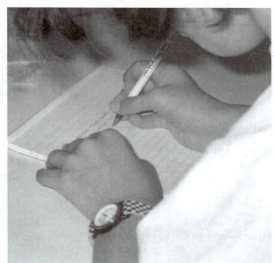

(top left) The young school-aged child holds the marker in a static tripod grasp.

(top right) The older school-aged child gradually develops a dynamic tripod grasp, using fine opposition of the thumb and index finger to position and move the pencil.

(bottom left) Some children prefer to hold the pencil in the position shown here, called a quadrupod grasp, as three fingers and the thumb are used to hold the pencil. This grasp works for this child.

(called the "palmar pronate" grasp), while other children hold it close to the little finger (called the "palmar supinate" grasp).

Gradually the fingers extend out onto the shaft of the pencil, while it is still held in the palm. This is sometimes referred to as a "radial palmar," or "digital pronate" grasp.

Next, the pencil is brought out from the palm to between the thumb and fingers, and the thumb and fingers hold it in a somewhat clumsy-looking grasp. Most of the movement comes from the wrist and arm. This is called a "static tripod," or "immature tripod" grasp.

Finally, children begin using the mature grasp, with the pencil positioned between the tips of the thumb and first two fingers, using small movements of the hand joints to move the pencil. This is called the "dynamic tripod grasp."

In *Clinical Perspectives in the Management of Down Syndrome,* the authors described the average age ranges for achieving these pencil grasps for children with Down syndrome (27):

- Palmar Supinate .... 13–36 months
- Digital Pronate .... 24 months–5 years
- Static Tripod........................4–8 years
- Dynamic Tripod................... 5–12 years

Helping Your Child Develop Pencil Grasping Patterns

When your child is a toddler, he will naturally hold a crayon or marker in a palmar grasp. He will either turn his hand thumb-side down to color ("palmar pronate"), or thumb-side up ("palmar supinate"), or will alternate between the two. The important point at this stage is to have fun with crayon and marker activities; don't worry about how your child is holding the crayon, or what he is drawing.

Showing interest and pleasure in any marks and scribbles your child makes will encourage him to continue.

Within the next year or so, your child will be ready to begin to extend his fingers on the shaft of the pencil ("digital pronate"). This will coincide with him using a tripod ("radial-digital") grasp on objects during play, as he begins to focus on using his thumb and fingers in a more coordinated fashion. Following some of the activity suggestions in Chapter 8 (page 87) to help him develop this kind of coordination during play will likely generalize to his grasp of a crayon as well.

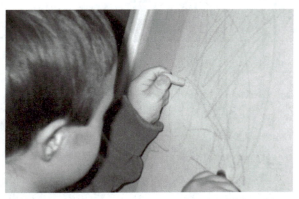

A small piece of crayon or chalk can help the child use his finger and thumb more actively, rather than holding a longer piece in his palm.

The next stage of pencil grasp development is switching from this digital pronate grasp, in which the pencil is positioned in the palm, to a tripod grasp. This involves changing the entire position of the pencil. It is now out of the palm and is held and controlled by the thumb and the first two fingers, and rests against the side of the hand. This is the biggest switch developmentally in the progression of pencil grasp. It is quite common and normal to see frequent switching back and forth between these two pencil grasps as your child experiments with the new feeling. Your child may begin to use a tripod grasp anywhere from about three and a half years on. Here are some suggestions that I have found helpful when encouraging your preschool or school-aged child to bring the pencil out of a palmar and into a tripod grasp:

1. Sometimes children need the sensory cue of something in the palm. "Finger crayons" can help. These consist of a round bulb, which is held in the palm, and a pointed end, which encourages a tripod grasp.
2. Use short stubs of crayons or chalk rather than a long piece. With a regular length your child may use a palmar grasp, but when given a short piece that won't fit into his palm, he will use the thumb and fingers in a tripod grasp.
3. Triangular or similarly shaped crayons can help cue the child to hold it with a tripod grasp.
4. Thick markers, as opposed to thin, may encourage the child to use a tripod grasp.

Children with Down syndrome commonly anchor the pencil with the base of the thumb against the side of the hand, rather than using the tip of the thumb. This is sometimes known as a "thumb wrap" grasp. This is an early tripod grasping pattern seen in many children. It can persist in children with Down syndrome, probably due to difficulty holding the pencil with the tip of the thumb, due to hypotonia, lax ligaments in the thumb, and the tendency of the thumb to "collapse." This type of tripod grasp is adequate for the first few years of printing. However, if expectations of quantity and speed of written work increase, this type of grasp will hold your child back. The small finger and thumb movements necessary for quick printing and legible cursive writing can be achieved with a dynamic tripod grasp.

Your child has the potential to develop a dynamic tripod grasp of a pencil if he can pick up and release small objects with a superior pincer grasp (tip to tip opposition). The activities described in Chapter 8 on pages 88-91 to develop and strengthen *(left) A pencil grasp pattern commonly seen in children with Down syndrome, in which the pencil is anchored against the side of the hand by the thumb.*

(right) A pencil grip helps this child position the pencil in a static tripod grasp.

pincer grasp and thumb control will prepare your child for making small, controlled movements of the pencil using a dynamic tripod grasp.

The progression of pencil grasp development may not come naturally to all children with Down syndrome. Your child may have to be shown how to hold the pencil the "new" way. This may mean repositioning the pencil in his hand to give him the idea. Commonly he will initially reject the new grasp in favor of the old, less developed grasp. Be aware that when he does try holding his pencil in a new grasp, he may not have as much control with the pencil at first. If he was able to draw circles with a palmar grasp, he may only be able to scribble when first shown how to hold it with his thumb and finger extended down the shaft of the pencil. However, if you consistently help him to position the pencil the "new" way, letting him readjust it after a try, he will eventually feel comfortable and adopt this grasp position all the time. For some children, the use of a pencil grip will help him to position his fingers in a tripod grasp on the pencil. Pencil grips are discussed in more detail on page 132. Occupational therapists use a variety of techniques to help children remember how to hold their pencil. For example, an elastic band or hair elastic can go around the wrist, then cross and go over the pencil, to hold it resting between the thumb and index finger.

If you look around a regular primary classroom, you will see children using different variations of the tripod grasp when printing and writing. A child does not have to hold the pencil in a perfect tripod grasp to be functional in printing and writing. Don't worry if your child doesn't hold the pencil in a perfect dynamic tripod grasp by grade 1! Children need time and practice.

Children Who Resist Holding Pencils

Some children with Down syndrome do not like to hold anything in their hands. This may not be recognized as a challenge until the child enters school, where he is expected to hold crayons and pencils, scissors and paintbrushes. This child often holds things by his fingertips to avoid holding them in his palm. If the child demonstrates other avoidance behaviors (not exploring with his hands, not wanting to touch or hold anything, avoiding all sensory play) he may be overly sensitive to touch. Sensory over-responsiveness can lead to these types of behaviors. Strategies for helping a child deal with sensory over-responsiveness, in this case, hypersensitivity to touch in the hands, are discussed in Chapter 11.

All of the ability areas already outlined in this book contribute to a child's ability to master fine control of the pencil for printing, and, eventually, cursive writing. These are very precise skills that many children, with or without Down syndrome, find a challenge.

Helping Your Child Get Ready to Learn Printing

PREPRINTING SKILLS

At first, young preschool children experiment with colors and strokes on the paper that usually do not "look like" anything in particular. They are experimenting with their ability to direct their hands, and the end result doesn't really matter. Children at this stage benefit from lots of opportunity to experiment, such as painting or drawing on paper at an easel; on a paper or memo board on the fridge; on a blackboard, or on a large paper taped to a table or floor.

Drawing at an easel can help develop eye-hand coordination and shoulder stability.

At this stage some parents find artwork on their walls! Set up a place for your child that is always available, and clearly let him know that it is acceptable to draw or paint there, but not on the walls, furniture, etc. It is best to keep the supplies handy and available. Usually a child spends only a few minutes at a time at these activities, which only becomes frustrating for the parent who takes everything out and then has to put it all away again a few minutes later.

I suggest often placing the paper up at eye level (on an easel or blackboard, or taped to the fridge) for several reasons. First, positioning the activity so that the hands come up in front of the eyes is beneficial for eye-hand coordination when your child is first learning how to direct a pencil on paper. Second, it helps the continued development of shoulder stability and wrist positioning. Your child begins using large strokes, with movements of his whole arm.

If using paper on a table or floor, you can tape it down so it doesn't move around. When your child has developed more control, he will be able to stabilize the paper with his other hand.

This is the developmental progression for printing and coloring abilities:

1. Scribbling: making random marks on the paper;
2. Separate strokes: vertical and horizontal lines;
3. Circles: continuous circular strokes;
4. Strokes become more controlled and precise; e.g., a closed circle;
5. Simple combination of circles, lines, and dots; e.g., a variety of forms on the page or combining vertical and horizontal lines to make a cross;
6. Coloring without much regard for the form on the page; may use primarily one color;
7. Diagonal lines;
8. Strokes with changes of direction; e.g., corners;
9. Coloring with some attention to the form, but unable to stay inside the lines and color not always appropriate;

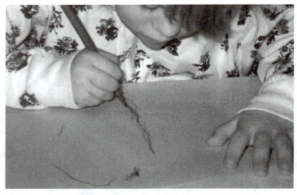

The non-dominant hand should automatically hold the paper steady in paper and pencil tasks.

Preprinting skills: Lines and circles are the preparation for printing letters and for drawing representational pictures.

10. Simple shapes; e.g., square, triangle;
11. Simple representational pictures; e.g., face, person, sun, tree, rainbow;
12. Coloring with more attention to detail of the form, attempts to stay inside the lines, some attention to appropriate color;
13. First letters: Usually children first learn to print their own name in capital (upper case) letters. Reversal of letters and numbers is common initially;
14. Coloring with attention to the detail of the picture, choosing appropriate colors; more success at staying in the lines.
15. Letters: Children are usually taught to print upper case letters first, then lower case. In my experience, letters with simple linear combinations are easier to learn to print at first. Letters that combine curves, lines, and diagonals are the most difficult initially. For example, I, L, T, O, E, H are easier to learn to print than R, S, M, N, B, W, f, j, g, K, Y.

DETERMINING YOUR CHILD'S READINESS FOR PREPRINTING ACTIVITIES

Your child is ready to participate in preprinting activities when he:

- has an interest in toys and manipulative materials beyond banging, throwing, and mouthing them;
- can follow simple, one-step instructions (e.g., "hands up");
- watches others;
- makes some attempt to imitate;
- has an interest in scribbling and marking on paper.

HELPING YOUR CHILD DEVELOP PREPRINTING CONCEPTS

Based on the developmental sequence described above, here are some ideas that I have used in a preprinting program in an integrated nursery school setting. These activities introduce the basic perceptual concepts involved in printing letters. The concepts that are introduced and reinforced through fun movement and rhythmic games are:

- spatial attention and localization: pointing, touching target with marker;
- up/down;
- scribbling: getting a "feel" for paper and crayon/marker;
- vertical orientation: standing up tall;

- "top": starting at the top; going from top to bottom;
- horizontal orientation: lying down; "sleeping line";
- same/different;
- left to right;
- bottom; middle;
- circles;
- start and stop;
- combining lines: cross.

Spatial Attention and Localization: Your child learns how to focus his visual attention on a specific item. This is necessary in order to be able to imitate or copy a printed letter when learning to print. This skill begins very early, when you are pointing to and naming objects for your child. When your child begins to point himself, you will reinforce his visual attention by also pointing at and naming the object. For example, "Ball. That's a ball. Do you want the ball?" Pointing is very important, as it helps your child direct his visual attention to an object, and brings your attention to it as well.

Targeting stickers on a paper develops eye-hand coordination.

Next, you and your child point to specific people or things in photos and books. Naming and developing little conversations around what your child's visual attention is focused on reinforces his ability to zero in on one part of the picture or photo at a time.

From pointing, you progress to targeting one object on the page or picture and using a marker to indicate it. For example, in a simple coloring book, your child can put his crayon or marker on Barney to begin coloring, thus directing his hand to one particular spot on the page that he is visually focused on. As he gets better at this, he can target increasingly smaller details, such as Barney's mouth, eyes, etc.

At this stage, your child's grasp of the marker is not as important as being able to localize and direct his hand to a particular spot. He can use any kind of writing tool: marker, crayon, chalk, paint brush, etc. Other activity suggestions for this skill are:

- Scatter stickers randomly on a large paper; your child "zooms" in (like an airplane) to each sticker, first with his finger, then with a crayon or marker.
- Jan Olsen, in her *Handwriting without Tears* program, has developed a preschool workbook, which devotes several pages to this targeting and visual attention skill. (See Resources.)

Up/Down: Your baby learns that when he lifts up his arms to be picked up, you pick him up. Simply saying the words "up" and "down" when you pick him up and put him down introduces the language long before your child hears them in relation to paper and pencil activities. Simple games such as bouncing up and down on your knee, tossing up and down in the air, and bouncing up and down to the rhyme "The Grand Old Duke of York" help your child feel what up and down mean spatially.

"Hands up. Hands down" is a transition chant we use at the nursery school to help the children stop what they are doing and make the transition to the next part

The baby learns up/down through imitative games.

of the day. "Up" and "down" are often among the first words we hear a child say at nursery school. Up and down become fascinating when the child learns to go up and down stairs, and parents know how many times a child will repeat going up and down over and over again! He is practicing his gross motor skills, and also feeling the movement of up and down in space.

Other activity suggestions for preschool-aged children are:

- Reach way up in standing (such as trying to reach a hanging streamer or balloon), then crouch down low to touch the ground.
- Jump up high, then down low.
- Climb up on a platform and jump down.
- At a large blackboard or easel, direct the chalk/paintbrush up and down.

Scribbling: Scribbling is an important first step in the visual motor skills of coloring and printing. All children scribble before they learn to isolate strokes on a paper. Even though it doesn't look like much, your child is developing control of arm and hand movements and visual attention through scribbling. It is exciting to be able to mark up a paper with color by scribbling! Initially, scribbling is very random, but as your child develops, you will notice that the scribbling will assume definite directional orientation, such as vertical scribble vs. circular or horizontal scribble. This is the precursor to developing directional strokes. Children usually first color with scribbles, with gradually more and more localization to the picture on the page. At first, many children use large arm movements without good control, and need large pieces of paper if you want to avoid marks on your floor, table, or wall. Gradually, your child will be able to refine his arm movements to keep his scribble to a smaller space.

Vertical Orientation: Most printed letters have one or more lines with vertical orientation. You can reinforce your child's recognition of "vertical" long before he is ready to print through games and activities:

- Draw a vertical line down your child's back (starting at the top) with your finger, small brush, small toy, etc., so he feels "vertical."
- Place long felt strips vertically on a felt board.
- Move streamers up and down through the air.
- Tape vertical strips of paper on the wall as a measure of your child's height.
- Stand up a rectangular block in a vertical orientation; the block is "standing up tall."
- Stick wooden sticks with Velcro on the back to a felt or carpet board in a vertical orientation (the sticks are "standing up tall"). The wooden sticks I use in these activities are from Jan Olsen's *Handwriting without Tears* program. Other sticks could be used (such as popsicle sticks) to teach the same concept.

Top: "Top" is an important word for children to understand in a motor context before they begin to learn to print, as we begin printing many letters at the top and move the pencil down. Some games and activities to reinforce this concept are:

A preschool child has placed stickers at the top and middle of the stick, and placed it in a vertical position.

- Have your child put something on top of his head (sometimes looking in the mirror can help).
- Use wooden sticks with Velcro on the back and have your child stick them in a vertical orientation on a felt board. He then places a sticker at the top of the stick.
- Have your child orient a tall narrow block into a vertical ("Standing up") position; then place a small toy on top.
- Hang a large piece of paper on the wall for drawing vertical lines. A visual cue can be placed along the top to remind your child to start drawing his line at the top.
- Let your child draw hair on top of a stick figure drawing on the wall.
- Any activity in which your child places something on top will help him understand this concept.

Horizontal Orientation: Again, you will notice your child's scribbling becoming more differentiated, sometimes being more horizontal, sometimes more vertical, sometimes more circular. There are many ways that the horizontal orientation can be reinforced. Here are a few ideas:

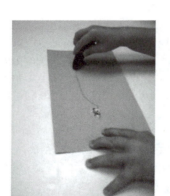

Joining dots involves targeting, left to right, start/stop, and horizontal concepts.

- Draw a "sleeping" line across your child's back.
- Have your child place long blocks end to end to make a long horizontal block path. Then he can walk along the path.
- A rectangular block can be placed lying down, or sleeping.
- Lie down on the floor ("sleeping"). Sometimes children can understand the words "lying down" or "sleeping" in relation to a horizontal line more easily than the word "across," which gets confusing when drawing a "cross."
- Wooden sticks with Velcro on the back can be placed on the felt board in a horizontal position.
- Streamers: moving the arm back and forth will move the streamer in a horizontal direction.
- Place a long narrow strip of paper horizontally on the floor or wall; your child can stroke lines in a horizontal direction across the strip.
- Name cards are horizontal. Children can stick their name cards on a board.

Same/Different: As your child participates in the above activities, you will be able to tell if he recognizes the difference between vertical and horizontal. To reinforce "same," use the word to describe anything your child does in imitation. For example, if you are playing with rectangular blocks, placing them vertically "up tall," point out that they are standing up the same way.

Matching is a concept that children develop as they understand that objects are "the same" or "different." During the preschool or early school years, children learn to match colors that are the same, shapes that are the same, pictures that are the same, etc. This is a visual discrimination and cognitive ability that will develop when your child is ready. If your child has this understanding, you can reinforce it in relation to visual motor skills by:

- taking turns placing felt strips the same way on a board (e.g., all horizontally);
- taking turns imitating each other's strokes on paper;
- matching letters and numbers;
- differentiating big/little: use the language that your child is used to hearing (big/little, or large/small). (Matching and sorting by size introduces the concept that he will need to form big vs. little strokes in printing letters);
- finding two pictures/shapes on the page that are the same.

Left to Right: In English, reading and writing move across the page from left to right. Children eventually need to learn to print and read from left to right across the page. Also, most letters are printed starting with the left stroke and then doing the right stroke. It is normal for children to make strokes and do activities in both directions, and I am not suggesting that you must *always* move from left to right. Children who are left handed will often draw horizontal lines from right to left initially, as this is more natural for them. However, there are ways to help your child recognize the left to right orientation for reading and writing in our culture:

- When you are reading to your child, point to the words on the page.
- Let him watch as you print his name on his drawings and paintings.
- Slide his finger across his name card as you say or spell out his name.

Bottom/Middle: As your child begins to make vertical strokes, you talk about starting at the top and going down to the bottom. Just as your child placed a sticker at the top of the vertical wooden piece, so he can place a sticker at the bottom. As he begins to learn to print, if the concept of starting at the top is reinforced, the idea of bottom will develop naturally. Middle is a more abstract concept that will probably develop later than "top" and "down."

"Middle" comes into play in letters such as E, H, F, P, A, B, R, where a horizontal or curve stroke starts/stops at the middle of the vertical stroke. We can introduce "middle" through some of these games and activities:

- Run to the middle of the room (with a mark on the floor).
- Step into a hoop and pull it up to the middle of your body (stomach); everyone can try to do the hula!
- Place an elastic band tightly around the middle of the wooden stick; your children can roll it up to the top, back to the middle, down to the bottom, back to the middle.
- Play "monkey in the middle": one person stands in the center between two or more people playing catch and tries to intercept the ball; when he does so, the person whose throw was caught then becomes the "monkey in the middle."
- Stick a sticker in the middle of a vertically oriented wooden stick, or a long vertical strip of paper on the wall.

Circles: Children scribble in a circular direction early in their visual motor development. It can be another one to two years, however, before they draw a closed, single circle. At this early stage of visual motor development, introducing circles helps them to discriminate between straight and circular objects and strokes on paper. Some circle activities are:

- Peek through small rings or discs with holes.
- Put bracelets/rings on over hands and feet.
- Crawl/step through hoops.
- Crawl through a tunnel.
- Place round stickers inside a big circle drawn on a paper.
- Place round stickers on paper, then draw a circle around the sticker.
- Make circular shapes with streamers by moving your arm in a circle.
- Many treats are round circles, such as Cheerios, Froot Loops, and Life Savers; these can be used in creative activities.
- Draw eyes on an incomplete face picture.

Start/Stop: Another concept that children develop is the ability to begin a pencil stroke at a defined spot, and to stop at a defined spot. For example, when your child changes from making continuous circular strokes to a single circle that comes back to where he started, he is developing this concept. The same is true for simple shapes. In order to be able to attempt a corner—for a square or triangle, for example—your child has to stop the stroke to change direction. Your child needs to understand these concepts to be able to learn to print letters and numbers. Here are some suggested activities for the concept of start/stop:

- motor activities, such as marching and stopping on command; dancing to music and stopping when the music stops;
- running and stopping to a visual or sound cue;
- music activities with instruments, such as shaking bells in a song and stopping at the end;
- tapping and clapping activities, stopping and starting on cue.

When your child understands the concept of start/stop through these types of motor activities, visual motor start/stop activities can be introduced, such as:

- starting a vertical or horizontal line on a green dot, stopping at the red dot;
- matching worksheets, where the child draws a line to join the two pictures that are the same;
- dot-to-dot activities to reinforce the idea of a definite start/stop point, and number and letter sequencing;
- visual motor worksheets (see Appendix 1);
- mazes, which can help a child learn to begin a stroke, then stop and change direction. Look for simple mazes at this early stage of visual motor development, with a simple path that clearly indicates the starting and finishing points, with one or two changes of direction.

Combining Lines (e.g., Cross):
Typically developing children begin to combine a single vertical and horizontal line to form a cross around the age of three. At this stage, we are introducing the concept of combining lines that go in different directions, and encouraging imitation of these movements in motor activities.

- Trace two long blocks in a cross pattern on a paper. You place one block on the pattern and have your child place the other block in the other direction to form the cross. If you demonstrate and then place the block in your child's hands in the proper orientation, he will almost always place it down to form a cross, thus experiencing success. This is your starting point! Next time, you can demonstrate placing both blocks down to form the cross.

- Have your child hold one wooden stick in each hand and tap them together. Get him tapping in rhythm ("tap, tap, tap… and stop"), stopping with the sticks crossed over each other, so he can experience making a cross with two sticks.

- Walk along a large cross on the floor, made of low benches or balance beams.
- Place felt strips on a felt board in a cross pattern, starting with the vertical strip.

At this stage, children usually combine a variety of strokes and forms on paper. They certainly should be encouraged to do this! They will put circles and lines together (sun, stick person, animals), lines going in different directions (house, car), and usually will add dots. Some demonstration by adults is okay, but it is important that your child experiment and discover for himself how these combinations can represent something, not that he can copy your drawing.

This sequence shows some of the activities used in a preschool preprinting group: Exploring the letter T using blocks, the Handwriting Without Tears wooden pieces , a gross motor activity using benches, and finally, tracing T on paper.

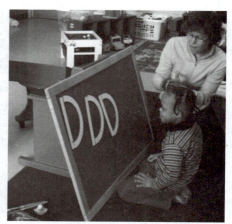

Learning the sequence of forming the letter with the wood pieces helps prepare the child for learning the sequence to print the letter.

DRAWING, PAINTING, AND COLORING

Drawing is the child's first experience of expressing a thought or idea on paper. You may want to show your child how combining forms on paper can represent something in real life. For example, a circle with lines coming out all around represents a sun. Experiment together to give your child more ideas. Representing ideas on paper with pictures may help prepare your child for representing ideas and information on paper with words.

As children commonly include a person or people in their drawings, there are actually developmental norms for this. The face is first to be represented, with simple circular or linear features for the eyes, nose, and mouth. When children begin to represent the body, it is usually as a "stick person," with a line or circle for the body, and single lines representing the arms and legs. As children get older, they add more dimension and shape to the body and limbs, and more detail to the facial features.

Painting is a fun way to explore form and color, and to develop grasping patterns.

When your child begins to learn to color in pictures, he will use large arm movements across the page to fill in the spaces. Often there isn't much regard for color choice, and he may even use only one color. You may see abrupt changes of direction of the crayon stroke: he may begin with a vertical arm movement, then switch to a horizontal movement. As your child matures, he will attempt to define different parts of the picture by using different colors, but he won't yet be able to stay in the lines. As he gradually develops the stability at the shoulder, elbow, and wrist and uses the small joints of the hand for movement of the crayon, his coloring will become more refined. His attempts at staying in the lines will be more successful, and he will be able to contour his strokes to the outline of the picture. Color choice usually becomes more varied and appropriate.

Appendix 1 has visual motor worksheets that I have developed to use with Sarah and other children. These can be used as a fun exercise to improve refinement of pencil strokes, from a preprinting to cursive writing stages.

PREPRINTING DEVELOPMENTAL CHART

The Preprinting Developmental Chart outlines the stages of visual motor development, the developmental skills that are emerging concurrently, and activity suggestions for reinforcing these emerging skills.

STAGE AND DESCRIPTION	DEVELOPMENTAL SKILLS	SUGGESTED ACTIVITIES FOR PREPRINTING PREPARATION
1. mouthing crayon, crinkling paper 2. banging crayon on paper 3. scribbles randomly, watches others	Child: ■ takes things in-out; on/off ■ attends to books ■ holds crayon in palmar grasp ■ sits independently ■ attends to others drawing ■ picks up using thumb ■ points to objects	■ sensory play & hand rhymes for sensory awareness ■ point to pictures in books ■ provide exploration with crayons, markers, etc. ■ balance activities, with free arm movement ■ cause-effect play ■ encourage thumb use in picking up objects
4a. scribbles spontaneously in vertical direction, watching direction of movement of crayon on paper 4b. scribbles spontaneously in horizontal direction 5. scribbles spontaneously in circular direction	■ develops better control with hands (can stack a few blocks, insert pegs) ■ begins to match (single shape) ■ begins to join in with actions in simple familiar songs (e.g., "Wheels on the Bus") ■ understands up/down ■ opposes thumb to index for small objects (pincer) ■ begins to identify body parts ■ often switches hands during visual motor play	■ tabletop activities (puzzles, Duplo, blocks): learns about form in space, and language used in teaching printing, such as "on top," "middle," "bottom," etc. ■ encourage imitation in action songs and, if appropriate, simple signs ■ finger feeding for pincer grasp ■ begin spoon feeding for control of wrist ■ sensory visual motor play; e.g., finger painting, paint with brush, chalk, coloring
6a. imitates a vertical & horizontal direction 6b. imitates a circular scribble direction 7a. imitates vertical & horizontal lines 7b. imitates a circular line	■ holds crayon in palm with fingers extended, or in crude tripod grasp ■ completes simple sorting & puzzle activities ■ picks up scissors, often with 2 hands, attempts to snip ■ understands 1-2 part directions ■ actively participates in action songs/signing	■ use different surfaces for visual motor play (easel, table, floor) ■ encourage visual discrimination skills in sorting activities ■ offer child scissors (loop or squeeze initially) ■ sensory play for hand strengthening (play dough, dry sensory for scooping, etc.) ■ finger songs/rhymes

STAGE AND DESCRIPTION CONT.	DEVELOPMENTAL SKILLS CONT.	SUGGESTED ACTIVITIES CONT.
8. copies vertical & horizontal line 9a. copies circle 9b. imitates a cross 10. imitates a right/left diagonal	▪ adds lines, circles, and dots spontaneously to drawings ▪ understands up/down, on/off, in/out ▪ uses touch to identify and manipulate objects ▪ engages in pretend play ▪ snips with scissors (often thumb down) ▪ usually a dominant hand is becoming evident ▪ recognizes some letters ▪ draws simple representational pictures	▪ imitation in visual motor and game activities ▪ encourage tripod grasp if necessary by providing small pieces of crayon/chalk ▪ manipulative play that strengthens grasping patterns (e.g., stringing beads, foam puzzles, Duplo) ▪ snip play dough, straws, heavy paper (e.g., paint chips, cards) ▪ introduce concrete preprinting materials, such as the wood pieces in "Handwriting without Tears" program ▪ complementary worksheets for pencil control (such as in Appendix 1) ▪ introduce to computer, begin to use mouse
11. copies a right/left diagonal 12. copies a square 13. copies a left/right diagonal 14. copies an X; imitates a triangle 15. copies a triangle	▪ adds shapes to drawings ▪ attempts to imitate some letters (usually name) ▪ names some letters ▪ understands simple directionality (top to bottom, left to right) ▪ cuts with continuous snips ▪ uses a tripod grasp ▪ colors with more attention to the detail of the picture	▪ multi-sensory visual motor activities, such as Magna Doodle, chalk on carpet, finger in sand, etc. ▪ cut along progressively longer lines on heavy paper; add corners and curves when ready ▪ use mouse to make choices on computer ▪ introduce printing program

Stages revised from: Dunn Klein, Marsha. Pre-Writing Skills. San Antonio, TX: Therapy Skill Builders, 1990.

Printing

Developing the ability to direct a pencil on paper in preprinting practice prepares children to learn to print letters. The preprinting activities help your child to learn how to form the "parts" of the letters. These activities give him lots of practice making lines, circular strokes (going in both directions), and diagonals. He also comes to understand the concept of a starting point and a stopping point, and has an idea of the meaning of letters and numbers. The next step is for your child to integrate his motor control with a pencil with his visual perceptual development; that is, the understanding that certain forms represent a concept (a letter or number).

Learning to print is a complex process involving the integration of visual, sensory, and motor learning. All children benefit from watching someone else print the letter, so they can observe the movements involved. Over time, the movements become automatic as the pathways are established in the brain. If the child learns incorrect letter formation due to lack of models and coaching, it will be more difficult to "undo" the learned movement patterns and re-teach correct formation. If the child is expected to learn to print before he is developmentally ready, he may develop incorrect patterns of letter formation to compensate for the lack of visual motor foundation skills. A focus on building strong preprinting foundation skills for the child with Down syndrome will provide the groundwork for learning to print *when he is ready*.

Determining Your Child's Readiness for Printing

So when is he ready? These are some of the questions I would consider when deciding if a child is ready to learn to print:

1. Can the child hold a writing tool, preferably a pencil? The development of pencil grasp was discussed earlier in this chapter. Printing requires control of small movements in the hands. If a child is using a palmar grasp, he is not usually ready to learn to print. However, there are exceptions to this, as some children have developed the perceptual and cognitive readiness for printing but are delayed in fine motor control. For most children, holding a pencil in an immature tripod grasp is the starting point for learning the pencil control necessary to print functionally in workbooks and on worksheets.

2. Can the child imitate in visual motor activities? For example, if you draw a horizontal line, can he imitate it? Can he imitate more complex patterns, such as a cross, closed circle, diagonal line? If the child is not yet able to imitate some of the preprinting strokes, he is probably not ready to learn to print. I usually begin with the easiest upper case letters before a child can consistently copy or even imitate diagonals and a square. There are differences of opinion on this.

3. Does the child display an interest in and attention to visual motor activities? Is he motivated to participate in drawing with markers and crayons, coloring, painting, and using a pencil? If he is

motivated, then he is more likely to have the attention necessary to learn to print.

4. Does the child spontaneously draw some or all of the preprinting stokes, such as directional lines, circles, dots, zigzags, and combinations of these? In other words, does he initiate some of these strokes himself when painting, coloring etc., without any adult direction?

5. Does the child have the body stability to sit in a chair at a table and direct the movement of his hand with the pencil?

6. Does the child have the cognitive level to understand the meaning of printing? If the child understands that letters form words that symbolize objects and people, he will be much more motivated to participate in a printing program. Otherwise, it becomes a meaningless fine motor exercise. Sound-letter recognition (understanding the sounds each letter can make) will develop over time, while the child is learning to read and print.

PRINTING HIS NAME

Usually the first word that children learn to print is their name. As mentioned above, your child will be motivated to print if it has meaning for him. First your child recognizes the sound of his name, later he recognizes his printed name, and then he learns to print it himself. Often, even if the child is not really ready to begin a *printing program* as such, he will be taught how to print his name. This is fine, as usually the child is motivated and is pleased with any attempts, even if they aren't exactly correct.

Profile: Sarah

At five years old, Sarah was having difficulty mastering diagonal lines. I found that using a calendar helped. Every day she would take the calendar down from the bulletin board, removing the thumb tack, and would put an x through the date. I showed her how to start in the top corner and go across to the opposite corner. We started doing only one line, from the top left corner to the bottom right. When she was able to do that consistently, we added the other diagonal line from the bottom left to the top right corners. Putting the calendar back up on the bulletin board with the thumb tack helped strengthen her pincer grasp. After doing this for a couple of months, she was able to make diagonal lines anywhere. This activity also helped reinforce the days of the week, number recognition, and the months of the year.

Helping Your Child Learn to Print

POSITIONING

Positioning for printing is very important. It helps provide the stability that is one of the building blocks for developing pencil control. According to some researchers, however, many children with Down syndrome lack this stability. In observing children with Down syndrome doing handwriting activities, the researchers noted that most assumed a slouched posture after a short period of time, and some "hitched" their writing arm shoulder in an attempt to stabilize (5).

When your child has developed the early preprinting skills on larger paper at an easel or similar setup, and he is ready to begin working at a desk or table, keep in mind the following positioning considerations:

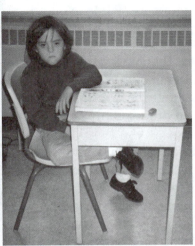

It is important for your child to have a comfortable table or desk to work at. The desk and chair on the left are the right height. Those on the right are too high. When the chair is too high, the child may twist in her chair to be able to reach the floor.

1. The chair and desk should be the right size for your child. Although this seems basic, it is often overlooked. Knees should be in line with hips, or slightly higher, but not lower, and feet flat on the floor, directly under the knees. If the available chair is too high, place a sturdy footstool under the feet. Elbows should rest comfortably on the desk, without the shoulders being elevated (desk is too high), or hunched (desk is too low).

2. Sometimes children with lower muscle tone find it difficult to sit up straight for long periods at a desk, even with correct desk size, and end up leaning their head down on their other arm while they work. Sometimes working on a slanted surface, something like a drafting table or slanted writing board, can help. I have used an empty binder, two inches wide or more at the spine, on the desk, slanting up away from the child. When I used this with Sarah, she was better able to maintain an upright sitting posture while printing, and didn't put her face down as close to her work. Another strategy for children with low tone who tire quickly is to offer a variety of printing positions and techniques. Doing some work at the computer, some at the desk, some at the blackboard, some on the floor, each for shorter periods, may enable them to complete more written work.

3. Consider your child's desk position in the classroom or at home. Factors such as lighting, position relative to the teacher, and nearby distractions will all affect how your child works at the desk.

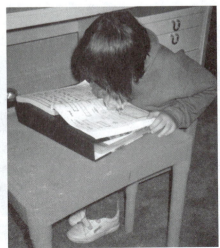

A slanted writing table can help some children with low muscle tone to keep an upright sitting posture when printing. A binder can also be used.

4. Providing a cushion that allows for some movement and sensory input can help activate the muscles for maintaining an upright position. Some suggestions are:

- Try placing a small beach ball with a tiny bit of air in it on your child's chair, just enough to allow for a little bit of movement input.
- Put a "Movin' Sit" or Disc'O'Sit cushion on his chair (see Resources).
- Sitting on a therapy ball with feet on the floor: Therapy balls can be purchased with a base to prevent them from rolling around (see Flaghouse and Sammons Preston Roylan on page 233). This can be used at a desk instead of a chair.

An example of a cushion (Movin' Sit) which stimulates a little bit of trunk movement while sitting. For some children, this can assist with posture and provide the sensory input that can help them sit longer.

<table>
<tr><td>PRINTING SEQUENCE</td></tr>
</table>

Children with Down syndrome usually learn to print by following the sequence outlined here:

1. imitating,
2. tracing and copying,
3. printing independently, and
4. printing on lines.

IMITATING

Your child watches you make the letter, then either traces on top of yours, or makes his own. By watching you, your child learns how the letter is formed, and learns how to break it down into its parts. It may also be helpful to describe what you are doing as you do it. For example, for a capital D, "First I draw a straight line down, then I jump back to the top and make a big curve around to the bottom." Talking your child through it may be more successful than showing him hand over hand. By talking through it, you give your child another sensory message (auditory) to help him remember. You also give him a little more independence than with hand-over-hand assistance.

TRACING AND COPYING

After your child has mastered making a letter by imitation, he is ready to attempt tracing and copying. When tracing, he makes his strokes directly over the model. In copying, the model is there for him to see, but he has to remember how to make it. He has to remember the process of breaking down the letter into its parts and putting them together. This is obviously harder than imitating. Also, copying from the blackboard is harder than copying from a sample right in front of him, such as an alphabet strip on his desk.

Some markers change the underlying color when traced. Crayola's "Color Changeables" are markers that change color when traced over with another marker, and there are other similar markers available. When your child traces over your printing with his marker, the color changes, or an interesting effect appears. This makes tracing more motivating for many children.

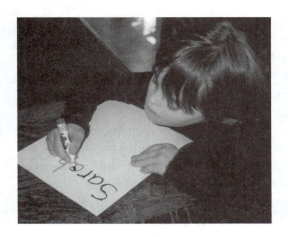

I do not recommend tracing as the first step in teaching a child to print. All children will learn better printing habits if they are taught how to form the letters, and then have supervised printing practice, during which they use the correct patterns. If a child is given worksheets to trace before he knows how the letters are formed, he is likely to be inconsistent in the letter pattern. This will make it more difficult for him to progress to independent printing. Tracing can be one method used to practice printing once your child knows how to form the letters correctly.

Copying is often used with children with Down syndrome in the classroom. Usually the educational assistant or teacher prints out the lesson and the child copies it underneath. This is called "underwriting." Again, this should only be used once the child has learned how to print well enough that he can form the letters automatically. Adults must remember to leave extra space between words so that the child, whose printing is usually larger, can continue to copy directly underneath the adult's words. In the higher grades, when there are large amounts of written work in a day, the child with Down syndrome may be copying pages of printing. The challenge is to keep this written work meaningful for the child, so that he is reading and understanding the content as well as copying it. The goals in copying skills are:

1. looking at each letter and copying them one by one;
2. looking at a whole word and copying it without having to glance back up at it;
3. looking at a short sentence, and copying it without repeatedly glancing up at it.

The child's ability to progress through these stages depends largely on literacy development, rather than on fine motor skills. Methods of accommodating and adapting written language work in the classroom are described in detail in the book *Classroom Language Skills for Children with Down Syndrome,* by Libby Kumin (Woodbine House, 2001).

PRINTING INDEPENDENTLY

This is the next stage of learning how to print letters and numbers. Your child must be able to recall the visual image of the letter, and remember how to direct his hand to reproduce this on the page.

Thinking up imaginative anecdotes about particularly tricky letters or numbers may help your child remember how to form them. The cues and anecdotes you make up will be best remembered if they are interesting for your child. For example, in order to help Sarah remember how to form the number five, I used this visual image: There is a little man (straight line down) with a big round tummy (semicircle) and a hat (horizontal line on top). When she couldn't remember how to form a five, reminding her about the little man helped her remember how to get started.

Some letters and numbers are easily confused because the pattern is similar except for the initial starting direction. For quite a long time, Sarah printed her name beginning with an S or a 3, depending on which way her pencil began to move! Other letters that are easily confused are M & W, b & d, p & q, n & u. If your child has learned the pattern for each letter, he will probably have less trouble with reversals and inversions. For example, "b" begins with a vertical line down, and can be learned at the same time as the other letters that begin in the same way (h, k, l, p). If "d" is also taught by beginning with the vertical line down, it may cause confusion. Instead, it can be taught by beginning with the curved stroke, at the same time as the other letters that begin that way (a, g, q). At the end of this chapter, I give one suggested way of grouping lower case letters for learning to print. Other educators and therapists may use similar groupings when teaching printing.

When your child is ready to practice printing letters, there are many commercially available workbooks that provide direction and practice, some with wipe-off pages. Most of these books have arrows that show the child which direction the line or curve should go. However, your child with Down syndrome may have difficulty following arrows. Without supervision, he may randomly attempt to trace and copy the letters. It is generally thought to be best for the child to learn to print with consistent direction of his strokes (20). Until your child is consistently printing letters in the right direction, it may be best to continue with imitating (so he can see how you form the letter) and supervised copying. Once he has established the patterns of movement for printing the letters, he could use the printing workbooks for more practice. The book *Handwriting without Tears,* by Jan Z. Olsen, describes one program for teaching printing and cursive writing that is successful for many children. Workbooks are included in the program (20).

Here are some more examples of verbal cues to give your child to help him remember the visual image of the letter or number, and how to initiate the printing sequence. These are only a few examples. What works for your child will depend

Alternatives to Paper and Pencil

During these first three stages of printing development, offering a variety of ways to practice may help keep your child motivated, and keep it fun. Using a multi-sensory approach can help some children learn letter shapes more easily. Here are some ideas:

- finger painting letters, numbers, and shapes;
- drawing in sand with a stick;
- sidewalk chalk;
- Magna Doodle;
- colorful chalk for a blackboard;
- paint brush dipped in water: make letters, etc. on outside walls, fences, etc.;
- drawing with a finger in flour; powder; dry Kool Aid or Jello mix
- making letters, etc., with cooked spaghetti noodles;
- making letters, etc., with "Wikki Stix" (colorful string dipped in wax);
- rolling out a snake of play dough and forming a letter. (The last three activities will be easier initially if your child makes his letter on top of a large printed letter.)

partly on his interests. If he particularly likes trains, for example, you can talk about "n" being a single train tunnel, "m" being a double tunnel, etc. Even with this type of cuing, learning to print takes lots of time and practice.

- h: a tall line with a hump;
- r: a small line with a roof;
- s: a slithery snake;
- w: choppy waves;
- j: a fishing line and hook going down into the water.

PRINTING ON LINES

Once your child can print letters independently, he will gradually begin to refine his printing to be able to stay on lines, with consistent size and spacing. This stage may be as difficult as learning to print the letters themselves. It is hard enough to remember how to form all the letters, while retaining the understanding of the words and sentences being printed, without having to worry about staying on the lines! Recognize how challenging this is, and support your child in every attempt to print. If the demands are too great, he might refuse to keep trying.

Here are some strategies that may help your child develop the ability to print on the lines with consistent size:

1. Widely spaced lines should be used initially, as your child's printing will be quite large. You can draw the lines with a ruler on unlined paper.

2. When your child begins to reduce the size of his printed letters, he may benefit from using some specialized paper. Using paper with very dark lines may help direct the printing orientation. Jan Z. Olsen, in her book *Handwriting without Tears,* suggests using two lines, a top and bottom line, without the dotted or multicolored lines that some primary workbooks have. Also available in some educational stores is raised-line paper (such as Right-Line Paper, by Pro-Ed), so the child can feel where the line is. If your child doesn't always begin his printing on the left side of the page, you can put a small green dot there to remind him.

3. Another strategy sometimes used is to make boxes on the page for the child to fill in the letters; this helps him learn size and word spacing as well as staying on a horizontal line.

4. Leave plenty of space between words if your child is copying under someone else's printing. If there is not enough space between words, his words will run together. Children learning to print always need more space.

5. Underline the space under the word to be copied, to give your child a cue as to where to place his word and how to space his copying.

When your child is printing at school and is trying to master all these skills, it is best to discuss the type of approach to use with your child's teacher (and occupational therapist, if one is involved). Many children with Down syndrome will learn to print on lines with correct spacing without using specialized paper; it just takes a long time!

PENCIL PRESSURE

Sometimes a child may have difficulty with the amount of pressure he uses on the pencil. Pressure can be affected by position and posture (page 26), by the type of grasp used and where the pencil is held, the type of pencil or pen used, and by the child's experience with printing. If too much pressure is used, it may give him a tight, cramped hand, and he may rip the paper. More often, children with Down syndrome use too little pressure, resulting in printing that is very light and wobbly. A heavier lead in the pencil or a felt tip marker may help the child who uses too little pressure. A weighted pencil (a small weight that slides on and off a regular pencil) may provide more sensory input so the child can use appropriate pressure. A pencil grip or tactile cue can help him hold the pencil with a firmer grasp.

A pencil grip may also sometimes assist the child who holds the pencil too tightly and uses too much pressure. A child may hold the pencil too tightly in an attempt to stabilize, if he lacks stability in the body and shoulder. If this is the problem, activities as suggested in Chapter 5 will be helpful.

Pencil Grips: Sometimes a special grip on the pencil will help your child place his hand in the right spot, and also maintain a tripod grasp. There are several types of pencil grips available commercially. I have had the most experience and success with "The Pencil Grip" and "Stetco" pencil grips (see Resources).

Pencil grips can be helpful for the child who can achieve a tripod grasp on a pencil when it is placed there for him, but:

There are several types of commercially available pencil grips. The three on the left are available from educational or therapy suppliers. The coil and the Wikki Stix™ wrapped around the pencil can remind the child where to hold the pencil. A shorter pencil may be easier to position and control. A fine tip marker can help if your child lacks strength to print with enough pressure.

1. has difficulty remembering how to position the pencil in his fingers himself, or
2. uses the base of the thumb to hold the pencil against the side of his hand (the anchoring grip, described above).

However, for some children, pencil grips can be more distracting than beneficial. Because the child isn't holding onto the pencil directly, but onto the grip, some control of the pencil movement is lost.

Tactile and Visual Cues: If your child holds the pencil too far up the shaft, his writing hand is completely off the paper, resulting in light pressure and less control. A sticker, Wikki Stix, or pencil grip indicating where the pencil should be held can help your child position the pencil more effectively. Alternately, you can make a mark on your child's hand, between the thumb and index finger, to indicate where the pencil should rest against his hand.

Cursive Writing

Most children learn handwriting (cursive writing) in grade three or four. This is too early for most children with Down syndrome. Some of our children may never learn functional cursive writing. They will need to be able to print or write their signature, but may not need to learn more cursive writing skills. What they will need is some relatively efficient way to communicate in written form. This is often a combination of printing and/or cursive writing, and computer use.

Cursive writing demands continuous movement of the small joints of the hand as the letters are formed in a flowing, nonstop motion. There isn't the opportunity to stop after each letter and reposition the hand for the next letter, as in printing. The adjustments of position in the arm as it moves across the page have to be smooth for handwriting to be efficient. The child must also make small adjustments in posture to accommodate his arm movement. For children who have any difficulty with posture, balance, and stability, handwriting will be more of a physical challenge.

Prewriting exercises can be introduced prior to learning to write individual letters. This is a similar approach to the preprinting activities described earlier in this chapter. Prewriting exercises involve repetitive, flowing patterns that help the child gain control of the continuous, joined movements for writing. For example, making a line of joined loops will help your child develop the motion that begins the letters l, k, b, f, and h. As in the preprinting activities, it is often helpful to begin doing these patterns at a blackboard or easel, where the arm can move freely and the size can be larger. In appendix 1, I have included some prewriting worksheets which incorporate the five basic patterns found in most written letters. There are also commercially available handwriting workbooks and programs that incorporate pattern practice and letter formation. Some examples are: *Callirobics* (in which the exercises are done to music); *Neurokinesthetic Approach to Hand Function and Handwriting* (#3 in Bibliography); *Handwriting without Tears* (#50 in Bibliography). See the Resources section at the back of the book for sources of handwriting programs.

At school, your child may be taught handwriting with the D'Nealian or Zaner-Bloser methods. I don't feel that there is any right or wrong method of teaching handwriting. What is most important is that the child learn *how* to form the letters consistently and efficiently. To do this he must be shown and taught the correct way, otherwise he will devise his own method that will likely not lead to cursive writing success in the long term. Sarah has still not developed cursive writing that is automatic enough to replace her printing for efficiency. We have had to put the cursive writing program on hold for a couple of years, but when she was practicing it, it seemed that the *Handwriting without Tears* program was the easiest for her, as it is based on the printed letter.

Your child may be able to learn writing in the same way most children learn: practicing one letter at a time, going through the alphabet in order. Many children, however, benefit from learning the letters in groups with similar formations. For example, in cursive writing, the letters "a," "c," "d," "g," "o," and "q" all begin in the same way. Learning this pattern as a group of letters helps many children remember how to form them.

Cursive writing is the culmination of the development of all the areas described throughout this book. Good stability and control in the body, shoulders, and arms; hand stability and dexterity of the small joints of the hand; sensory awareness and memory of the feel of how to form the letters; visual motor control; cognitive ability; and motivation all contribute to the ability to learn cursive writing. Given all these factors that come into play, it is not surprising that many children, not just children with Down syndrome, find the process of learning cursive writing difficult. When setting goals for our children with Down syndrome, we need to consider the amount of time and effort that may need to be put into learning cursive writing. It is realistic to set a goal of cursive writing if it is expected that the child will be able to eventually use cursive writing as a functional skill.

Dictation to a Scribe

Dictation to a scribe is commonly used in classrooms for students with Down syndrome. The "scribe," usually an educational assistant, sometimes another student, writes down what the child says. For example, in journal writing, the scribe might first write down what the child describes about what he did last evening. Then usually the child writes underneath, copying the words above. Scribes are also used to write down information dictated or written on the blackboard by the teacher. Again, often the student copies underneath. Scribes can also be used to assist students during testing situations, if the child knows the material and is able to verbalize it, but doesn't have the fine motor skill to write it all down.

When printing independently, the child has to think about the content, the spelling of the words and the construction of the sentence. If printing or writing is not yet fully automatic, the child will also have to think about the formation of the letters, the spacing, etc. *If* the goal is printing development, he should not always use a scribe, but may have an assistant to verbally help him with spelling and sentence composi-

Profile: Mark

Seven-year-old Mark is "underwriting" in his journal at school; that is, his educational assistant prints what he dictates, and he copies underneath. As the lines in the small notebooks are too small for his printing, his assistant draws lines on unlined paper for him to print on. One day, Mark says he wants to try. Holding the ruler down while drawing a line promotes stability, as he has to hold it steady, and bilateral coordination, as one hand is using pressure to hold the ruler and the other hand is drawing the line. His assistant also encourages him to pick up his pencil with only his dominant hand, without helping to position it with his other hand. This helps him use small movements in his fingers to orient the pencil in his hand to be ready to print.

tion. *If* the goal is spelling, grammar, and content, he should have a scribe to help him organize the fine motor aspect of putting the information down on paper. There is no magic age when a child should stop using a scribe. High school students with Down syndrome may have a peer tutor to assist with taking notes in order to keep up with the information being presented.

Some schools are now adopting the use of laptop computers for note taking for all students. Students with Down syndrome can also learn to use a keyboard for written work. This is discussed in detail in the next section.

Computers

In this age of computers, many of us find that keyboarding skills are as important as handwriting. In fact, the ability to understand how to access technology using a keyboard will be crucial for our children in their everyday lives. We all now access library information through a keyboard; we use bank machines and e-mail, etc., etc. I hope that all children with Down syndrome will have the opportunity to learn some basic keyboarding skills in school to augment their printing or handwriting skills, and to increase their opportunities for independence in their daily lives.

Laura Meyers, in "Using Computers to Teach Children with Down Syndrome," reports that children with Down syndrome often get less frustrated and are more enthusiastic about written communication when they are using a computer than when they are printing or handwriting (44). Printing and cursive writing is usually a slow and laborious process for our children due to the difficulties with pencil grasp and visual motor control. Learning the keyboard also takes time for children with Down syndrome, but the physical process may be less difficult than writing.

As with printing and writing, positioning is important: correct work height, back support, feet flat on the floor. With the elbows bent at 90 degrees, the keyboard should be level with or slightly below the hands. The monitor should be at eye level; your child should not have to look up to see the monitor. If your child is doing a lot of typing on a regular basis, I recommend wrist supports, which are readily available in office supply stores. These firm wrist support cushions reduce strain and fatigue on the muscles.

Computers are used in most elementary and high schools as instructional tools, for data management, and for word processing. In this section, the access to and use of computer hardware and software to assist written communication will be briefly discussed. Decisions about computer options are best made in consultation with a computer expert, either someone within the school board, or someone from an augmentative communication clinic or program. Companies that sell accessible technology provide consultation and training in the use of the technology. This is a field that is growing all the time, and experts in the field can provide the most up-to-date information about computer access and options.

The information presented here covers three broad areas:
1. accessibility options built into computer operating systems;
2. hardware options;
3. software options.

Built-in Accessibility Options

Most computers have built in accessibility options in the control panel. For example, if you use Windows, you can access these through "My Computer," then "Control Panel." Those that may be helpful to the child with Down syndrome include:

- Mouse speed: the speed that the cursor moves on the screen can be slowed down.
- "Sticky keys": two or more keys that are usually pressed simultaneously (such as shift and a letter) can instead be pressed in succession with this option.
- Keystrokes, or onscreen keyboard: rather than using the regular keyboard, the mouse is used to choose letters on the screen.
- "Filter keys": the length of time a key needs to be pressed down can be adjusted. If your child unintentionally touches another key, it will not type it. The computer will type the key that is held down for the specified amount of time. Also, it helps to avoid the problem of typing repeated letters if your child can't release the key quickly enough on the normal setting.
- Double click: double click speed can be slowed down.

Hardware Options

"Hardware" refers to the physical components of the computer. Discussed here are the computer screen, the mouse, and the keyboard. Hardware options can be used to circumvent language, cognitive and fine motor difficulties that can interfere with a child's ability to use a computer effectively. In this section, only hardware options related to the fine motor aspect of written communication will be discussed.

Although some school systems do have hardware options available, many do not. Parent or teachers may have to consult with assistive technology experts, either through a company that sells the hardware, or through a hospital or clinic that offers this service. If a trial of a hardware option proves successful, the parents and school may want to include it in the IEP, if it helps the child to meet his educational goals.

TOUCH SCREEN PROGRAMS

Touch screens are separate screens that mount externally on the computer monitor. Any software program can then be activated by directly touching the computer screen rather than using a mouse. The child makes choices by touching the screen with his finger. This adaptation is beneficial for a child of any age who cannot use a mouse (or alternative) or keyboard. It teaches choice-making, cause/effect, pointing skills, visual attention, and gives the child early exposure to computers. Two such screens are Magic Touch from Keytec, and TouchWindow from ProEd (see Resources: Mayer-Johnson, Inc.)

MICE AND ALTERNATIVES

Using a computer mouse is a good example of an activity that involves using our sensory and perceptual system to guide our fine motor movements. The sensors in our muscles and joints direct our arm movement on the mouse while our eyes track this movement on the screen. Computer mice vary in their design, number of buttons, sensitivity to movement, and degree of fine motor control required.

As mentioned above, the cursor speed can be slowed down through the control panel, making it easier for your child to learn to control the mouse. Also, look for software programs that do not require the cursor to be in a precise position to make a selection. Some software allows for a broader area of selection, so that when the cursor gets close, it selects that item. This is known as creating "hot spots." This feature can be helpful for children who have difficulty moving to and stopping on a precise spot, but can get close. There are also some preschool computer programs that respond positively to any movement of the mouse or touch of the keyboard (e.g., *Jumpstart Toddlers; Reader Rabbit Toddler*).

Two examples of trackballs and a trackpad.

Many children need hand-over-hand assistance to learn how to move the mouse and to click a selection. "Double clicking" to open a program can be tricky and takes practice. There are mice available that have separate buttons for single clicking, double clicking, and dragging, thereby eliminating the difficulty some children have combining two movements, such as clicking and holding while dragging. There are various sizes and shapes of mice now; keep in mind that your child's hand is smaller when you are buying a mouse for your computer.

TASH makes switches (called Switch Click, Mini Click, and Buddy Buttons) that can be used instead of a mouse to activate programs. (See Resources.) These may be helpful for a young child with Down syndrome who would like to use simple games for learning, but who has difficulty with a mouse. As they grow up, many children with Down syndrome do learn how to use a regular mouse for their computer activities.

TRACKBALLS

Trackballs may offer greater control than a traditional mouse. The hand moves the ball, which in turn moves the cursor, while the rest of the unit stays in one position. Trackballs also come in a variety of shapes, sizes, sensitivities, and options. Some have speed settings (e.g., Roller Plus Trackball by Infogrip). Most trackballs have separate buttons for the click and drag functions.

JOYSTICKS

A joystick is another alternative to a mouse that some children may find easier to control. The joystick is grasped with the whole hand and moved in the desired direction. As with trackballs, there are a variety of speeds, sensitivities, and sizes available.

TRACKPADS

Trackpads are now often used with laptop computers instead of a mouse. The user moves his finger across the trackpad (which looks like a miniature screen) to direct the cursor.

Most computers in homes, schools, and public places are accessed using a mouse. Therefore, I recommend teaching the use of a mouse. Only as a last resort would I recommend using a joystick or a trackball. Most laptops that have a trackpad also have the option of using a mouse. Personally, I find a mouse easier to control than using a trackpad.

KEYBOARD ADAPTATIONS

KEYGUARDS

A keyguard is a metal or plastic cover with holes that sits over the keyboard, isolating the keys so that the finger hits only one key at a time. It can be helpful if your child inadvertently hits more than one key at a time, or tends to lean his hands down on the

A keyguard separates the keys. Here, the letters of the keyboard are enlarged so they are easier to see.

Two examples of adapted keyboards.

keyboard. However, it may make the letters on the keyboard slightly more difficult to see. To make the letters more visible, high contrast letters (such as "Zoom Caps" and "Keyboard Seels") can be stuck onto the letters of choice, making those letters easier for your child to see. For example, if your child is learning to "log on" to the computer, but can't always find the letters of his name, you can try sticking these adhesive letters to the keyboard until he learns where they are located.

ALTERNATE KEYBOARDS AND WORD PROCESSING DEVICES

Some computer equipment companies have designed keyboards to allow computer access for children with disabilities. Because these keyboards are usually simplified and require less physical skill, they may be helpful for children with Down syndrome. Some examples of alternate keyboards are the Discover Board by Don Johnston Incorporated, and Intellikeys by IntelliTools, Inc. Overlays for particular software programs can be custom designed to be used with these keyboards. Another example is Big Keys LX Keyboards, which is a regular keyboard with oversized letter and number keys.

Smaller, portable word processing devices are now available. These devices can be used by the student who has handwriting difficulties but can use a smaller keyboard to type. Examples are the Writer, by Advanced Keyboard Technologies, and Alphasmart.

Software Options

There are many readily available games and software programs that help children learn keyboarding skills and develop academics. As well, there are specialized software programs to assist students with special needs. A few of these specialized programs will be highlighted here, to give an idea of the types of programs available. See Resources for manufacturers and distributors.

- **Picture processors:** These programs provide pictures with text. Examples are Boardmaker, Writing with Symbols, and Clicker. Boardmaker is commonly used to aid many students with communication difficulties who use picture communication. The software produces representational black and white or color pictures depicting many common words. The pictures and words can be customized for the individual.
- **Talking word processors:** These programs provide auditory feedback, as the words are spoken as they are typed. Examples are Intellitalk and Write OutLoud.
- **Word Prediction Programs:** Word prediction programs provide word options after one or a few letters of the word are

typed in. They can speed up writing for students who need help with spelling but can read. The software can be customized to provide options of words frequently used by that individual. Once the word is displayed, it can be chosen with a click, reducing the need for typing individual letters. An example of a word prediction program is "CO:Writer" by Don Johnston, Inc.

Learning Keyboarding Skills

As with printing, learning the keyboard is a process that will take time and *practice.* Some preschool-targeted computer programs include games that help the young child become familiar with the keyboard (one example is *Playroom,* from Broderbund software). The instant feedback to the child from these types of programs can be very motivating.

Some specialized keyboards offer an ABC order option for keyboards. "Qwerty" is the commonly used letter setup on all computers found everywhere in North America. For this reason, if possible, it is recommended as the keyboard of choice.

Most commercially available keyboarding programs stress using all the fingers on the keyboard. Although this is ideal, it may be too difficult for children with Down syndrome because of the individual finger movement required. It has been suggested that it is more functional for children with fine motor problems to use one or two fingers on the keyboard, rather than trying to learn to use all their fingers. I would rather see children with Down syndrome learn where the letters are on the keyboard and gain confidence in written communication, even if they use one finger to type. The coordination of all the fingers on the keyboard can come much later, if at all.

Summary of Computer Options

In summary, there are many options available for customizing a computer for your child's individual needs. Since your child will grow up to use computers in different environments (home, school, and work), it is best if he can learn to use a computer without alternate hardware. Software and accessibility options can be accessed from any computer, and are easier than hardware options to try on a trial basis. Schools have some access to some specialized software and options, and most school boards hire personnel who load and set up this software.

Most children with Down syndrome will not need specialized hardware to use a computer to assist with written communication, but will benefit from some of the software picture and/or word processing programs, such as those described above. This field is evolving very quickly and there are often new programs on the market. Start with the computer resource staff in your school and school system. If you need more help, agencies and organizations that market assistive technologies can be helpful in determining what is best for your child (such as Mayer-Johnson). In some areas, augmentative communication or assistive technology clinics or institutions are also available to help you sort through the choices.

Incorporating Fine Motor Goals into Your Child's Educational Program

For many children, kindergarten is their first introduction to a structured learning environment. Most children with Down syndrome, however, will have participated in some early stimulation and/or preschool or daycare program, where they will have had exposure to fine motor and early learning tasks. This helps to prepare them for the curriculum-based programming that they have once they start school.

Teachers take some of these factors into consideration when assessing a child's learning in a classroom setting:

1. The child's ability to express himself verbally and on paper are the primary means by which a teacher can observe a child's understanding and retention of taught material. Most children with Down syndrome have delays and difficulties with both verbal and written communication. It is important to take fine motor abilities and goals into consideration when setting up educational goals, so that the child can do written work in the classroom to the best of his potential.

2. The child's ability to focus and pay attention and to initiate and complete tasks indicates his readiness and ability to learn in an academic environment.

3. The child's ability to follow routines and organize himself and his work space throughout the school day helps to indicate his overall maturity level.

The classroom is obviously a prime place for children with Down syndrome to continue to develop their fine motor skills. In the early school years, children do a lot of concept-oriented play, manipulative play for early math and spatial skills, drawing, coloring, and cutting, and begin to learn to print. As children progress through school into the higher grades, classroom activities become focused primarily on fine motor skills (printing, writing, drawing, and computer use), auditory skills (listening), and verbal skills (answering questions, expressing ideas, etc.).

Most children with Down syndrome in the public school systems in North America have an individualized education plan written up, usually annually. These plans identify short- and long-term educational goals, and the strategies and resources to be used in meeting those goals. In the U.S., the plan is called the Individualized Education Program (IEP); in Canada, the Pupil Education Plan (PEP). Each child's education plan will reflect his own level of development and individual needs within that particular classroom environment. In order to establish *fine motor goals* for the educational plan that are appropriate and realistic for your child, keep the following points in mind:

1. Know your child's fine motor developmental level. The teacher can observe the manner in which your child participates in the fine motor activities that go on in the classroom. You, as parents, can supplement this with information about what self-help skills and play activities he is able to do at home. A comprehensive fine

motor assessment by an occupational therapist can give more information on the quality of fine motor movements, development of grasp and other fine motor patterns, and visual motor skills. Once the developmental level of your child's fine motor abilities is known, goals can be set.

2. Set goals in small steps. If activities are broken down into small steps and goals set one step at a time, there is a greater chance of success, everyone can see progress, and your child will probably be more motivated.

3. Reevaluate goals at set intervals. If no change or progress is seen after a set period of time, the goal should be reevaluated. Perhaps the presentation or materials need to be changed, or the goal itself changed.

4. Keep the goals relevant to your child. If he can see the point of working towards a goal, and the activities used to reach that goal are of interest to him, he will be more motivated to keep at it.

GOALS FOR CHILDREN IN INCLUSIVE SETTINGS

For children who are integrated into regular classroom settings, fine motor goals on their educational plan will usually reflect an adaptation of the fine motor activities that the class participates in, and additions to those activities already going on in the classroom. Here are some examples of goals with specific classroom activities that could be incorporated into the educational plan of a child with Down syndrome in a regular classroom:

KINDERGARTEN—GRADE 1

Goals	Strategies
Mark will use a tripod grasp of a pencil and marker.	Pencil grip; small pieces of chalk at blackboard; drawing at easel and at table.
Mark will demonstrate improved control of pencil movement.	Making connecting lines on matching worksheets. Circling pictures on phonics worksheets. Drawing and painting at easel. Completing preprinting worksheets.
Mark will be able to print his name.	Mark prints each letter after demonstration by EA (educational assistant). Mark prints whole name after demonstration by EA. Mark traces the letters of his name. Mark copies his name from his name card.

Mark will cut along a line with scissors.	Mark will hold scissors in the mid position (thumb on top) with help. Mark will cut two or more strokes starting close to his body and cutting out. Mark will cut along dotted lines to cut out sentence strips to match with pictures.
Mark will organize his work to take home.	Mark will roll up his paintings. Mark will fold his work papers in half and put in his backpack.
Mark will improve his fine finger dexterity.	Mark will insert his attendance card into the slot on the attendance board. Mark will put a sticker beside every activity in his activity record book upon completion. Mark will complete a 10-piece interlocking puzzle. Mark will stack and count 10 math counting blocks. Mark will unscrew the glue stick and apply glue in cutting and pasting. Mark will unzip his lunch bag and open his juice box at lunch/snack. Mark will use his index and third fingers to use arrow buttons for selection on the computer. Mark will take a handful of pencils and distribute one to each child.

GRADES 2-4

Goals	*Strategies*
Katie will print independently.	Katie will practice printing the individual letters of one letter group each day to reinforce letter formation. Katie will print her first and last name at the top of her journal entry each day. Katie will copy two sentences, that she has dictated, into her daily journal, with 1/2" dark spaced lines. Katie will leave a finger space between each word when printing. Katie will check off subject areas completed by class at the blackboard.

Katie will stay in the lines
    when coloring.

Katie will color in her own drawings.
Katie will pick one part of the
    worksheet picture to color,
    doing it slowly and concen-
    trating on staying in the lines.
Katie will color in block letters
    on headings of worksheets.

Katie's arm and hand strength
    will improve.

Katie will open and hold the school
    door for the class after recess.
Katie will help erase the blackboard.
Katie will attach her completed
    work papers to her activity chart
    using a colored clothespin.
Katie will open and close her
    pencil box to take out and put
    away her pencils/pencil crayons.
Katie will erase errors in printing.

Katie will improve her fine
    finger dexterity.

Katie will collect the library sign-
    out cards from her classmates and
    place them in the sign-out box.
Katie will help distribute worksheets to
    the class.
Katie will attempt to zip up her coat.
    After three tries she will receive help.
Katie will count out groups of 10
    popsicle sticks and put a rubber band
    around each in math.
Katie will insert a tape into the
    tape player at the listening center.
Katie will use individual finger
    movement to count out answers
    in math addition and subtraction.

Katie will cut out simple shapes
    with scissors.

Katie will cut out a large square
    with red dots at the corners to remind
    her to stop and change direction.
Katie will cut a semicircle out of
    a folded piece of paper (when she
    opens out the fold it will be a circle)
Katie will cut out shapes and glue
    to a math geometry worksheet.

Katie will be able to use a language
    computer program with minimal
    assistance.

Katie will control the cursor for
    selections using a trackball.
Katie will learn the keyboard position
    of 2 new letters per week (which will
    be highlighted on the keyboard).

GRADES 5-8

Goals	Strategies
Tim will be able to do a page of legible written work in his journal and math book daily.	Tim will print and underline his name and the date at the top of his journal page.
	Tim will print on regular lined paper, double spacing the lines.
	Tim will use a ruler to draw a red line down the middle of his math workbook page to help him organize his work on the page. He will do one math problem on each side of the red line, so that his work remains separate and easy to read.
	Tim will erase errors in pencil or will use white-out for pen errors.
	Every second day Tim will use the computer to type his journal entry.
Tim will learn to sign his name using cursive writing.	Tim will do daily prewriting activities at the blackboard.
	Tim will practice each letter of his name individually.
	Tim will write his name on the blackboard when he has completed listed activities.
Tim's hand strength will improve.	Tim will be able to open his binder to insert papers, then close it.
	Tim will use a hole punch when necessary, to insert worksheets into his binder.
	Tim will gather up the class assignments and attach them together with a large clip or paper clip.
	Tim will thumbtack art work up onto the class bulletin board.
Tim will improve in fine finger dexterity.	Tim will open and insert pages into a Duotang notebook cover.
	Tim will break off pieces of masking tape and will tape art work up on the walls.
	Tim will plant individual bean seeds in a class gardening activity.

Tim will be able to pour liquids without spilling.

Tim will water the class plants.
Tim will pour exact amounts of liquid into measuring containers for science experiments.
Tim will pour his soup into his thermos lid at lunchtime.

Tim will be able to cut a variety of shapes and sizes with scissors.

Tim will cut out and fold three-dimensional geometric shapes (cube; pyramid; cylinder).
Tim will cut out block letters for a project heading.

HIGH SCHOOL

Goals	Strategies
Jodie will use the computer to make journal entries.	Jodie will use a word prediction program to assist her with spelling as she fills out a formatted journal entry page.
Jodie will expand her computer use.	Jodie will independently type in her name and password to access programs. Jodie will remember the location of all the letters and punctuation on the keyboard.
Jodie will practice her written signature.	Daily, Jodie and her classmates will sign the attendance list.
Jodie's dexterity will continue to improve.	Jodie will assist in the construction of hallway bulletin board displays, including tacking or stapling up photos and lettering. Jodie will collate and staple together handouts. Jodie will sharpen some drawing pencils for art class. Jodie will open her combination lock.

These goals and strategies are just a few examples of how your child can work toward fine motor skill goals in the classroom. After each goal is accomplished, refer to Chapters 8 and 9 to help you define the next goal in the developmental progress of that particular skill.

Grandma's and Grandpa's List

- Magnetized letters and numbers
- Foam letters for bathtub play
- Paint, brushes, paper
- Easel; table easels
- Large memo board
- Chalkboard, chalk
- Sidewalk chalk
- Finger crayons
- Crayons, pencil crayons, pencils
- Markers (various sizes and types)
- Changeables (markers) by Crayola (for tracing)
- Fun erasers (to make the inevitable erasing more fun)
- Simple coloring books with clear, simple, undetailed pictures
- Simple maze books (where the child has to follow a very simple path with his pencil)
- Simple dot-to-dot activity books
- Preschool workbooks: activity books with concepts of shape and color; same and different, etc.
- Squeeze/loop (self-opening) scissors
- Good child-sized scissors with a decent cutting blade, e.g., Fiskars
- Tweezer/tong games (e.g., Operation)
- Wikki Stix
- Magna Doodle (with tracing cards, alphabet stencils)
- Stencils
- Construction paper
- Computer software
- Sticker books

CHAPTER 10

Daily Living Skills: Self-Help Skills, Household and Leisure Activities

Daily Living Skills
Self-Help: Dressing, Eating, and Drinking; Grooming
Household Chores
Leisure Activities

Dexterity
Precise movements of hands and fingers;
Individual finger movements;
Strength of finger and thumb pincer grasp

Stability
Positions the body
and arms

**Bilateral
Coordination**
The hands work together

Sensation
Sensory awareness of body
and hand position;
Motor memory of sequences
(e.g., tying shoelaces)

Figure 18

SELF-HELP SKILLS

Children are very busy in their first years of life, establishing the building blocks of fine motor skills and gradually gaining the movements that will develop dexterity. Self-help skills play a special role in hand skills development:

EATING   DRESSING   GROOMING

DEXTERITY

Figure 19

To understand the relationship between the development of dexterity and self-help skills, it may help to think about the electrical wiring that runs through a house; the current travels in both directions. It isn't necessary for a child to have developed good dexterity before she begins to do self-help activities. Practicing and doing these activities over and over will improve your child's dexterity. For example:

- Finger feeding helps to develop pincer grasp.
- Putting on socks helps to develop finger and thumb strength.
- Doing up a zipper helps to develop finger coordination, with both hands working together.

Your child will practice these tasks many, many times before they become "easy," but all that practice will develop the dexterity that she will need for other daily living skills.

Dressing

It takes years for children to become independent in dressing. Your child will gradually learn, step by step, how to undress and dress herself, do up fastenings, and make choices about her clothing. Remember the progression of learning new skills discussed in Chapter 2. Also consider these basic strategies while your child is learning dressing and undressing:

1. **Positioning:** Your child needs to be in a stable position in order to hold the clothing and put it on/off. This may mean sitting with her back against the wall to put on socks and shoes, or on a stair to push her foot into a boot.

Sitting in a corner or against a wall can give a child more stability to reach down and use both hands to take off shoes and to put on socks.

2. **Step by Step:** As discussed in Chapter 2, a child moves gradually from being dependent to independent in dressing. Remember all the steps, letting your child do more for herself as she is able. When she is beginning to learn a new skill, you can begin the

task, then let your child finish the last step, or help her to finish. (This is called backward chaining.) For example, you put the sock on over her toes, and she pulls it up over her heel. Some children respond better if you do it in the reverse order, with her starting and you finishing the task.

3. **Hand-over-Hand:** Hand-over-hand assistance works well with some children, and not with others. Use gentle movements to help guide your child's hands. Sarah wasn't always keen on hand-over-hand, but couldn't do it by herself, yet wanted to be independent. I have found that talking about our hands working together as a "team" helped her accept my physical guidance when it was necessary. As they get older, most children need less and less physical assistance.

4. **Expectations:** Don't expect too much, but do expect your child to participate in some way.

5. **Timing:** Dressing in the morning rush may not be the best time to expect your child to attempt to learn the next step in the task. Try to find a time that isn't rushed and that is motivating, such as getting changed for swimming.

6. **Modeling:** Letting your child watch you or her siblings dress will help her through imitation. Dressing together may be more fun for her than on her own.

7. **Choice of Clothing:** Choose easy clothing: loose, comfortable fabrics, elastic waist bands, Velcro shoes. Avoid fastenings on clothing for young children when possible; e.g., pullover shirts rather than button-up shirts, elastic-waist jeans rather than zipper- and button-closing jeans.

8. **Sequencing:** Sometimes children can manage the physical skills required in dressing, but may have difficulty planning how to carry out the step-by-step sequencing required. In this case, visual cues may help. A strip of picture symbols (such as those available through the Boardmaker software program) showing the correct sequence for dressing can be used. For example, the pictures could say: 1. underwear 2. T-shirt 3. pants 4. socks 5. shoes 6. sweater. If the Boardmaker program is not available, you can use pictures cut out of magazines, or actual photos of your child's clothes.

Removing socks introduces this young child to dressing activities.

Usually, children learn to take off loose clothing before they learn to put it on. Babies often frustrate their parents by continually taking off their hat, mitts, or socks! If your baby doesn't do this on her own, help guide her hands to do it when you come in from outside, or are getting ready for bed. This stage is important for your baby to develop a sense of body parts and the first steps of dressing independence.

As your child develops, you gradually increase the expectations during the daily routine. Here are the main steps in dressing skills that our children learn. They are outlined in approximate order of difficulty, but your child will usually be learning several skills at once:

- Taking off hat; mitts;
- Taking off socks and shoes;
- Putting on hat;
- Taking off jacket (after it is undone);
- Pulling down pants and taking off;
- Pulling shirt on/off the head;
- Pulling zippers up and down (once started);
- Putting on jacket using the flip method (described below);
- Taking off loose pajamas;
- Putting legs in pants and pulling up;
- Putting arms in sleeves of shirt (once over head);
- Putting shoes/boots on;
- Putting socks on;
- Pulling arms out of sleeves;
- Putting shirt over head and putting arms through;
- Putting on jacket (usual method);
- Putting on a front-opening shirt/blouse;
- Buttoning;
- Zipping up (including starting);
- Tying shoelaces.

COMMON DRESSING CHALLENGES AND ADAPTED METHODS FOR CHILDREN WITH DOWN SYNDROME

PUTTING ON A JACKET

The flip method is often taught to young children in nursery schools, as it is easier for them to do than the usual method. Your child sits or stands on the floor. Lay the jacket down on the floor, with the top of the jacket label/hood closest to your child and the inside of the jacket facing up. Your child pushes her arms into the armholes, then flips the jacket up over her head.

Another approach is to place the hood of the jacket on your child's head. The jacket is then in position for her to put her arms into the sleeves. This technique can be a good transition between the flip method and the regular method, as your child has to reach behind to slip her arms in.

When helping your child learn the regular method, she holds the jacket with one hand above the arm hole of the other side. (For example, I hold the jacket with my left hand above the right armhole.) She then slips that arm in. That part is easy, because she can see where to put her arm. She then has to rotate her other arm in and behind her, find the hole, and

Young children can learn to put on their coats using the flip method.

slip her arm through, all without being able to see. During this step, you can help by lightly positioning the jacket so she can more easily find the sleeve behind her. Once the motor pattern becomes automatic, she will be able to find the sleeve with that arm. Most of us always put on our coat or jacket the same way, starting with the same arm. (It seems that most right-handed people put their right arm through first.) If you try doing it with the other side first, you will find it more difficult. When you are helping your child learn, make sure she always starts with the same arm. With repeated practice, the movements become automatic.

BUTTONS

Fortunately, clothing for children is not encumbered with as many buttons as in years past. Elastic waist pants are popular with young children, even in blue jean styles, as are pullover sweatshirts and T-shirts. However, as your child gets older, she probably

Stable positioning, a vertical buttonhole, and clear view of the button will make buttoning easier.

will want to wear some styles with buttons, as her peers do. In helping Sarah learn to manage buttons, I have found that it is much easier initially to both do up and undo buttons with a vertical buttonhole, as opposed to horizontal. With a vertical buttonhole, the button just slips straight into the hole, without the wrist movement required of a horizontal buttonhole. Larger buttons and buttonholes are easier than smaller buttons.

If your child is practicing on a doll or a practice button board—often found in kindergarten classrooms—it will help your child more with her own clothing if the doll or practice board is on her lap facing out. This way the buttons are facing the way they would be on her own clothing. It may be fun for your child to have "dress up" clothes with buttons, such as an old adult shirt or vest with the sleeves cut short, the buttonholes enlarged, and larger buttons sewn on.

ZIPPERS

Children can practice zipping and unzipping on backpacks, pencil cases, etc. These provide practice and strengthening opportunities.

We all know how tricky zippers on jackets and coats can be for many children! When buying a coat or jacket for your child, look for a sturdy zipper, with a stable end that is large enough to be grasped firmly. A young child will likely need help connecting the zipper to start it, then she can pull it up. Sometimes a small key ring or other attachment to the zipper tab is useful if her pincer grasp is not yet strong enough to pull up the tab.

Trying a different position while putting on the jacket may also help. Sitting on a chair or step when connecting the zipper may be easier than standing up. Here are some possible alternatives to use while your child is learning to do up zippers:

1. Look for a pullover jacket with a zipper neck closure that avoids the difficulty of connecting the zipper to start it.
2. Use a one-piece snowsuit.
3. Look for a coat with loop and Velcro tab closures.
4. Have your child connect the zipper with the coat on her lap, and zip it up just a bit. She then steps into the coat and pulls

it up and on, then completes the zipper. (It is easier to connect a zipper when you don't have to bend forward and look down.)

5. Purchase a jacket with snap closures. Usually I find snaps more difficult than zippers, but some children may find them easier.

A zipper ring can make zippers easier if your child has difficulty grasping the tab to pull it up and down. (The dangling shoe accessory isn't necessary!)

For Sarah, the most difficult part about learning to do up a zipper was getting the feel of the zipper being properly connected at the bottom, and continuing to hold the inserted side in while she pulled up the tab. When you begin to teach your child to pull her zipper up and down, it may be easier for her in the long run if she does this with her left hand, even if she is right handed. The way most zippers are designed, it is usually the right hand that has to hold the base of the zipper in place while the left hand pulls up the tab. If you don't hold the base while beginning to pull up, the zipper usually gets stuck or comes disconnected.

Acquiring the ability to start a zipper independently takes a lot of practice. Remind your child that often a zipper doesn't start on the first try!

SHOELACES

Fortunately, children these days can get by without knowing how to tie shoelaces, with so many styles of Velcro closing shoes on the market. There are also elastic shoelaces available in different styles. These can be found in drug stores; a medical equipment supplier usually carries a more extensive selection.

Even though a child may have good fine motor skills, she still may not be able to tie shoelaces. As with many more complex daily activities, the task requires more than just dexterity. The child has to remember each step, and how to sequence the steps in order. She has to be able to plan the sequence of steps until they become automatic. A lot of attention, concentration, motivation, and persistence are necessary. When I wrote the first edition of this book, Sarah couldn't yet tie her shoelaces completely independently, but she did part of the process, needing help to finish. Eventually she did learn the whole sequence, and she can also double knot them so they don't come undone. Now she is a typical teenager, tying them loosely and slipping her feet in and out of her shoes without touching the shoelaces. This ruins the back of the shoe, but it is how it is done at this age!

Remember, tying shoelaces is optional in our world, and we sometimes have to decide that it isn't worth the energy required to teach a skill that your child can get by without. That being said, if you do want your child to learn to tie shoelaces, remember to take it step by step. There are different ways to tie shoes, and you may need to experiment with your child to find out which way will work. I would *not* attempt learning to tie shoelaces if your child cannot yet do up buttons or start a zipper. It isn't necessary to know right from left, however. Tying shoelaces is a motor sequencing activity, and once the motor pattern is established your child will be able to do it automatically.

1. The first step, crossing one lace over, then under the other lace, is probably the easiest part, and is a useful thing to know how to do. Your child can practice tying on larger materials initially, such as a housecoat belt, the sash on an apron, the handles of a plastic bag, or a ribbon around a stuffed toy's neck

2. Then she can practice on a shoe that is on the table in front of her, facing out, as if it were on her foot. (Bending down to tie laces when the shoe is on the foot is more difficult for balance and stability.) When she knows how to tie the laces together, she can attempt to do so when her shoe is on!

3. After the initial tie is accomplished, the next steps can be approached in different ways:
   - Your child can either make two "bunny ears," holding one loop with each hand, which she then crosses over and under to tie together, or
   - She can make one loop and hold it, while her other hand wraps the remaining lace around and tucks it under. This method is probably more difficult perceptually.

4. Some strategies that may help:
   - Remember that wide, flat laces are easier to hold and manipulate than thin, round laces.
   - Much of the difficulty with tying laces is the sequencing and the perceptual differentiation of which lace goes where. You can try using two different-colored laces, tied together at the base of the holes (you will probably have to cut them or they'll be too long). This way, your child makes one bunny ear of each color, then makes a tie with one color going over and under the other. Or, using the other method, she makes the loop with one color and wraps around and through with the other color.

Inserting two different colors of shoelaces may help the child who is learning to tie shoes.

   - When helping your child, try to help from behind or beside her, so that your hands are oriented the same way as hers, and you are not demonstrating in reverse.
   - There is a method of teaching called backward chaining that is successful for many children. In this method, you begin the activity and complete all but the last step. You let your child do the last step—in this case, pulling the two bows to tighten the knot. Your child learns the sequence one step at a time, beginning with the final step and proceeding backwards through the sequence. With this method, the child feels the success of completing the task.

PUTTING SHOES ON THE RIGHT FEET

We are advised not to worry about our kids putting their shoes on the wrong feet. After all, how many thirty-year-olds do we see walking around with their shoes on the wrong feet? However, I know that many parents *would prefer* that their child learn to put shoes on the correct feet, especially if they have just paid for good orthotics for the shoes. Marking the shoes with an R or L doesn't usually work, because many kids can't consistently tell their right from left foot. I have found that putting a mark of some kind (e.g., a red dot) on the inside of each shoe at the heel works for many children. The child then puts the dots together (most children understand the concept of apart/together from about age 3 on), and the shoes are then lined up on the correct side.

REMOVING CLOTHES

When taking off their clothes, some children pull from the top of their sleeve or pant leg. They are usually successful at removing it, but the clothing is then inside out for the next time it has to be put on. This can be frustrating, if every time your child has to put on her jacket, the sleeves are inside out and have to be turned for her. Teach her to grasp and pull from the bottom of the sleeve or pant leg.

PUTTING CLOTHES ON BACKWARDS

The easiest way to get around this challenge is to choose clothes that look the same whether they are on forwards or backwards. Track pants, T-shirts, and sweatshirts with either no pattern or with a pattern both front and back fit this bill. The key to getting clothes on the right way is to get started with the leg/arm going into the correct opening. I used to lay Sarah's clothes out for her to help her with this. She didn't care when things ended up on backwards, so I had to decide how much I cared! (It depended on where we were going.) As she got older, she began to identify the tag as being at the back, and was able to figure out the orientation of the clothes that way.

Eating and Drinking

FINGER FEEDING

Children with Down syndrome can begin to feed themselves with their fingers from about the age of ten to twelve months. Initially, they will hold a cracker or teething biscuit to chew on. During the next few months, they can develop the ability to pick up small pieces of food using a pincer grasp. Although a neat pincer grasp usually develops later in the child with Down syndrome, do not hesitate to place small pieces of food on the highchair tray for your child once she is able to chew and swallow and does not choke on solid pieces. Babies can manage soft solid pieces (such as soft cheese and bits of banana) before they have teeth. If your baby can't pick up the pieces off the tray initially, hand her small pieces that she can grasp with her thumb and fingers and put in her mouth.

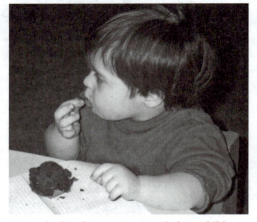

Finger feeding from a young age helps a child learn independence and self-help skills, as well as finger dexterity.

USING A SPOON AND FORK

By approximately twelve to eighteen months, your child will be ready to hold a spoon. At first, just let her hold it and bang it on the highchair while you feed her. As she becomes more interested in the process, you can gently assist her in the scooping motion and in bringing the spoon to her mouth. Gradually reduce the amount of assistance you provide. Child-sized spoons with easy-to-grip handles are best to begin with. Some spoon handles curve inward, which reduces the amount of wrist movement required to get the spoon in the mouth, and are easier for very young children. In addition, spoons with flat, shallow bowls are easier to eat from.

It also may help initially to use the child dishes that have raised sides, so your child can scoop against the sides. Textured foods that will stay on the spoon will be best to practice with initially, such as pudding, porridge, thick stews, yogurt, and pureed baby foods.

Children usually hold their spoon or fork in their palm with a palmar grasp for a few years at least, before they switch to holding it with the more mature

This child is learning to feed himself with a spoon. A slightly larger handle on the spoon may be easier for him, as in the photo to the right.

tripod grasp that most adults use, with the thumb up. The palmar grasp may persist longer in children with Down syndrome, but when they have been able to use a dynamic tripod grasp on a pencil for some time (see page 111), they should be able to use the more mature grasp of cutlery as well. Sometimes it is just habit that causes earlier patterns to persist. Also, the type of grasp used on cutlery has cultural and regional variations. Many adults hold their forks in a palmar grasp. If it is important to you to help your child learn to hold cutlery in the tripod grasp with her thumb up, try putting a sticker on the end of the handle of the spoon or fork, and help her hold it so she can see the sticker.

Examples of drinking and eating utensils for young children. Left: a cut-out cup makes room for the nose, so the child doesn't have to tip his head back as far. Right: a cup weighted on the bottom doesn't tip as easily. The angled spoon (shown second from the left) accommodates the lack of wrist movement in the young child.

Learning to hold and use a fork involves the same process as a spoon. Introduce using a fork with mashed or soft chunky foods that are easy to stab and will stick to the fork, such as mashed potatoes, squash, scrambled eggs, or thick stews. Progress to soft foods that can easily be stabbed to be picked up, such as pancakes, macaroni and cheese, tender chicken, or fish. Foods that are hardest to eat with a fork are those that need a firm stab to stay on the fork, such as salad, vegetables, and meat.

DRINKING

When your child is beginning to make the transition from bottle to cup drinking, a cup with a spout may help. You can then progress to a lidded cup without the spout, with small holes in the lid. Your child may find it easier to grasp a cup with handles at first. As she develops better control of picking up and placing down the cup, you may wish to try a small child's cup without handles, to help strengthen the thumb joint and "cupping" position of the hand.

Your child will gradually gain skill with cup drinking if she can practice it at every meal. Initially, your child may tip too much liquid into her mouth at once, resulting in sputtering and coughing. You can slow the liquid flow down by using nectars instead of juice, or by adding a bit of gelatin powder or infant cereal to thicken it.

It is not unusual for children to take some time to adjust to drinking from a cup when they are used to the bottle. Your child with Down syndrome may display some typical patterns:

Biting the Cup: This makes for messy drinking, as the liquid can't enter the mouth if the teeth are clenched on the cup. Rest the cup on the lower lip; don't put the cup in as far as the teeth. Tell your child to "use your lips" while you gently bring her lips together on the rim of the cup.

Protruding the Tongue: Often, a child with Down syndrome will rest the cup on her tongue rather than on her lower lip. Although it is effective, it is probably not a pattern you want to encourage. Before offering a drink, tap your child's lower lip to increase sensory awareness. Remind your child to keep her tongue in and use her lips on the cup. We used a mirror with Sarah and she became good at self-monitoring herself while drinking.

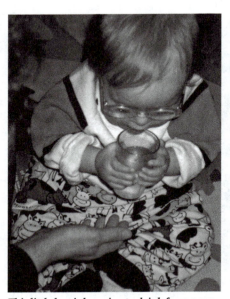
This little boy is learning to drink from a cup.

CUTTING AND SPREADING

Cutting and spreading with a knife are good practice opportunities for developing finger coordination and strength. The index finger guides the knife while the rest of the hand holds it stable. Complete independence in cutting of foods may not happen until your child is in late childhood or adolescence. Often before children are given knives to cut their food, they have practiced cutting skills with play dough. Then your child can begin practicing with a small, dull table knife on soft foods, such as pancakes. Encourage your school-aged child to spread her own bread or toast with butter/jam, etc., or to help you spread frosting on cupcakes. Not only will she be one step closer to making her own lunch, but this spreading practice will help her develop better control for gluing, printing, and writing at school.

As your child gets older, she will learn to cut foods such as meat. You may need to point out visual cues to help her remember which side of the knife is for cutting (the food side), and which side is for holding. There may be a serrated, bumpy, or rounded edge on the cutting side.

Using a knife to cut and spread helps the school-aged child develop control, which carries over to paper and pencil activities.

ORAL MOTOR CONTROL

It is not unusual for children with Down syndrome to experience some difficulties with oral motor control when eating and drinking. Hypotonia in the tongue, lips, and throat muscles, and a protruding lower jaw—which can make biting and chewing more difficult—can all contribute to delayed oral motor control. Some problems that are sometimes seen are:

- difficulty coordinating suck-breathe-swallow pattern;
- choking, gagging, and/or aspirating (when liquid enters her airway);
- difficulty making the transition from pureed to lumpy and solid foods;
- tongue protrusion;
- poor lip closure;
- lack of complete closure of the *velum* (soft palate) during a swallow, causing some food to enter the nasal passages.

If your child has difficulty with the oral motor aspects of eating or drinking, consultation with a speech-language pathologist or occupational therapist who has experience in feeding issues is recommended. Both professionals can specialize in feeding issues; it varies among communities and health centers.

Grooming

As with dressing and eating, children gradually develop independence in grooming and bathing over several years. Being able to care for body hygiene, teeth, hair, and toileting needs requires a combination of sensory awareness, dexterity, and social and emotional development.

TOOTH BRUSHING

A note of caution about tooth brushing. Sarah was eager to brush her own teeth, and I was keen to let her. Somewhere I had read that children with Down syndrome were less prone to tooth decay, but more prone to gum disease. As a result, I felt that she could brush her own teeth when she developed the interest and could move the toothbrush around her teeth herself. Unfortunately, not all children with Down syndrome are less prone to tooth decay, as I quickly discovered. This fact, in combination with Sarah's less diligent brushing, resulted in several cavities and extensive dental work. Tooth brushing is one self-help skill that I supervise closely. Sarah now uses an electric toothbrush, but needs supervision to brush for an adequate length of time.

You may find that your child has decreased awareness of bits of food stuck in the mouth, and difficulty removing bits with the tongue, resulting in food sitting in a spot until the teeth are brushed. Brushing after meals and snacks is clearly the ideal situation.

After your child brushes her teeth, an adult should go over them to make sure they are cleaned thoroughly.

Even before your baby has any teeth, you can get her used to the routine by rubbing her gums with a damp cloth or baby toothbrush. Nuk makes a toothbrush that is suitable for this purpose. Check with your dentist about the best toothbrush for your older child. An angled brush may make it easier to reach tricky spots. An electric toothbrush may be easier for the older child.

Although you may need to supervise your child's brushing, as I do, she can still participate in the routine of brushing her teeth. You can let her brush first herself, then go over her teeth again when she has finished. She can unscrew or uncap the toothpaste tube, squeeze the toothpaste onto her brush, turn the water on and off, and prepare the cup of water. These aspects of the toothbrushing routine can help develop and reinforce fine motor skills.

TOILET TRAINING

Toileting is usually learned very gradually, over a long period of time. I found a consistently timed toileting routine helped Sarah learn the necessary skills. She learned that she was taken to the toilet at frequent, specific times every day, and thus initially became "schedule trained." This method may not work for every child and every family.

Balance and stability may affect a child's comfort on a toilet. The child should have some support for her feet when sitting on the toilet, and something close by to hold on to with her hands. It is usually easiest to provide a small potty for the young child. There are now potties available that can be used either as a separate potty or as an insert for a regular toilet. Some have stepstools and grab handles. Examples are:

- Graco Soft Seat Potty and Stepstool
- Safety 1st 3 in 1 Potty 'N Step Stool
- The First Years 3 in 1 Toilet System

Examples of potty seats.

If you use an insert on the regular toilet, try to choose one with grab handles and use a footstool for your child's feet. Be aware that it may be difficult for the older child who is on a regular-sized toilet to reach for and break off the toilet paper without feeling unbalanced. It may be easier for your child to prepare the toilet paper before sitting on the toilet.

Wiping effectively after a bowel movement can be difficult for some children and adolescents with Down syndrome. Possible reasons for this are:

- difficulty with the body and arm rotation (turning) required to reach;
- decreased sensory feedback (knowing when she feels clean);
- weak grasp, resulting in not enough pressure used through the hand and arm to wipe effectively.

If this is happening for your child, the following suggestions may help:

- Have her stand up and hold the counter or some other surface (or grab rail) with the other hand. This will help her feel more balanced and secure for turning and reaching behind.
- Teach your child to use three (or more, as necessary for your child) separate wads of toilet paper and to wipe three times. This should be adequate to clean.

- Moist disposable wipes may be more effective for your child to use. They are also more comfortable than several wads of dry toilet paper, especially if your child has sensitive skin.
- The ideal solution is a toilet used in some parts of the world that provides a cleaning flush of water. These are obviously not standard issue yet in North America!

When you begin teaching your child to wipe herself, teach wiping front to back, so that you will not have to re-teach later on.

BATHING AND SHOWERING

Because independent sitting and good sitting balance develop late in children with Down syndrome, you may find it helpful to invest in some kind of a sitting support for the bathtub, such as a ring seat. Even with this support, do not assume that your young child is safe to be left, even for a minute. *Never* leave your young child unattended in the bathtub.

The bathtub can be a fun place for you and your child to play together, while improving fine motor skills:

- scooping and pouring with various sized containers;
- dropping toys into the water (to develop release);
- using squeeze/spray bottles (hand strength);
- squeezing a puffer under water to make bubbles (hand strength);
- wringing out a washcloth (hand strength and wrist movement);
- pouring liquid soap/shampoo into your child's palm (wrist rotation, hand cupping);
- body awareness and naming body parts;
- bath mitts or puppets (sensory awareness; opening/closing movement of thumb and fingers);
- playing with foam letters/numbers that stick to the tiles when wet;
- making the shoulder movements needed to wash the opposite shoulder and the back of the neck develop shoulder mobility that will help your child when dressing herself;
- briskly drying with the towel, which gives sensory input to the muscles that can help activate them.

Older children and teenagers should be taught how to take a shower. It is much easier to wash your own hair in the shower than it is in the bathtub. Independence in showering will be a great asset for participation in school physical education programs, swimming, and other sports programs. If your child has difficulty with balance in the shower, you can use a bath mat, install a grab bar, or use a bath bench in the shower stall. These are available at medical supply stores. It is usually easier to squeeze some liquid soap onto a cloth or sponge than to use a bar of soap.

HAIR CARE

When washing your child's hair, she can practice her fine motor skills by pouring or squeezing the shampoo into palm. Rubbing the shampoo into her hair encourages individual finger movement and sensory awareness. A small mirror suctioned onto the wall of the shower may help your child check to see if all the shampoo has been rinsed out.

Brushing hair develops wrist and shoulder movement control, especially when reaching for the back of the head. As much as possible, it is best for your child to participate in her own hair brushing. As with all of the self-care routines, try to find a pattern or rhythm to the activity that can help your child remember to complete the activity. You may want to teach her to count out a specific number of strokes for brushing each section of the hair. For example, "Brush 1, 2, 3 in the front, 1, 2, 3 in the back, 1, 2, 3 on one side and 1, 2, 3 on the other side." Also, you can use visual cues, such as pictures of all sides of the head being brushed in sequence.

I have found that hair care can be difficult for many families, especially as children get older. If you work on these skills when your child is younger, hair brushing may go more smoothly as she gets older. Choosing an easy-to-manage hair style is sometimes necessary to make life easier, especially if your child resists brushing. Use of a softer bristle brush may be somewhat helpful. Resistance to hair brushing and hair cuts may be a sensory response, and is discussed in Chapter 11.

It is beyond the scope of this book to cover the full range of self-help skills our children need to learn, and all possible strategies that can help them. What I have hoped to do is provide a framework for understanding some of the motor aspects of learning these skills, which can be improved through practice and adaptations. There are several resources for parents to turn to for detailed approaches to teaching self-help skills to children with developmental disabilities. Some are listed at the end of this chapter.

Profile: Michael

Five-year-old Michael had just started kindergarten in a regular class. It soon became apparent that he wasn't participating in the routine of coming into the classroom and removing his outerwear with the other children. When he came in, he simply stood at the door, waiting for someone to assist him. His teacher, rather than helping him immediately, attempted to determine how much he was capable of doing. When she asked him to unzip his jacket, the zipper tab slipped out of his fingers and he quickly gave up. When she handed him his coat to hang up, she noticed that he lost some control of his balance when he lifted his arms to reach for the hook, so that he couldn't get the coat on the hook.

After a meeting with the parents, teacher, and consultant occupational therapist, a few strategies were put into place to help Michael be more independent in this routine. He was given a zipper ring, which is easier to grasp than the zipper tab, and enabled him to unzip his jacket. The coat hook was lowered and put at the end of the row so he could easily reach it, and he wasn't jostled as much by the other children. When winter came, Michael was given a low bench to sit on so he could remove his boots (slip-on style, without laces), and put on his shoes (Velcro closure running shoes). With these adaptations, Michael soon became independent as he came into school, and gained confidence in greeting and interacting with his classmates. By first grade he no longer needed the adaptations.

HOUSEHOLD TASKS

Another role that we hope our children will begin to assume as they mature is that of helper in our home. Encouraging your child to participate in household tasks from a young age has many benefits. Your child learns that every family member has a role to play in household chores, and that she can make a meaningful contribution. Just don't expect a perfect job! She will not be able to make the bed as neatly as you can, but what is more important is that she develops the confidence to do it, and the positive self-esteem from having completed a task.

Many young children go through an imitative stage (at about two to four years), during which they love to imitate their parents around the house. Later, they often go through a helpful stage, in which they actually want to help and genuinely enjoy doing the task for you. As they get older, however, you are probably more likely to face resistance to household chores!

In the chapters on stability, sensation, and bilateral coordination, several references were made to household activities. Activities such as sweeping, folding towels, vacuuming, dusting, etc., are all good ways to improve these building blocks of fine motor skills in your child. Whenever she participates in these activities with you, she is improving her stability, bilateral coordination, and sensory awareness in her hands, arms, and body. Many of these activities will also help your child develop dexterity, the fine movements of her hands and fingers.

Chores Your Child Can Participate In

Examples of appropriate household activities for a child with Down syndrome include:

1. **Tidying Up Toys:** You can start teaching your child to tidy up when she is very young, and is learning to grasp objects and release them into containers. Putting away toys can help your child learn to identify same/different and to sort as she puts them into the appropriate container. Toddlers and preschoolers can practice throwing skills by tossing blocks into the bucket.

2. **Setting the Table:** Your child learns to count the correct number of utensils needed and to hold them in her hand while placing them down one at a time on the table. She learns spatial organization when making a place setting. Carrying plates is good for wrist and hand strength and wrist rotation.

3. **Assisting with Meal Preparation:** When assisting you with baking or cooking, your child can:
   - Practice control of scooping and pouring both dry ingredients (e.g., flour, sugar), and wet ingredients (e.g., water, oil).
   - Stir and mix, which develops control and strength of grasp and wrist movements. The other hand holds the bowl steady (bilateral coordination).

■ Knead dough, which develops strength in the hands and wrists. Shaping cookie dough into balls helps the smaller movements of the fingers. Sensory awareness in the hands is enhanced when working with dough.

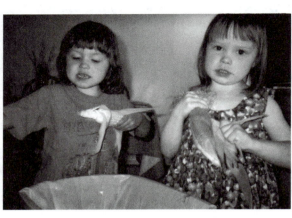

   ■ Vegetable preparation can include activities such as opening and removing fresh peas from the pod (bilateral thumb and finger control; pincer grasp); breaking the ends off green beans (pincer strength); or husking corn. The older child can cut soft vegetables, such as cucumbers or cooked potatoes, and can attempt to peel carrots.

   ■ Adolescents can rip and wash lettuce for salad, as well as cutting vegetables for a salad. They can also be involved in opening packages and cans, measuring using measuring cups and spoons, and pouring. There are endless opportunities in the kitchen to use and develop fine motor skills!

4. **Gardening:** Children of all ages love to get their hands in the dirt in the garden! Digging helps develop strength and stability, one of the foundations for finer movements.

5. **Raking Leaves and Shoveling Snow:** Both of these activities develop upper body strength and stability and bilateral coordination. Adjusting to the weight and resistance of the snow or leaves also helps develop sensory awareness through the muscles and joints in the arms.

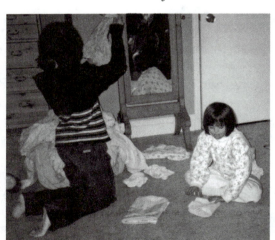

Children take pride in being able to help around the house. By participating in chores, they learn important life skills and develop their hand skills.

6. **Sorting and Folding Laundry:** Young children can learn about same/different by helping to sort socks. Folding flat items, such as pillowcases or towels, is a good bilateral coordination activity for young school-aged children. Folding a towel helps your child with the control needed to bring the two sides together with a fold in the middle. This skill will help her learn to fold papers in half for putting into her backpack at school.

7. **Sweeping and Vacuuming:** Vacuuming and sweeping develop body and shoulder stability, as your child moves her arms in all directions while maintaining her balance.

8. **Hand Vacuuming ("Dust Buster"):** Pushing and holding the Dust Buster button while vacuuming develops strength in the thumb.

9. **Cleaning Windows and Mirrors; Dusting:** Spraying the window cleaner or dusting cleaner helps develop hand stability and index finger control, not to mention aim! Wiping with the cloth enhances shoulder movement and body stability.

10. **Washing and Drying Dishes and Unloading the Dishwasher:** Your child uses sensory discrimination skills to sort out dishes, silverware, etc. in the soapy water. In addition, both washing and drying are good bilateral coordination activities. And your child develops strength as she holds dishes, lifts items out of the dishwasher, and scrubs dirty pots.

11. **Putting Away Groceries:** As well as teaching organizational and sorting skills, your child learns to adjust her grasp and movement to the size and shape of the item when she helps you put away the groceries.

12. **Making the Bed:** Bilateral coordination and stability are used as your child pulls up the covers and smoothes out the bed.

LEISURE

Leisure activities are those we do for fun and recreation. Developing leisure interests early in life promotes a sense of well-being and an active and participatory lifestyle that will result in many enjoyable hours of free time in adulthood. Full-time employment and family responsibilities may not fill the days of our children with Down syndrome when they are adults. Thus, it is crucial for them to begin to develop interests and pastimes that are rewarding and meaningful while they are young. These may include volunteer work, group social activities, music, dance, sports, outdoor pursuits, pets, gardening, art, theater, reading, collections, crafts, etc. The list is endless! For the purposes of this book, a few possible leisure activities as they relate to your child's developing fine motor skills will be discussed.

Sometimes traditional sports are too difficult and frustrating. Here my daughters have made up a "balloon badminton" game.

Helping Your Child Develop Fine Motor Skills through Leisure Activities

Much of the teaching and assisting we do as parents must be structured to be successful. However, it is also important for your child to learn to initiate fun activities herself, so she can amuse herself without always needing structured entertainment. From an early age, encourage her to develop the ability to play freely, without constant adult structure. (This does not mean without adult supervision!) Below are some ideas to get you thinking about involving your child in leisure activities at home and in the community.

Community Programs: Involvement in community programs, such as Girl Guides or Scouts and Boy Scouts, is valuable for building a sense of community and involvement, and for developing social skills in an environment outside of school. Most of these programs include craft activities as part of their regular schedule.

Telephone Use: Learning how to use the telephone to call cousins, grandparents, and friends is a positive social ability that will help your child interact with peers as she gets older. Pushing the buttons on a touch tone phone or dialing a dial phone can help develop individual finger movement and strength.

Sports: Sports activities also offer opportunities for children with Down syndrome to develop in many areas. Overall movement control may be enhanced, which helps lay a good foundation for fine motor skill development. Self-esteem, emotional development, and social interaction skills can all flourish in the right environment. Many children with Down syndrome participate in community recreation programs and sports teams. Others find the Special Olympics programs to be inspiring and rewarding.

Gymnastics programs can help the child improve overall strength and endurance, which will enhance her physical well-being.

Children and youth with Down syndrome will vary in their interests, just as all children do. One child may love basketball, another soccer, and another rhythmic gymnastics. Swimming and gymnastics are particularly good for developing strength and stability. Children with Down syndrome **must** be examined medically for atlanto-axial instability (with a neck x-ray) prior to participation in contact sports, skiing, and gymnastics. If atlanto-axial instability is present, it may be recommended that your child not participate in these sports, although medical opinion seems to differ on this matter. There are many sports and recreational activities that are appropriate and can be mastered by people with Down syndrome. The challenge for parents is matching the child's interests with the programs available in their community.

Creative and Imaginary Play: Keep supplies available for creative and imaginary play (e.g., dress-up clothes, art and craft supplies). Art and craft activities usually focus on dexterity, and require a lot of small finger movement and coordination. For this reason, children with Down syndrome may shy away from these activities. However, crafts and art can be both beneficial and rewarding for children with Down syndrome. The secret is to know your child's abilities, and adapt or prepare the activity ahead of time so that she will be able to participate successfully and to feel a sense of satisfaction, not frustration. Sometimes, having the "perfect" model in front of her to try to copy is not the best idea. She will not be able to produce the same result. Creativity, and the process of doing it, is what is important.

Arts and craft activities that are openly creative and do not require a precise duplication of the model will probably be more rewarding and successful for most children with Down syndrome. Some examples are:

- Making a frame or wreath: Paste decorative pieces of foam, sequins, etc. onto a pre-cut shape to make something such as a picture frame or a wreath.
- Thread decorative beads with large holes onto pipe cleaners, which can then be bent into different shapes.
- Make plaster mold kits, in which a plaster mixture, mixed with water, is poured into a plastic mold.
- Stamping activities: Press the rubber stamp on the stamp pad and then onto the paper; this is a good activity for strengthening the thumb and fingers in the tripod grasp.

- Crayon rubbings: Place flat, textured items (e.g., coins, textured placemat, leaves, tiles) under a piece of paper and rub the side of a crayon over it.
- Black magic pictures: Color an entire piece of paper with different colors of crayons in a random pattern. Color over top with black crayon, completely covering the other colors. Take the blunt end of scissors and scratch a drawing through the black crayon to reveal the other color underneath.
- Another way to make black magic pictures is to color a picture with crayons (fluorescent show up best), then paint over the entire paper with black poster paint. The paint will fill in the uncolored areas of the paper, but will not stick to the crayoning, which shows through.
- Torn tissue design: Rip pieces of tissue paper of different colors and place them around a piece of sturdy paper, overlapping the colors. Paint over all with a mixture of white glue diluted with water. This will hold the tissue paper in place and the color combinations will show up nicely. Tearing paper is a good activity for coordinating the wrist movements of both hands. Tissue paper has a grain and will only rip well in one direction.
- Fold and dye dipping: Fold a piece of absorbent paper (like a sturdy paper towel) many times to make it into a small square or triangle. Dip the corners into little bowls of food coloring. The dyes will spread and mix, giving a beautiful effect. This is a good activity to practice folding paper.
- Bird feeder: Attach a string at the top of a pine cone, for hanging up your bird feeder. Put peanut butter all over the pine cone, then sprinkle and cover with bird seed. Hang up outside!
- Sticker art: Stick precut stickers onto a paper in a random or specific design. Peeling the sticker off the backing is good for pincer grasp.
- Vegetable print designs: Cut fruit and vegetables in half (e.g., apple, onion, orange, cabbage), dip the cut side in a bit of paint or dye, then stamp onto a paper. Don't use too much paint or the textured effect of the vegetable will not show through.
- Chinese lanterns: This is a good craft activity for children who can cut straight lines. Fold a paper in half lengthwise. Starting at the fold, cut straight lines about one-half inch apart about two-thirds of the way across the paper, along the length of the fold. Open the paper and glue the sides together, then hang up.

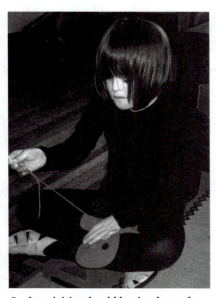

Craft activities should be simple, preferably with repetitive steps, allowing the child to improve during the activity and to feel successful.

Music and Dance: Music is another creative and leisure activity that can have many benefits for a child with Down syndrome. Involvement in music programs enhances listening skills, rhythm, speech, and coordination. Children and young people with Down syndrome can benefit from music therapy as well as learning specific music skills. Learning to play an instrument develops self-discipline, finger control and speed, timing, and motor control. Listening to music, and learning how to choose and put on their own tapes or CDs, is a relaxing and rewarding leisure activity for many children with Down syndrome.

I have yet to meet a young person with Down syndrome who does not love to dance! Sarah and her friends get together once a month for DJ dances; nobody sits out even one dance! Dance is a marvelous way to achieve exercise in an enjoyable way. Like music, it can be enjoyed purely as a recreational activity, or can be an instructional activity where remembering a dance sequence, developing timing, paying attention, etc. are goals.

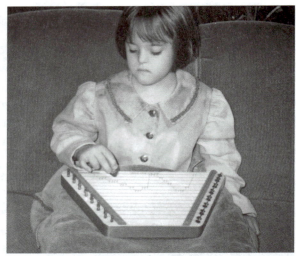

A Music Maker is Sarah's introduction to a musical instrument.

Self-Help Resources

Baker, Bruce L. and Brightman, Alan J. *Steps to Independence: Teaching Everyday Skills to Children with Special Needs.* 4th edition. Baltimore, MD: Paul H. Brookes, 2003.

Klein, Marsha Dunn. *Pre-dressing Skills.* San Antonio, TX: Therapy Skill Builders, 1999.

Wrobel, Mary. *Taking Care of Myself.* Arlington, TX: Future Horizons, 2003.

Grandma's and Grandpa's List

- Dress-up clothes
- Old Halloween costumes
- Streamers for dancing
- Child's kitchen and dish set; tea set
- Toys that promote dressing skills (such as puzzles with fastenings; dolls; a snake on the market that has buttons, snaps, zippers, etc.)
- Child-sized broom and dust pan
- Child-sized shovels, rakes, and gardening set
- Doll with long hair for brushing
- Stuffed toys with ribbons for tying
- Toy lace-up boots/shoes for lacing and tying
- CD player
- Child-sized basketball net

CHAPTER 11

Sensory Processing

In Chapter 7 I discussed sensation and how it contributes to the development of fine motor skills. This chapter will go into more detail about sensory processing—that is, the integration of sensory information from all the sensory systems, and how this affects development and behavior. Motor skills are the end result of sensory processing; therefore, sensory processing contributes to fine motor and other motor skill development. Part of the foundation of self-help skills is body awareness, which develops through the sensory systems. Many other skills and aspects of your child's development are also affected by sensory processing.

In this chapter, I would like to discuss sensory processing first in general terms and then in relation to children and adolescents who have Down syndrome. My observations and discussions with other parents have led me to believe that at least some people with Down syndrome have differences in how they process sensory input. This chapter may therefore be useful in helping you understand behaviors in your child that may be related to sensory processing, and may give you some strategies to help your child deal more effectively with his sensory needs.

What Is Sensory Processing?

- Sensory processing is keeping a balanced posture while seated at a desk in class, writing spelling words dictated by the teacher, all the while not paying attention to the other noises around the room.
- Sensory processing is stepping aside as someone brushes against you in the hall, keeping up the conversation with your friend.
- Sensory processing is enjoying playing on the playground equipment at recess, then being able to stop and line up when the bell rings.

Technically, sensory processing refers to the ongoing activity in the brain to register, modulate, interpret, and integrate all this information that is coming in through the senses, so that we can organize a response. We respond by moving, by speaking, through our behavior and/or emotions, and by learning.

More simply, sensory processing is tuning in and tuning out, responding to and not responding to, adjusting energy levels up and down, being appropriately still or appropriately active: basically, it is being in a calm, alert state in order to respond in a productive manner to others and the environment.

This process has historically been called "sensory integration." In the past few years, the term "sensory processing" has been used in the literature to describe the entire process, with integration being one component. "Sensory processing disorder" is now the term being used to describe dysfunction in any or all levels of sensory processing.

We can expand the House Model to include sensory processing and other aspects of motor development.

Figure 20

An analogy of a home heating system may help understand how sensory processing fits into the house model. The house has a thermostat, which regulates the temperature. If the temperature goes below the setting, the heat comes on. The thermostat is like the threshold for the nervous system. At a certain level, the nerves will "fire" impulses with greater frequency and/or intensity, to alert the brain to the sensory information. Below the threshold, the nervous system is still registering the information, but is not firing with the frequency or intensity to alert the higher brain centers to the information. Your nervous system modulates the thresholds by turning up or turning down your receptivity to different types of sensory input. Many home heating systems have a filter, which removes dirt and dust particles so they don't interfere with the efficiency of the system. Likewise, the lower areas of the brain act as a filter, screening out unimportant information so that the higher brain centers can be more *efficient*.

The home heating system regulates the temperature continuously to all levels of the house. Likewise, sensory information flows continuously to all levels of the brain, with connections between the levels and parts of the brain.

This analogy is, of course, very simplistic. The way the brain registers, modulates, interprets, and organizes sensory information is very complex, and it is also very individual. Everyone has somewhat different thresholds for sensory information, which vary according to the situation and our internal state (how tired or hungry we are, etc.) Sound is an experience that we can probably all relate to in terms of our own variable thresholds. When I am feeling "just right," high pitched sounds (such as a baby crying) or monotonous sounds (such as a tap dripping) would not bother me. However, if I have had a long, busy, stressful day and need to concentrate on completing more tasks before I can rest, a baby crying or a tap dripping may drive me crazy. My threshold for sound has been lowered, so I am getting more information about these sounds than I need, but my nervous system is not efficiently screening them out as it normally does.

Therefore, having a "low threshold" means that it doesn't take much sensory stimulation for the nervous system to fire, and to pass the information into the conscious levels of the brain. Having a "high threshold" means that it takes a lot of sensory stimulation for the nerves to fire, and pass the information along to conscious awareness.

What Is the Difference between "Sensation" and "Sensory Processing"?

Sensation refers to the specific sense of touch, and our ability to discriminate using touch. In Chapter 7, the development of sensation in your child's hands, and the contribution of this discriminative ability to fine motor skill development, was discussed. Touch sensation is one part of sensory processing. Sensory processing includes all the senses:

1. vision;
2. hearing;
3. taste;
4. smell;
5. touch;
6. proprioception (awareness of posture and movement provided by nerves in joints, muscles, and tendons);
7. vestibular system: (awareness of head and body position in space and movement provided by nerves in the inner ear; important for balance).

Sensory Modulation

One part of sensory processing is sensory modulation, which enables us to pay attention to what is important at any given time. It helps us to screen out background noises and other sensory information that is not important for the situation right now. It also brings to our attention sensory input that is important. Modulation controls how intensely we notice any particular sensory input, "turning up" or "turning down" the information as necessary (74). A person with sensory modulation difficulties either over- or under-responds to ordinary sensory experiences. This person is either too sensitive or not sensitive enough to one or more types of sensory input.

For example, a child in the classroom turns his head to every background sound and is irritated by the feel of his socks, causing him to scratch and fidget. This sensory input is not being modulated to allow him to pay full attention to the teacher.

Our brain modulates much of the sensory information around us, which allows us to focus our attention on what is important. Otherwise, we would feel bombarded and exhausted by the constant information. The nervous system "habituates" to a lot of the stimulation around us, which means that we don't always pay attention to all the information coming from every sense. For example, because we hear the hum of the fridge every day, we don't notice it anymore. Or we may not be able to recall the color of something we see every day. Some people with neurological disorders do not filter the sensory stimulation coming in very well, and it is very difficult for them to focus attention on a task when other information is constantly demanding a response.

Profile: Danny

Six-year-old Danny is taking swimming lessons at a time when several other groups of lessons are going on simultaneously in the pool. When his instructor explains the next activity, Danny has to screen out the voices of the other instructors and all the other pool noise, and focus on listening to and understanding the directions. He watches his instructor as she demonstrates the starfish float. When he attempts the float, his vestibular sense gives him feedback about the position of his head in the water, and his proprioceptive system gives him awareness of the position of the rest of his body. The tactile system (touch) sends information about what it feels like to have the water supporting his body and face. Danny's brain is integrating:

- what he has **heard** in the instructions (auditory sense);
- what he has **seen** the instructor demonstrate (visual sense);
- what he **feels** in his body (proprioception, vestibular, and tactile senses).

This is sensory processing. Once Danny has learned how to float, this skill will gradually become automatic. Sensory processing will continue to occur, but he will not have to focus his attention on the sensory experience. He will be able to build upon his ability to float to learn a new swimming stroke.

Nervous System Development in Down Syndrome

As your baby grows, his brain also grows and changes. Of significant importance to brain development is the process of myelination. Myelin is a sheath that forms around nerves in the central nervous system, and facilitates the quick and efficient transmission of information. This process of myelination is typically complete by two years of age. Research has shown that the process is delayed in infants with Down syndrome (69).

As the child grows and develops, established nerve networks are readily accessed as the foundation for new learning. New nerve growth continues as the result of ongoing sensory experiences, integration in the brain, and the connection of information in new ways. New nerve growth expands the capacity of the brain for learning and thinking. Children demonstrate their new learning through gross and fine motor movements, speech and language, and behavior. Our unique, individual genetic makeup guides our responses to the world around us, and it is through our responses that we interact with others, learn, and develop ideas.

Nervous system development occurs more slowly in children with Down syndrome. Learning also usually occurs more slowly. Repetition is vital for learning for everyone; more repetition over a longer period of time is usually needed for the child with Down syndrome.

When trying to understand behaviors that may seem inappropriate, it is important to consider all aspects of nervous system development and medical factors that may be having an impact on the child. These include:

- medical considerations,
- sensory impairment,
- developmental delay,
- sensory processing.

MEDICAL CONSIDERATIONS

If difficulties with sensory processing are suspected as a contributing factor in your child's motor development and behavior, it is important to rule out any underlying medical factors. There are several possible medical reasons for some of the behaviors that will be described in this chapter. For example, lethargy and low energy may be due to thyroid dysfunction, rather than due to sensory processing. Dehydration and sleep issues are other possible causes of lethargy. Some medical journal articles report an incidence of sleep apnea as high as 45 percent in individuals with Down syndrome. As children with Down syndrome enter adolescence, lethargy and low energy may be related to depression, which is treatable with medication.

Teeth grinding is another behavior that could be due both to sensory processing or to medical issues. For example, sinus pain, tooth decay, jaw instability, and ear infection could all lead to teeth grinding.

Sensory impairment can result in similar behaviors. For instance, if a child is unable to get enough sensory information by looking at and touching an object, he may put it in his mouth, one of the most sensitive areas of the body. Likewise, a child whose hearing is impaired will obviously not be very responsive to his name being called. But the child might also fail to respond due to sensory processing issues.

All children with Down syndrome should have regular monitoring of their medical status, using the Health Care Guidelines published by the Down Syndrome Medical Interest Group (*Down Syndrome Quarterly,* Vol. 4, No 3, Sept. 1999). These are available online at www.dension.edu/collaborations/dsq/health99.html.

SENSORY IMPAIRMENT

Some of the sensory input going into the brain may be somewhat different for children with Down syndrome. Therefore, the child's ability to respond may also be somewhat different. The chart on the next page describes some of the differences that may be present in sensations going in, and describes how this may affect the child's ability to respond. Again, some of these differences may result in behaviors similar to those caused by sensory processing disorders.

SENSE ALTERATION OR IMPAIRMENT	IMPACT ON THE CHILD
Hearing: 1. Fluctuating hearing loss due to fluid buildup in the inner ear (caused by inflammation or infection); called conductive hearing loss. 2. Permanent hearing loss. 3. Research has shown that speech that is heard is processed more often in the right hemisphere, which is the opposite of most people (70).	1. When fluid is present, the child will hear muffled or distorted sounds, making it difficult to interpret all that is said to him. Inconsistent responses to verbal requests and ability to follow instructions. Sometimes inattention to noises; sometimes over-sensitivity to them. 2. Child may need hearing aids. Some sound may be distorted and sound perception altered. 3. More difficult to listen and respond verbally (left hemisphere motor function) because input and response areas are on different sides of brain.
Vision: 1. Near and far sightedness 2. Nystagmus (continuous rapid movement of the eyes from side to side)	1. Can be corrected with glasses; therefore little or no impact on the child's ability to see. May affect the child's level of caution in trying new activities. 2. May cause blurry vision and difficulty focusing. Difficulty with visual tracking. Children may outgrow this condition.
Proprioception: *(Nerves in the joints, muscles, and tendons that provide awareness of position and movement.)* 1. Research suggests that hypotonia leads to altered proprioceptive input because of the greater degree of stretch on the muscles and tendons (33).	1. More difficult to use the exact amount of muscle force and adjustments necessary for precise and sustained movements. Greater need to watch hands while doing activities; to watch feet on stairs.
Touch: 1. Nerve conduction tests have shown that touch perception is transmitted more slowly in people with Down syndrome. 2. Delayed and often decreased reaction to pain and difficulty pinpointing where the pain is (12).	1. Slower reaction to touch information. May have difficulty making fine adjustments in hands to accommodate a variety of objects. 2. Delayed reaction to getting hurt.
Vestibular: *(The sense located in the inner ear that responds to head position, tells us about the speed and direction of movement and contributes to the development of balance skills. It is strongly connected to the visual system.)* 1. The literature does not clearly discuss differences in the vestibular system in people with Down syndrome.	1. Balance can be delayed (more than developmental age expectations) in adolescents with Down syndrome (33). This is likely due to a combination of factors, including low muscle tone.

DEVELOPMENTAL DELAY

As mentioned above, the process of maturation of the nervous system is slowed down in children with Down syndrome. This is *not* a problem of sensory processing—it is a developmental delay. It is important to remember that **the primary deficit of children with Down syndrome is a genetic disorder causing developmental delay affecting cognitive, motor, language, and social development.** *There may be a sensory processing component, but sensory processing is not the root cause of all the child's delays and challenges.*

During the process of maturation, a child may develop learned patterns of behavior that persist over extended periods of time. Sometimes these learned patterns are associated initially with sensory experiences, or with other factors, such as stranger anxiety. In response to a sensory experience or situation, the child establishes a behavior pattern. For example, a baby may dislike being placed lying down on a change table. He becomes fearful and quite distressed. This could be due to difficulties processing the vestibular and visual information about where he is in space, or because he doesn't like the feel of cold baby wipes on his skin. This behavior may continue, even as he gets older, in situations such as a doctor's examining table. He may not be experiencing the same sensory experience now that he is older, but he has learned to associate the situations of being placed lying down on a high table with a fearful response. In other words, some behaviors may have had a basis in a sensory processing delay or deficit, but they persist as learned behavioral responses (74).

With a developmental disability such as Down syndrome, there is likely less flexibility in the nervous system to adapt to changing situations and new demands. Expecting the child to be able to frequently adapt to changing situations and new demands will result in a lot of *stress*. Physiologically, chronic stress changes the chemical situation in the nervous system, thereby making the nervous system even less able to respond and adapt (24). When under stress, we are all less able to learn and retain learning, and it is the same for children with Down syndrome.

It is also important for us to remember that it takes more energy for our children to meet the normal demands of a day. Obviously, when more energy is required, a child will get tired more quickly.

As a parent, I know how much we want our children to be integrated into school classrooms and community activities as their siblings and school peers are. We also know it is important for them to receive specialized services, such as speech and language, physical, and occupational therapy, at various stages of their life. There may also be other programs available to our children that we feel we must take advantage of so that our children can "reach their potential." All this can mean a very full plate for our children, with activities scheduled throughout the week, all demanding energy and focus.

As parents and educators, we have to be aware that constantly trying to "keep up," "cooperate," and "comply" with the expectations in all these activities over the childhood and adolescent years may lead to a buildup of stress. Yet, we certainly don't want to deny our children these opportunities. I find it is a real dilemma. I try to be open to Sarah's responses as my gauge for how she is able to handle everything. Her behavioral and emotional responses are what I have to go on, as she can't clearly articulate her feelings about things. My older daughters would have been able to say something like "I don't like that dance class. There are three girls who are mean to everyone and the instructor doesn't do anything about it." The situation could then

Stress and Behavior

Stress triggers responses in our autonomic nervous system. Think of a time when you have had to speak or perform in front of a group of strangers. You may have felt butterflies in your stomach, your heart racing, your breathing becoming faster and shallower, your hands shaking, and you may have started sweating. You may have appeared calm and collected to others, but you were probably feeling some or all of these things inside.

Physical and/or emotional stress triggers an immediate "fright, fight, or flight" response in the autonomic nervous system, with some of these physical signs:

- pupil dilation (not due to visual impairment or lighting conditions),
- shallow, quick breathing,
- fast heart rate,
- sweating.

Extended stress over long periods of time can cause more chronic behavioral and health issues, including physical ailments (e.g., stomach aches), and mental health concerns. Stress and anxiety can reduce the chemical receptiveness of the brain to memory.

be dealt with by discussion with the instructor, etc. Sarah, however, is unable to verbally articulate such feelings, and therefore shows us through her behavior that she is uncomfortable and under stress.

SENSORY PROCESSING DIFFICULTIES

If medical problems, sensory impairment, and developmental delay are ruled out as primary causes of problematic or odd behavior in your child, difficulties with sensory processing should be considered. Some children *may* exhibit some behaviors that *could* be partly due to the way their nervous system is processing sensory information.

Behavior can be due to a number of causes. It is important to gather as much information as possible in order to try to figure out what could be causing, triggering, and reinforcing the behavior. As discussed above, you will want to consider possible causes related to developmental delays or medical or sensory impairment. Determining whether the behavior is used as communication is also important. Here are some questions to ask yourself:

- *Is a medical condition causing the behavior?* For example, a skin condition can cause discomfort and over-reaction to touch; obsessive-compulsive disorder may cause a child to need to have things a certain way all the time.
- *Is there a deficit of one of the senses causing the behavior?* For example, does fluctuating hearing cause inconsistent attention and responsiveness to verbal instructions in the classroom?
- *Is the behavior considered to be within the range of typical for your child's developmental age?* For example, a three-year-old child with a developmental age of eight months who puts everything in his mouth is exhibiting typical behavior for his developmental age.

- *Is the child using the behavior to communicate?* For example, perhaps he wants to have a turn to be first in line going out for recess, but because he is slower getting his coat on, he is always near the end of the line. He tells you this by balking and refusing to put his coat on to go outside.
- *Is the behavior a learned response (such as an avoidance technique)?* For example, does he repeatedly drop his pencil on the floor to avoid doing written work?
- *Is the behavior meeting a sensory need of the child?* If you take away the behavior through behavior modification, does the child replace it with another behavior that also may be meeting the sensory need? For example, if you teach your child not to chew on his fingers, does he chew on his shirt?

As you can see from this list, there are *many* possible explanations for understanding behavior. It often takes work and the help of professionals to sort it out and reach solutions that work for our children. The chart on the next page describes examples of typical behavior for many children with Down syndrome, in contrast with behaviors that are more extreme and may indicate sensory processing difficulties.

This chart describes some of the behaviors that may be considered to have a sensory processing component. Earlier in the chapter I described **sensory modulation,** the ability of the brain to "turn up" or "turn down" the sensory information coming in. We can now look at the examples above in terms of sensory modulation difficulties.

OVER-RESPONSIVENESS

A child who is **over-responsive** will exhibit behaviors like:
- significant sensitivity to clothing,
- significant distress over self-care routines,
- an inability to wear socks or long sleeves,
- an inability to tolerate background noise,
- distress and fear with movement,
- responding aggressively to light touch; can't stand being in a crowd or lining up,
- extremely picky about food, tolerating a very limited number of foods,
- intolerance of changes in routine or environment.

For these children, a small amount of sensory information causes their nervous system to overreact, placing them in an increased level of alertness. The brain perceives normal amounts and intensities of sensory input as first uncomfortable, and if they persist, as threatening and stressful. Children who are in this heightened level of alertness all the time are on edge, and because the focus of the brain is on survival and protection, they have difficulty learning new skills.

Over-responsiveness can result in "sensory defensiveness." In order to protect himself from what is perceived as harmful sensory experiences, the child develops defensive behaviors, such as those listed above.

TYPICAL BEHAVIOR FOR MANY CHILDREN WITH DOWN SYNDROME	BEHAVIOR THAT MAY INDICATE SENSORY PROCESSING DIFFICULTIES
Displays clothing preferences, and wants to make his own decisions about clothes	Is extremely picky about clothing, wearing only specific types of clothing, tugs at clothing, etc., seems irritated by different materials, tags, etc.
Approaches new gross motor activities cautiously; sticks to familiar activities; doesn't take motor risks	Becomes distressed or is very fearful of movement; resists many playground activities
Dislikes self-care routines because they interfere with play time, TV time, etc.	Consistently resists self-care routines; may become distressed and pull away or hit out
Seems unaware of danger; misses clues in the environment to danger (e.g., doesn't notice the curb, and trips over it)	Seeks dangerous situations (e.g., always climbing up on tables and jumping down)
Likes strong flavors, salty foods	Will only eat a limited selection of foods; extremely picky about texture, consistency, flavor, etc.
Likes to be barefoot	Either has to be barefoot (can't stand socks or shoes), or hates being barefoot
Has to watch his hands closely while doing coordinated skills, such as doing up zippers or tying shoelaces, or using a keyboard	Has to watch hands closely during ALL activities, even those that have been learned for a long time (such as scooping food onto spoon or fork); always seems awkward with hands
Tires easily in physical activity (e.g., can't run for as long as typical peers)	Seems unable to get up enough energy to initiate or complete activities
Has trouble with transitions	Is very rigid in the routines and the way things have to be done (e.g., food has to be presented a certain way); becomes very distressed over any changes in routine or environment
Needs his name called and instructions given more than once; benefits from visual cues	Can't tolerate background noise and is distracted by it; or needs physical prompts to initiate when given instructions

UNDER-RESPONSIVENESS

A child who is **under-responsive** will exhibit behaviors like:

- seeming very slow, lethargic, and unmotivated,
- being difficult to engage in interaction; unresponsive,
- lack of awareness of changes in the environment, people coming and going, etc.

When a child is under-responsive, it means it takes more of that sensory information to make his nervous system fire in order for him to respond. He has a *higher threshold.* He may not notice when someone calls his name or enters a room, when everyone around him gets up to go for lunch, when his face is dirty, or when his clothes are all twisted on his body. He may not notice because his nervous system is not passing along that information through the firing of the neurons.

SENSORY SEEKERS

A child who **seeks sensory stimulation** will exhibit behaviors like:
- taking unsafe risks in movement activities,
- purposefully crashing into things,
- spinning himself around for a long time without seeming to get dizzy,
- always moving; unable to be still,
- excessive touching of people and things,
- excessive chewing on toys, hands, or clothing,
- constantly making a sound.

The behaviors listed for children who are "sensory seekers" are often typical of very young children. One-, two-, and three-year-old children often lack the ability to delay their own impulses, are unable to attend for very long, seem to constantly be on the go, and seem uncoordinated as they develop new motor skills. Thus, it is important always to consider the developmental and cognitive age of the child before interpreting behaviors as sensory processing issues.

When a child is a "sensory seeker," he craves and seeks out sensory input beyond normal expectations for his developmental age. Often these children are under-responsive, and are seeking the amount of sensory input they need to meet the higher threshold needs of their nervous system. However, conversely, sometimes these children are actually over-responsive to sensory input, but instead of avoiding it, they seek one kind of input in excess to "drown out" the over-stimulating and uncomfortable effects of all the other input. For example, a child may constantly hum to drown out other sounds if he is over-responsive and hyper-sensitive to sound. Or, he may crash into walls and furniture to over-ride his hypersensitivity to light touch.

COMBINATIONS OF SENSORY PROCESSING PROBLEMS

Often children do not fall neatly into one category, and may show components of all three sensory modulation difficulties. This is because a nervous system that is "out of sync" is going to swing more in its responses to sensory input (62). From my experiences and those of other parents who have responded to a sensory questionnaire, it seems that *some* children with Down syndrome do exhibit sensory modulation difficulties. What seems to be most common is an over-responsiveness to light touch during self-care routines, and a seeking for certain types of sensory input, such as deep pressure touch, touching of objects, and chewing on objects.

Strategies for Coping with Sensory Processing Difficulties

The chart on pages 178-182 looks at some examples of sensory processing difficulties that seem to sometimes occur in children with Down syndrome, and strategies to help your child cope.

EXAMPLES OF SENSORY PROCESSING DIFFICULTIES	EXAMPLES OF STRATEGIES TO COPE
Over-responsiveness to Light Touch 1. Child is over-responsive to light touch. He may withdraw from being close to others, or may hit out if he feels threatened.	1. Approach your child from the front so he can see you and can anticipate your approach and touch. Check out the lining up, cloakroom, and seating arrangements in the classroom. Your child may be less anxious about unexpected touch if he is at the front of the line (perhaps holding the door, which provides pressure through the arms), or at the back of the line, where he can see everyone else. He may have less difficulty if his coat hook is at the end of the row or if he can go a minute ahead of the other children to put on his coat. He will feel more comfortable if no one sits right behind him. ■ Proprioception activities (heavy work through the muscles) is calming and organizing and reduces the impact of light touch on the nervous system. Examples of such activities include pushing and pulling a wagon, cart, or heavy doors; carrying heavy items; and most jungle gym activities. ■ Deep pressure touch also overrides the feeling of light touch. Tight clothing, massage, joint compressions, lying under a heavy blanket, using a weighted lap board or neck wrap, and wearing a weighted vest are examples of deep pressure touch. ■ The Wilbarger Protocol (p. 184) can help modulate the effects of light touch (75).
2. Child is extremely particular about clothing; some children don't tolerate long sleeves or socks.	2. Constant pressure input from tight Lycra clothing helps some children who are hypersensitive to the touch of clothing (e.g., exercise or bike shorts and a lycra tank top under other clothing). Certain materials are more comfortable against the skin (e.g., soft cotton, fleece). The suggestions above for touch sensitivity may also help.

3. Child avoids, resists, or fights self-care routines, such as teeth brushing, hair washing, face washing, cutting nails.	3. Encourage your child to do as much self-care himself as possible even if he doesn't do a great job. The sensory input is much more tolerable when you do it yourself, as you can anticipate the pressure and location.
	■ If this is not fully possible, do self-care routines in a consistent manner, at same place and time each day—included in visual schedule, if child uses one.
	■ Reduce impact of light touch through deep pressure; e.g.:
	  • child hugs a large stuffed toy while hair is being brushed;
	  • child is wrapped in a "comfort blanket" while face is washed,

SENSORY PROCESSING DIFFICULTIES CONT.	STRATEGIES TO COPE CONT.
	having hair brushed, etc.; • child squeezes a ball or pulls a thick band during self-care; • child wears exercise weights on his wrists and ankles. Cut nails while your child is in a warm bath. The warm water softens the nails, and diminishes the impact of light touch. If cutting hair is difficult, try: ■ holding your child on your lap; ■ having child sit on a low chair with his feet firmly on the floor; ■ brushing or combing out tangles yourself before starting (some hair stylists can be a bit rough); ■ washing hair at home just before the appointment; ■ using the deep pressure touch suggestions listed above; ■ providing your child with a visual schedule of the steps involved; including when each step is finished; ■ using a Social Story to frame the experience in positive language (see Resources); ■ providing a visual distraction (such as showing a video during the haircut). Hair salons that cater to children are more likely to offer this option.
Over-responsiveness to Food 1. Child is extremely picky about food; tolerates a very narrow range of textures and types of food.	1. Remember that many younger children have limited food preferences for a few years; picky eating doesn't always indicate a sensory problem. If over-sensitivity is severely limiting child's nutrition, consider: ■ defocusing attention on food; try to make mealtimes important for social value; ■ including child in preparation of food (touching food, opening packages, etc.) ■ letting child touch and smell new food without any expectation of tasting it initially; ■ beginning with what your child will tolerate and gradually adjusting texture/flavor and presentation; ■ doing oral-motor activities outside of eating times to desensitize the mouth (blowing whistles and bubbles in front of a mirror, blowing bubbles through a straw, playing body parts games such as "Head and Shoulders"); *(continued on next page)*

SENSORY PROCESSING DIFFICULTIES CONT.	STRATEGIES TO COPE CONT.

General Over-responsiveness
1. Child seems to be easily over-stimulated by the environment. Too much of any type of sensory input for him to process is disorganizing and he seems unable to cope behaviorally and emotionally.
	1. Change the environment by reducing the stimulation:
	  ■ unclutter a busy room full of toys
	  ■ put away toys/activities not in use
	  ■ muffle sound by putting tennis balls or felt pads on chair legs, placing area rugs down, hanging banners, etc. on the walls
	  ■ have the child wear headphones to reduce the sound volume
	
	Use calming and organizing activities
	  ■ a quiet room without intense lighting
	  ■ soft, soothing music
	  ■ rhythmic rocking, such as in a rocking chair, swing, or hammock
	  ■ warm water (such as a warm bath, or playing in warm water)
	  ■ hugs; cuddling with a pillow and stuffed animals
	  ■ chewing activities (gum, chewy foods)
	  ■ provide a "quiet space," such as a corner full of pillows or a small tent, where the child can retreat and reorganize himself if he feels overwhelmed
	  ■ visit a Snoezelen room (described on p. 190)

2. Difficulty with sleep routines; may have difficulty falling asleep and sleeping through; dislikes blankets.	2. Establish a bedtime routine that includes techniques such as:
	  ■ quiet activity leading up to bedtime
	  ■ cuddles; deep pressure massage
	  ■ a bath
	  ■ reading a book with a bedtime theme in bed or a rocking chair
	  ■ low lighting
	  ■ singing a lullaby
	
	Try wearing warm pajamas with feet so a blanket may not be needed.

Under-responsiveness
1. Child needs more sensory input to be able to respond. He may seem lethargic and slow to respond. He may need more movement and sensory input before doing a focused activity to bring his nervous system up to where he can be more responsive.
	1. Prior to beginning a cognitive or motor task, try:
	  ■ oral-motor activities: blowing bubbles or blowing through a straw; eating Popsicles or a snow cone; sucking on something sour; eating crunchy food such as carrot sticks or an apple
	  ■ quick movement activities
	  ■ brisk walking, running, jumping, bouncing
	  ■ lively singing; listening and clapping to lively music; dancing
	  ■ feeling textured toys or materials, such as Kooshballs, rubber toys, texture books, etc. (Do not give anything your child could bite off if he is still mouthing toys)
	  ■ cold water on face and hands

SENSORY PROCESSING DIFFICULTIES CONT.	STRATEGIES TO COPE CONT.

Sensory Seeking
 	
1. Child seeks deep pressure by seeking frequent hugs, crashing into furniture, crawling in tight spaces, etc. Deep pressure can override the nervous system effects of hypersensitivity to light touch. Many children with Down syndrome seek frequent hugs; this doesn't always reflect a sensory need but may be a learned social behavior.
 	
2. Child may seek excessive movement, such as swings and spinning tires. He may have difficulty sitting still because his body craves movement.
	1, 2. These children need regular opportunities for movement and sensory play in a structured, predictable part of their day.
	
	■ Provide structured times for the child to engage in sensory activities, trying to meet the same sensory need as those activities he craves.
	■ Repetitive activities that provide a lot of proprioceptive input are most calming and organizing. See examples under "Over-responsiveness to Light Touch."
	■ Other gross motor activities to try:
	   • doing modified push-ups (on hands and knees)
	   • wheelbarrow walks (holding at knees)
	   • repetitive pushing, such as a swing
	   • tug-of-war
	   • carrying heavy items, such as a stack of books
	   • jumping
	(Take care not to place excessive strain on the joints. If your child is not able to hold his joints steady and/or if joints hyperextend beyond normal range, do not have child perform these activities.)
	
	■ Household activities that provide proprioceptive input:
	   • moving laundry from the washer to the dryer
	   • carrying a full laundry basket or recycling bin (for an older child)
	   • pushing a shopping cart at the grocery store
	   • vacuuming, sweeping, and shoveling
	   • carrying a tray with heavy items on it
	■ Provide sensory play and sensory discrimination activities for the hands (as described in Chapter 7).
	■ Offer oral-motor activities at certain times during the day (such as blowing whistles, chewing gum).
	■ Provide opportunities for some movement during circle time at preschool/school, such as sitting on a rocker board, or an inflated cushion, putting feet on a rocker board or cushion.
	■ Allow the child to hold and play with a fidget toy or resistive elastic (such as Theraband) during listening times. (A fidget toys is a small toy the child can squeeze, pull, roll around in his hand, etc.).

(continued on next page)

SENSORY PROCESSING DIFFICULTIES CONT.	STRATEGIES TO COPE CONT.
Motor Planning Difficulties 1. Child has difficulty learning any new motor skill, needing more practice than expected for a child with Down syndrome. A skill that he does know can't be generalized to a new situation. These children seem very disorganized in their approach to motor activities; they don't seem to know how to start and they use a haphazard approach to getting through the task. Note that cognitive skills clearly contribute to a child's ability to quickly learn motor skills. It is still unclear how significant the sensory processing component is to motor learning in children with Down syndrome. Many children with Down syndrome do seem more dependent on environmental factors for success, however.	1. Play that incorporates a lot of tactile experiences (see Chapter 7) can be beneficial for disorganized children. Body awareness activities such as "Simon Says" or obstacle courses can help child become more aware of body position and movement. Having child verbalize what he needs to do to complete a task can help. For example, saying "1, 2, 3, throw" helps to focus the attention on the movement of throwing a ball accurately. Help your child develop verbal strategies and cues to complete a task. Young children often use such verbal cues when learning to print. Structure environment so that familiar tasks are repeated and new skills are introduced in a familiar context.

DOWN SYNDROME AND AUTISM SPECTRUM DISORDER

Although relatively rare, autism spectrum disorder (ASD) is sometimes diagnosed in children with Down syndrome. The rate of ASD in people with Down syndrome has been estimated at approximately 2 to 10 percent. Autism spectrum disorder causes social and communication deficits that are significantly impaired beyond what would be expected in a child with Down syndrome. Although many children with Down syndrome have delays in communication skills, they generally have what is called "communicative intent"—they want to communicate with others, even though they may have trouble speaking. When a child with Down syndrome also has ASD, this communicative intent is often lacking.

Many children with ASD have sensory processing difficulties (75, 36). Thus, it is likely that children with Down syndrome who are also diagnosed with ASD will have sensory processing difficulties as well. The sensory processing difficulties associated with ASD often present as over- or under-responsiveness to sensory input. You can try the same types of approaches for handling these problems detailed in the chart. However, sensory processing challenges associated with a dual diagnosis will most likely also require evaluation and recommendations from an occupational therapist.

What Is a Sensory Diet?

When sensory processing difficulties have been identified in a child, and specific sensory strategies have been found to be helpful for that child, a "sensory diet" may be recommended. A sensory diet means providing the type, frequency, and intensity of sensory input that the child needs to maintain a calm, alert, and organized nervous system (75). Some of the activities described above may become part of a sensory diet for a child. *A sensory diet is developed individually for each child, to meet his or her specific sensory needs.* It is not a "recipe" approach, nor is it simply adding more stimulation.

An example of a weighted vest. Weights are inserted into pockets in the shoulder and pelvic areas. Weighted vests provide deep pressure input that can be calming and organizing for children who are over-responsive or who are sensory seekers. Guidance from a therapist regarding the design and amount of weight is advised.

This chair is available at Ikea. It can be a quiet place for the child who is easily over-stimulated. It can also be a safe and comfortable place for the child who is over-responsive to light touch.

A bolster swing is an example of a piece of equipment that provides vestibular input, which can help an under-responsive child to be more aware of and responsive to his environment.

Child-sized earphones can muffle sounds for the child who is over-responsive to noise. The brush pictured is the specific surgical brush used in the Wilbarger protocol.

Examples of oral-motor activities, including a chew toy, a "Nuk" toothbrush for chewing, whistles, bubbles, and a pinwheel. The deep pressure through the jaw and the breathing for blowing activities can be organizing for many children.

An example of a homemade sensory board, including items of different textures, appealing for the child who seeds sensory input. The strap on the right has Velcro, which many children enjoy opening and closing.

Examples of fidget toys, which are manipulated in the hands by squeezing, twisting, pushing and pulling, etc. These can be helpful for the child who needs movement to keep himself alert and focused, particularly during seated activities.

Indoor and outdoor playgrounds offer a multitude of movement and sensory experiences beneficial to all children.

Profile: Diana

Diana is an eleven-year-old girl who resists hygiene routines. She dislikes having her face washed, which must be done a few times a day because she is a messy eater. Upon reflection, her mother realized that her approach to face washing with Diana was inconsistent and unpredictable. Usually just before going out, in the rush to leave, her mom would notice food on Diana's face, and would quickly moisten a cloth and swipe Diana's face. Diana always turned her head away and would try to push her mother away.

Her mom decided to try a new approach. She placed two Boardmaker pictures above Diana's placemat: Eat dinner; Wipe face. At the end of each meal, before leaving the table, Diana would take a face wipe cloth and wipe her face. A small handheld mirror was available to help her check. Diana responded well to this new routine that became a predictable expectation at every meal. She was happier to be able to manage this by herself, and to avoid the sudden unpleasant swipe during a transition time by her mom.

A sensory diet is usually designed by an occupational or physical therapist who has done a thorough observation and assessment of your child's sensory needs. A sensory diet includes:

- building sensory activities right into the daily routine;
- doing specific sensory activities (such as the Wilbarger protocol, discussed below);
- adapting the environment to include opportunities for the necessary sensory input;
- adapting your approach to the child to respect his sensory needs.

An occupational or physical therapist trained in sensory integration/sensory processing usually sets up a sensory diet or at least consults when it is being set up. National physical therapy and occupational therapy organizations (listed in the Resources section) can provide guidance in finding a PT or OT with this type of training.

THE WILBARGER PROTOCOL

The Wilbarger Protocol for Sensory Defensiveness is a method designed to reduce the effects of over-responsiveness (or "sensory defensiveness") in children and adults (75). It involves providing deep pressure to the skin of the arms, back, and legs at regular intervals throughout the day, using a special surgical brush, followed by joint compressions. Joint compression involves applying pressure through the bones into a joint. The protocol was developed by Patricia Wilbarger, an occupational therapist, and is based on sensory integration theory.

Although there have been many anecdotal reports of improvements in children with sensory processing disorder using the Wilbarger Protocol, it has not been studied in children with Down syndrome who have over-responsiveness to sensory input. Be sure to consult with an occupational or physical therapist who is trained in this technique before initiating such a protocol with your child. There are specific procedures that must be followed when using this protocol.

Profile: Andy

Andy, age fourteen, has a long bus ride to school every morning. He has to wake up early to catch the bus, and he is usually still sleepy as his mom prods him through the morning routine. By the end of the long bus ride, he is either asleep or very groggy. Andy can't get off the bus, walk into the classroom, and immediately focus on academic work. It takes him a long time to "get going" at school. Rather than coming in and sitting at his desk right away, his teacher has built a few routines into his arrival. First, he takes a pile of his classmates' workbooks from the teachers' desk and distributes them. Then he carries the attendance (put into a heavy binder) to the office. The teacher leaves one blackboard uncleaned from the day before so Andy can brush and wash it in the morning. These movement activities help Andy to become more alert so he will be more likely to be able to focus on his school work. He also keeps a water bottle with ice cold water on his desk while working. Cold drinks help us stay awake and alert (not to mention well hydrated!).

Sensory Strategies: Adapting the Environment

In Chapter 1 I discussed adapting the environment to provide more opportunities for trying out and practicing fine motor skills. The same principle applies in sensory processing: we can adapt the environment to accommodate our child's sensory needs and to provide the kinds of sensory input that help him be more organized. If he craves deep pressure through his jaw and is constantly picking up things and chewing on them, we can put a small container with a few oral-motor toys in each room, so that they are readily available to him. Examples might be a nubbed baby toothbrush, a textured chewing toy, gum(if he is old enough), and a whistle or blowing toy. If he is overly sensitive to certain sounds, such as the telephone ring, we can try to have a phone with an adjustable ring volume. Many of the ideas given in the sensory strategies chart are examples of adapting the environment.

Our children seem to do best in environments with consistency, structure, and clear communication of expectations. This is certainly true for all young children, but it is especially true for children with developmental and learning disabilities. Because children with Down syndrome have less flexible nervous systems, and delays in acquiring the cognitive strategies to problem solve and adjust their reactions, many seem to respond more dramatically to small changes in their environments. As discussed below, they may have difficulty with transitions, and with unexpected changes in routine.

As children with Down syndrome grow up, enter, and pass through adolescence into adulthood, they often develop patterns of behavior that they rely on to make their lives predictable and manageable. Sarah now is in high school and takes a bus home every day. She then has a snack and "down time." If any activity, such as an appointment, changes that routine, I have to be sure that she knows about it at least a day ahead of time, and even then she often has difficulty accommodating to the change. Unexpectedly changing the routine and placing different expectations on her never has a positive result.

Drs. Dennis McGuire and Brian Chicoine call this need for repetition, order, and sameness "the groove" (42). Having "grooves" seems to help adults with Down syndrome maintain some control over their lives, and can relieve some of the stress of the overwhelming world. We can run into problems with "grooves" when the person becomes very fixed and inflexible in their routines, and is unable to accommodate any occurrence out of the ordinary (such as a necessary trip to the doctor). The next section offers some strategies to help your child through transitions in a way that respects his need for "grooves."

TRANSITIONS

Many young children have difficulty with transitions; that is, stopping one activity and moving on to the next. When you tell your child to pick up his toys and come to the table for lunch, you are asking him to make a transition. Obviously, there are many transitions to be made throughout the day, and if your child resists at each transition, it can lead to frustration for parents and teachers. There are many possible reasons or combinations of reasons for a child with Down syndrome to have difficulty making transitions. They include:

- difficulty with self-regulation: it may be difficult for your child to change his level of activity and alertness quickly in order to meet the expectations of the next activity;
- difficulty processing and understanding the nature of the next activity and what is expected of him;
- difficulty communicating and making himself understood;
- inconsistent, unpredictable, or inappropriate expectations of the child;
- too many people telling him what to do;
- enjoying what he is doing right now and not wanting to stop;
- disliking the next activity.

MAKING TRANSITIONS EASIER

Here are some tips on how to make transitions go more smoothly for your child. These ideas involve a combination of sensory, behavioral, and cognitive approaches.

1. Use a picture schedule to help make the day more predictable, and, therefore, more manageable for your child. Often, Picture Communication Symbols© from the Boardmaker software by Mayer-Johnson are placed on a strip, showing a clear sequence of activities to help the child understand and remember the schedule. (Pictures can be arranged in a left-to-right or top-to-bottom sequence.) These pictures are particularly useful for children who have: a) difficulty understanding all that is said to them, and/or b) difficulty expressing themselves verbally. For example, a child can see from a series of pictures that first he picks up his sister, then he comes home and has lunch, and then he plays until naptime. He then has a sense of the sequence of activities and knows what to expect.

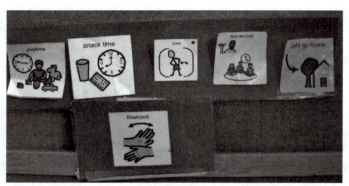

An example of a visual schedule for a preschool program, using Picture Communication Symbols© from Mayer-Johnson's Boardmaker™ software.

2. To prepare a child for a transition coming up, it is helpful to give him a warning, such as "in five minutes we have to put on our coats and go to pick up your sister." A visual cue, such as a picture card or the picture schedule, showing what is next, and/or an auditory cue, such as a timer going off, can also be helpful.

3. Be clear about your expectations. Help your child understand the steps of the process. Saying, "Now we're going to get your sister" may not be enough. He may need to hear the steps: "Now we have to stop what we're doing (wait for him to stop), put on our coats, and go in the car to get your sister."

4. In spite of all your preparations, it still may be hard for your child to leave what he is doing. Let him bring something from that activity with him to the next, such as bringing a small toy with him in the car.

5. Sometimes if a child feels he has an important role to play in the next activity, he will be more interested in stopping what he is doing and moving on. Try to find something that he likes doing. For example, perhaps he likes doing up seat belts in the car. He can do up his sister's and his own seat belt so that he feels he has a helpful role to play.

6. Children can manage transitions better if they are calm and alert. If a child with poor self-regulation is over-responsive or under-responsive at that particular time, he may not be able to make the transition on his own. You may need to plan an extra few minutes into the routine to help him calm down or "rev up." To calm down your child, you may want to try one of these suggestions:

   - Join him in his activity or play, match his energy level, and gradually try to lower his energy level by the use of your actions and voice (gradually slow down your movements and lower your voice level).
   - As he begins to calm down, a slow rhythmic song accompanied by rhythmic actions may help him regulate himself to make the transition.

   If your child can't seem to make the transition because he needs more energy, here are some ideas:

   - Join him in his activity or play, at his energy level, and gradually increase your own energy level and animation, encouraging him to join in active rhymes or songs that encourage more physical activity.
   - Light touch can bring up a person's level of alertness. Try non-threatening touch, like gently stroking your child's fingers, blowing on his hair, or touching his ears. Quick, brisk touch is also alerting, such as giving high fives and clapping.

7. There may be times when none of the above works, and you may have to resort to the Distract and Entertain routine. Take the focus off what you want him to do and put the focus on the two of

you interacting through singing, acting silly, putting on a funny voice, etc., and before he knows it, he will have cooperated with what you wanted him to do!

There are many ways we help ourselves through the day using sensory strategies without really thinking about them in that way. If we are getting drowsy on a long drive, we may turn up some loud music, chew gum, or sing to keep ourselves awake and alert. If we don't like the feel of wool on our skin, we simply don't buy wool clothing. The difference for our children is that they may not be able to identify what is making them uncomfortable or inattentive, or they may not be able to articulate it to us.

The first step for parents and teachers is to recognize that sensory input may be playing a role in your child's responses. If certain sensory inputs seem to cause your child to become more disorganized, you will try to reduce or eliminate those from his environment. If you find other sensory inputs that help your child be more calm and organized, you will try to build those into his day on a regular basis. Just as fine motor activities can be incorporated into everyday routines, sensory strategies and activities can become part of your child's daily routine. Sensory strategies help not only children with a sensory processing disorder, they help us all. Your child with Down syndrome may not have sensory processing issues, but he may still benefit from consideration of sensory strategies in his daily routines.

We all respond best to environmental demands when we are in a calm, alert state. Our "state" refers to how responsive we are at that particular time to what is going on around us. Our "state" is also referred to as our "level of alertness." This ranges from sleep, to the heightened state of awareness and responsiveness experienced in some situations, such as in combat. Sensory processing helps us to change our state as necessary for the time of day and what we need to do. For example, if your child is having speech therapy, he needs to be alert and attentive to the speech-language pathologist to benefit from the therapy. If he is drowsy and inattentive, or over-stimulated and excited, he is unlikely to get much out of the session. Many, if not most, young children need help learning how to regulate their state to the demands of their day. The bedtime routines we establish for our children can help them calm down gradually so that they will be able to fall asleep. For children who have developmental delay, medical concerns, sensory impairment, and/or sensory processing difficulties, maintaining an appropriate state throughout the day can be a challenge.

We all go through many levels of alertness throughout the day: drowsy first thing in the morning and at night, awake and responsive during normal daily activities, high level of alertness during a challenging sports activity, drowsy during a boring mid-afternoon lecture, etc. Our level of alertness is influenced by many internal and external factors. Fatigue, hunger, and physical activity level are internal factors. Medical conditions are also important factors affecting the state of our child, and must *always* be considered first. As mentioned earlier in this chapter, hypothyroidism, sleep apnea, respiratory infections, and dehydration are critical to monitor in children with Down syndrome. Many external factors, such as noise, visual stimuli, lighting, movement, type of food and drink, and many more influence the level of alertness.

"Self-regulation" refers to the ability to reach, maintain, and change one's optimal state (level of alertness) to match the needs of the situation (75, 71). For example, a child with good self-regulation would be able to play an active game of tag outside, then quickly come inside when called for dinner, sit at the table, and eat. A child with poor self-regulation may not be able to make this transition so quickly and easily, may be slow to respond, and may have difficulty settling down enough to be able to sit and eat. Knowing that it is difficult for him to change his level of alertness, he may learn to resist these transitions, especially when they are unexpected, and we may see behavior that is usually described as "stubborn." This behavior pattern can then become learned by the child, and may persist even as he matures and is better able to adjust his activity level more readily.

A program called "How Does Your Engine Run? The Alert Program for Self-Regulation," developed by occupational therapists Mary Sue Williams and Sherry Shellenberger, focuses on teaching school-aged children ways to recognize, understand, and implement sensory strategies to change and keep their energy level and alertness appropriate to their needs throughout the day (see Resources Section for information).

ALERTING AND PREPARING ACTIVITIES FOR CHILDREN WITH DOWN SYNDROME

Levels of alertness can be influenced by the tactile, vestibular, and proprioceptive sensory systems. If we are feeling lethargic and low in energy, often the best thing to increase our energy level and alertness is to do a movement activity, such as getting up and going for a walk. It is the same for children with Down syndrome. Self-directed movement in itself is alerting to the nervous system. Movement that involves changing the position of the head in space (vestibular input), such as going on a swing, and movement that provides deep pressure through the joints (proprioceptive input), such as jumping rope, can be particularly alerting and organizing for the nervous system.

These types of sensory input can *temporarily* change a child's level of alertness. They also provide good preparation for the body to learn a new motor task. Participating in vestibular and proprioceptive activities prepares the nervous system for a more challenging activity, such as one that is just being learned. I have a personal example of how this works. For a long time I tried to help Sarah learn how to ride a bike the usual way: by helping her get on and put her feet on the pedals, and holding the back of the seat of the bike while she rode. However, I never seemed to be able to let go of the back of the bike, as she wasn't getting the feel of balancing the bike. Finally, I tried putting her on a tire swing at the local park (which she loved); she swung and spun around for ten or fifteen minutes. When we tried the bike after the swing, she started catching on to the balancing of the bike right away, and I was able to let go. It seemed to me that the vestibular input helped prepare her for the more challenging task of balancing the bike. This may not work for every child, and every child may not need the input to learn to ride, but there seemed to be a correlation that worked for us.

Sometimes children with Down syndrome have difficulty with self-regulation in the context of environmental and social expectations. For example, they may seem lethargic and relatively unresponsive in the classroom, only to quickly become over-excited during a social interactive game. If there is physical contact in the game, they may overdo it, grabbing and holding the other children inappropriately. The adults watching aren't sure how to respond. They are glad that the child is finally interacting with the other children, but the child's difficulties understanding social protocol and regulating his interactions are limiting his success with the others. It seems that the child's "window" of optimal alertness and responsiveness is small, and that he is more

Profile: James

James is a twelve-year-old boy integrated into a regular classroom. Although quiet and somewhat non-interactive with his peers in the classroom, he "comes alive" at recess, running around randomly and trying to join games that are already going on in the schoolyard. Because he is moving around from group to group, and doesn't understand the rules of the game, he causes disruption and the other kids don't want him to join. His teacher recognizes his need for structured movement activities with heavy work input (proprioception) to help him be more organized in his play during recess. She organized a group of grade 8 students to set up a few activities to start off recess for James and some of his classmates. They begin with a tug-of-war on the lawn, then they play a game of dodge ball with a larger inflated ball (so the kids won't get hurt by the ball). They follow this up with a game of shadow tag (the kids step on each other's shadow to "catch" them in tag), so there is no reaching, touching, and grabbing that is hard for James to both tolerate and initiate appropriately. James becomes more organized during these activities, and is more alert and interactive afterwards in the classroom.

often under or over the optimum level. Because of the child's cognitive impairment, difficulty reading social cues, and responding accordingly, using a combination of sensory strategies and behavioral approaches will probably be most helpful.

SNOEZELEN

Snoezelen is a concept that was developed by occupational therapists in Holland. Snoezelen is a sensory environment which provides people with severe disabilities the opportunity to enjoy and control a variety of sensory experiences. Snoezelen is usually set up as a room or part of a room, and usually includes a variety of visual lighting effects (such as a bubble tube, fiber optics, and a solar projector), soft sounds, and comfortable cushions, and sometimes includes movement (such as a hammock), vibration, mirrors, and tactile activities. Some of the sensory experiences are soothing, while others are stimulating. Only those experiences that are appropriate for the individual's needs should be used.

Research into the effects of Snoezelen on people with challenging conditions supports the findings that it can have a positive impact on mood, behavior, and relationships. These changes are seen over time, as the child or adult spends time regularly in the Snoezelen room, and is free to enjoy and control the sensory experience without any expectations to perform or respond in any particular way. The white rooms, which have white floor and wall mats, can be calming and organizing and can help offset some of the more demanding aspects of a person's day.

A Snoezelen room, with fiber optics, light projector, and a bubble tube.

Snoezelen rooms are now available in some clinics, hospitals, schools, and residential and other facilities that service individuals with developmental and physical disabilities.

Supplies are available through Flaghouse. (See Resources.)

Behavioral Approaches

This chapter has focused on sensory processing issues in children with Down syndrome, and has described some sensory strategies to help. Sometimes, patterns of behavior have become learned over time and are difficult to change, even if the sensory environment is adapted to meet the child's needs. The child may be using the behavior for other reasons, such as to seek attention (either positive or negative), to get or avoid a particular activity or object, or to otherwise communicate. In these cases, the child often needs Intervention based on positive reinforcement of desired behaviors and structured activities that ensure his success. It is beyond the scope of this book to detail the types of behavioral interventions that can be used to help children with Down syndrome who have these needs. Psychologists, behavior therapists, child care workers, and teachers are among those professionals who develop and carry out programs based on behavioral principles.

Summary

Our ability to interact adaptively with our environment depends partly on the sensory information available, the processing and integration of that sensory information, and our own unique personality and genetic makeup. When faced with puzzling behaviors in our children with Down syndrome we must first rule out intrinsic factors such as hunger, thirst, fatigue, illness, or visual or hearing deficits. When these are ruled out, we can consider how the sensory environment may be contributing to the child's problematic responses, and what we might be able to change in the sensory environment to help him behave more appropriately.

If your child *overreacts* to certain types of sensory input (light touch and certain sounds are the most common), you will try to change the environment to reduce these types of input *and* provide deep pressure and proprioceptive input throughout the day. If your child *under-reacts* to certain types of sensory input, you will try to enrich his environment with the types of sensory input you have noticed help him to become more aware and alert (visual, touch, and movement inputs are the most common). If your child doesn't seem to overreact or under-react, but has a lot of difficulty organizing movement and learning new movement skills, you will ensure that he has an environment rich in tactile exploration and body awareness activities. You will also use verbal and visual feedback to help him.

As parents, we can take note of environments that help our child be most interactive, calm, attentive, and happy. We can also take note of environments that lead to more anxiety and disorganized or disruptive responses. Sometimes your observations may fall into patterns that indicate sensory needs or avoidances due to the way your child processes sensory information. Sometimes you can sort this out yourself and reach solutions that improve the situation for your child. At other times you may need the assistance of an occupational therapist or physical therapist trained in sensory integration/sensory processing. Remember: If there is not a pattern that seems to fit a sensory perspective, your child may be responding to other needs, such as the need for attention, to communicate, etc.

Grandma's and Grandpa's List

- Hop balls
- Inflatable punching bag
- Parachute
- Tether ball
- Beanbag chair
- Hammock
- Rocking horse
- Rocker/balance/"wobble" board
- Air mattress
- Ball pool
- Cloth crawl tunnels
- Vibrating stuffed toy
- Sit 'n Spin
- Fidget toys (small handheld toys that can be manipulated and/or have a pleasing sensory property, such as a bumpy surface)

CHAPTER 12

Hands Up!

Raising a child with Down syndrome presents an extra challenge to most parents. As with other unexpected life events, this challenge also opens the door for us to learn and to expand our own abilities. There is no doubt that I would not have written this book had I not had Sarah. Over the past fifteen years, as I have watched her, learned from her, and gained new insights, I began to think, "How can I *not* write this book?" Sarah has given me many new ideas and insights as an occupational therapist that I may not have had if I wasn't also a parent.

Having previous medical and therapy knowledge has been beneficial in many ways. I understand the terminology, the medical system, the philosophy of infant and child development, and can anticipate the developmental milestones and all the small steps in between. However, sometimes I have had unrealistic expectations of myself and Sarah. Although intellectually I can understand that Sarah has plateaus in her development, it is more difficult emotionally accepting that my therapy skills and experience can't change that.

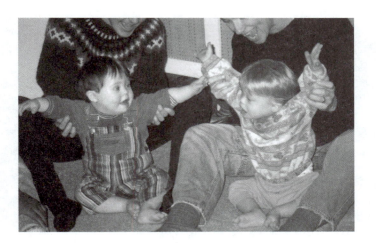

We all have limited time and energy. Some days Sarah and I connect well and I feel that we are making progress in an area of her development that we are pursuing, and other days it's all we can do just to get through the day. You may not have the time or energy to do many of the activities I suggest in this book. That is okay! The most important thing to do for our children is to be their parents. Loving them, caring for their needs, supporting them, and being there when they need us is the bottom line. The emotional commitment of parenting can make it difficult to act as a teacher and therapist to our own child.

As I have suggested in this book, helping your child develop fine motor skills and incorporating sensory strategies into your routine does not necessitate a special program. It does take some thinking about your own schedule so that some of the home activities can be incorporated into your regular routine.

All parents are concerned about their child's future. Fortunately, our society is demonstrating more awareness and acceptance of children with Down syndrome in schools and in recreational and employment situations than a generation ago. However, some parents still must advocate and struggle to ensure basic rights for their children. In addition, levels of function and independence vary greatly among adults with Down syndrome. Current research, books, and experience have shown that, given a chance, many children and adults with Down syndrome can manage aspects of their own lives that were previously thought unattainable.

It makes sense that if we help them prepare for adult life, our children will have a better chance. Our society is driven by the motivations and aspirations of the individual, by success, and by financial security. Our children with Down syndrome do not necessarily fit into this mold; they challenge us and all those in contact with them to develop new expectations of life. Our challenge as parents may not be so much to try to help our children fit into the mold, but to try to change and expand this mold, to help develop acceptance and inclusion, not just tolerance. At least in my case, I think part of the grieving process is an ongoing "letting go" of expectations that my child will be able to do all the things that her sisters and friends can do. It is not giving up hope, but changing the parameters of that hope.

I hope this book can be a help to parents. I know that often I find comfort in just talking to another parent who understands what it is all about.

Visual Motor Worksheets

Workbooks and programs that have activities for tracing and copying in preparation for printing are available through most toy and educational stores. I designed some of my own for Sarah based on her interests, and the types of pencil movements she would need to be able to print letters and numbers. The worksheets are divided into four stages:

STAGE 1

These worksheets are designed for children with Down syndrome who are making simple strokes on paper. For many children with Down syndrome, they will be appropriate from about age three to five. The worksheets can be used with different media, but the way the patterns are introduced should be consistent. The marker/paintbrush/pencil should always begin at the monkey's face, then follow the pattern. In all the linear patterns, show your child how to stop at the corner and change direction. For most children of this age, this will be a new concept. It is not important at this stage for your child to stay neatly within the lines. The points you want him to learn from these activities are:

- There is a definite starting point;
- He stops his stroke to change direction;
- There is a definite stopping point.

The direction and patterns are based on some of the upper case letter patterns that your child will first learn to print. The worksheets can be enlarged and used on an easel, with your child following the pattern with his paintbrush. Or, your child can take a thick crayon or marker and stroke along the pattern to fill the space with color. Your child can roll out a snake of play dough and lay it on top of the pattern, or do the same with a Wikki Stix. The inverted "V" pattern will be the most difficult for most children, as the monkey tells them to start at the top, draw down the left side, then pick up his marker, go back to the top, and down the other side. This exercise is included because several upper case letters are printed in this way, returning to the starting point to begin the next stroke.

STAGE 2

The next set of worksheets is for children who already have the ability to make vertical and horizontal lines and circles, and have begun to combine them in simple forms.

They may also be learning to print, as most children are introduced to printing their own name at about age 4 or 5. These worksheets will help your child refine his control of the pencil, in preparation for printing lower case letters. They will also develop these skills: starting and stopping the stroke at a defined spot; making smaller strokes within a defined space; and controlling the direction of the stroke more precisely. These worksheets can be appropriate for ages four and up, depending on the level of your child. The use of each worksheet is as follows:

- **CLOWN:** make horizontal lines across the clown's costume
- **TRAIN TRACKS:** make vertical lines across tracks; diagonal lines for crossing signs
- **PORCUPINE:** make short lines in various directions
- **HOUSE:** make a cross in each window
- **FISH:** make semicircles, starting at the top and going in a counterclockwise direction (top fish) and clockwise direction (bottom fish)
- **FISH BUBBLES:** make very small circles
- **FACES:** add eyes and mouth on each face

STAGE 3

One example of how letters can be grouped to teach printing of lower case letters is presented here. This example is given to help parents, teachers, and teacher assistants think about how a particular child will best learn to print using consistent patterns that will make it easier for him to remember how to form the letters. Other therapists and educators may suggest slightly different letter groupings. I don't advocate one method over another, but I do feel that children have more chance of success with printing if they are taught one method consistently, with attention to how the letters are formed. As mentioned in Chapter 9, a multi-sensory approach to learning letter formation can help some children.

Letter Groups:

1. a, d, g, q: These all begin with a curved (counterclockwise) stroke, then proceed into a vertical line. The line is retraced, continuing below the line for g and q.
2. c, o, e, s: Like group 1, these letters also involve a curved stroke in a counterclockwise direction. The letters "e" and "s" are a bit different, but are included in this group because the curved stroke begins in the same direction.
3. l, t, f, k: These letters all begin with a straight vertical line down (in the case of "f," it begins with a little hook and then proceeds down in a vertical line). The pencil is then lifted to make the cross stroke in "t" and "f," and the diagonal strokes in "k."
4. i, j: Like the letters in group 3, these also begin with a vertical line. The letter "j" ends with a little hook at the end.
5. h, b, p: These letters also begin with a vertical line down, which is then retraced partially to proceed into the curved (clockwise) stroke. The letter "p" is retraced back up to the top of the line.
6. n, m, r: These letters begin with a short vertical line, which is

retraced up to begin the curved stroke. The middle line is also retraced in "m."

7. u, v, w, x, y, z: These letters (except for "z") begin with a downward stroke: "u" curves, "v," "w," "x," and "y" are diagonals. The letter "z" includes a diagonal line, but begins with a horizontal stroke.

STAGE 4

The last set of worksheets provides prewriting patterns that will help children who are preparing to learn cursive writing. They cover the basic patterns of pencil movement that are found in most of the letters. Again, similar types of writing practice are available in other workbooks and programs. These worksheets are provided so that parents and teachers can photocopy them for repeated use with a child. Alternately, they can be placed in a plastic cover so that the child can practice with an erasable marker.

STAGE 1—DIAGONAL LINES (BEGIN DRAWING AT THE MONKEY FACE)

STAGE 1—CIRCLES (BEGIN DRAWING AT THE MONKEY FACE)

STAGE 1—DIAGONAL LINES (BEGIN DRAWING AT MONKEY FACE)

STAGE 1—STRAIGHT LINES (BEGIN DRAWING AT MONKEY FACE)

Stage 1—Curved (Begin Drawing at the Monkey Face)

STAGE 1—CURVED LINES (BEGIN DRAWING AT THE MONKEY FACE)

STAGE 1—DIAGONAL LINES (BEGIN DRAWING AT THE MONKEY FACE)

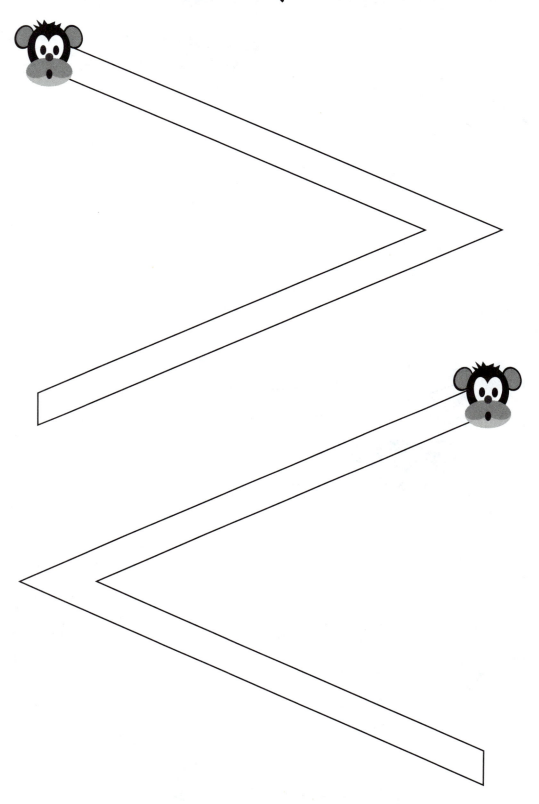

STAGE 2—CLOWN (DRAW HORIZONTAL LINES)

Sue J. Yurkewich

STAGE 2—TRAIN TRACKS (DRAW VERTICAL LINES)
CROSSING SIGNS (DRAW DIAGONAL LINES)

Sue J. Yurkewich

STAGE 2—PORCUPINE (DRAW LINES VARIOUS DIRECTIONS)

Sue J. Yurkewich

STAGE 2—HOUSE WINDOWS (DRAW CROSSING LINES)

Sue J. Yurkewich

STAGE 2—FISH SCALES (DRAW SEMICIRCLES CLOCKWISE & COUNTERCLOCKWISE)
BUBBLES (DRAW SMALL CIRCLES)

Sue J. Yurkewich

STAGE 2—FACES (DRAW FEATURES)

Sue J. Yurkewich

STAGE 4—ROLLER COASTER (FINISH THE RIDE ON THE ROLLER COASTER)

STAGE 4—CAMEL (FINISH THE CAMEL'S HUMPS; PRACTICE BELOW)

STAGE 4—SPIDER (FINISH THE SPIDER'S WALK ON THE TALL GRASS)

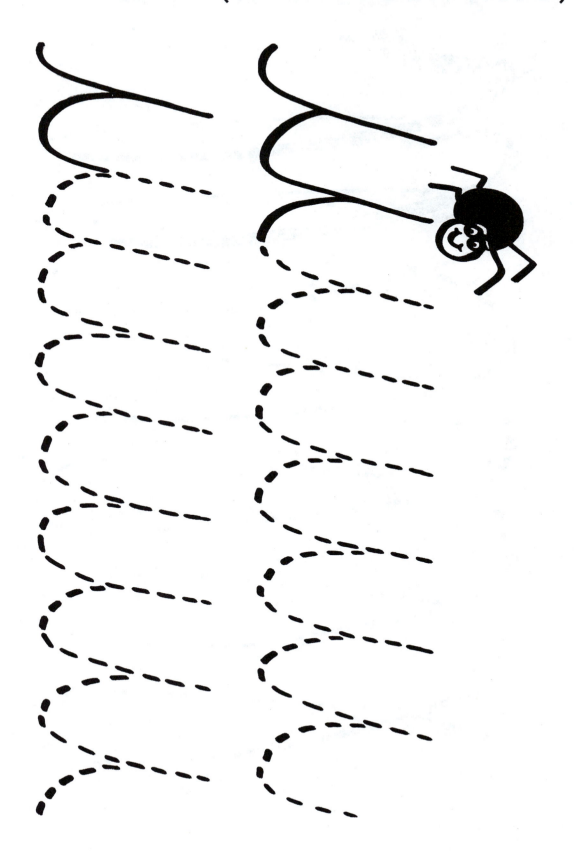

STAGE 4—BOOMERANG (FINISH THE BOOMERANG'S PATH)

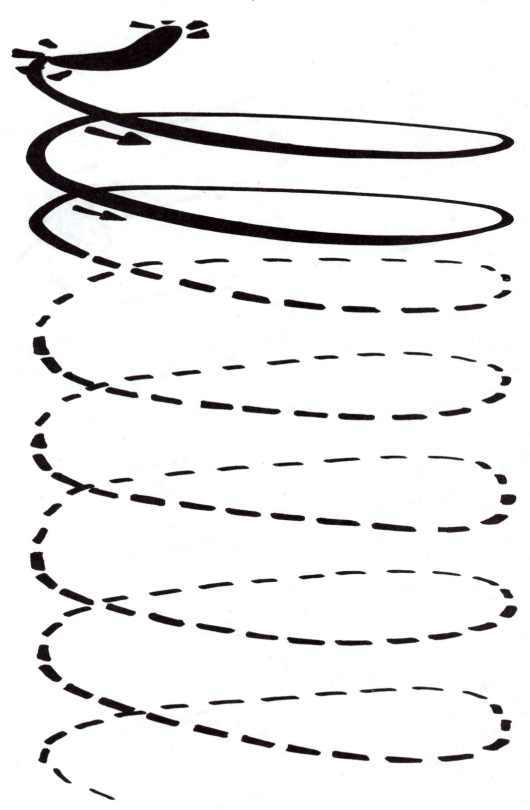

STAGE 4—BIRD (FINISH THE BIRD'S FLIGHT)

STAGE 4—WAVES (FINISH THE WAVES)

Don't Throw It Out!
Household Items to Use for Hand Play

It isn't necessary to spend a lot of money buying expensive toys. Young children are usually just as happy with whatever is lurking in your cupboards and closets. Here is a list of things families often have around the house, and their uses:

- Empty plastic pop bottles: Fill with colorful beads, marbles, or water—anything that will make a nice noise and catch your child's visual attention as she moves it around and picks it up. It's good for early bilateral hand skills, as the bottle has to be picked up with both hands.
- Empty plastic ice cream/yogurt containers: cut a hole in the top for dropping objects into; you can also cut out the center of the lids, leaving only the rims, to be used as rings to put on pegs (or empty paper towel rolls). Simple shapes can be cut out of a lid to make a stencil.
- Empty bleach containers: cut off the bottom of the container to make a "scoop catcher," which is held to catch bean bags or other tossed items.
- Paper rolls: a paper towel or toilet paper roll can be glued to a piece of cardboard and used as a peg. Put cut-out margarine container

Household playthings. Clockwise from tennis ball can: tennis ball container filled with smaller balls; measuring cups for separating and size sorting; salad spinner for bilateral coordination; film containers for stacking, filling, and shaking; yogurt container with slit in lid for inserting frozen juice can lids; colorful scarf; shoe boxes for stacking and filling; squeeze bottles; frozen juice cans; tissue paper; pots and pans; styrofoam block with holes for markers (an improvised peg board); empty toilet paper rolls; rings cut out of lids of plastic containers; string; buttons; single mitts and socks; wooden spoons; plastic "bubble" packing material; toothbrush holder; shape stencils cut out of plastic container lids.

lids or bracelets on it (rings on peg game). Paper rolls can also be used for making a variety of crafts.

- Empty squeeze bottles, such as dish detergent bottles: Wash out well and use in the bathtub for water play.
- Measuring cups: A set of measuring cups that fit into one another are good for learning concepts of taking apart/putting together, and size discrimination.
- Bangle bracelets: Guiding the hand through to put the bracelet on helps develop hand awareness skills for a toddler or young child.
- Empty orange juice cans (no rough edges): for paints; filling and pouring water activities; stacking.
- Orange juice can lids: good for thumb-finger grasp development; put into slots cut into lids of plastic containers; attach 2 together with Velcro for child to pull apart.
- Pots and pans: A favorite of all toddlers, practicing taking lids on and off, stirring with a wooden spoon, etc.
- Dried-up markers: Still good for pulling the caps on and off. Improvise a pegboard by cutting holes in a block of styrofoam that the markers can stand up in.
- Plastic "bubble" wrapping paper: This is the stuff many fragile items or electronics are packed in. It can be used for a different sensory experience, or to develop pinch strength when trying to pop the bubbles. Supervise closely; it is plastic!
- Plastic film containers: Can be used to practice taking the lid on and off; as shakers when filled with rice (the lids are quite secure); even as a sound matching game (fill 2 containers each with rice, beans, Rice Krispies, or other different materials, to get different-sounding pairs that your child can match).
- Cardboard boxes: Larger, sturdy boxes can be used as sitting stools, footstools, or as "tables" for children playing on the floor (cut out a semicircle for their legs). This may help the child who is just becoming independent in sitting by raising the height of the toys.
- Shoeboxes: Can be used as large building blocks.
- Tissue paper: Tissue paper is great for ripping or cutting into small pieces, scrunching into a ball and gluing on paper.
- Single socks or mittens: sew on buttons or wool to make hand puppets with funny faces, or make bean bags by filling them with beans or lentils.
- Buttons: Can be used to practice picking up and releasing small objects; also used for crafts.
- Scarves: An old scarf has many uses, such as playing peek-a-boo, waving in the air to music, wrapping up small objects, etc.
- Magazines, calendars. etc.: Have pictures for practicing cutting skills.

Glossary

Here is a brief compilation of terms you may encounter in this book, or in your contacts with various professionals involved with your child:

arches—the contours of the palm of the hand that position the hand for function.

assistive technology—a piece of equipment or system that is used to increase, maintain or improve functional capabilities of persons with disabilities.

asymmetrical—one side of the body is positioned or is moving differently from the other side.

bilateral— relating to both hands, or both sides of the body.

camptodactyly—a permanent bent (flexed) position of one or both of the small joints of a finger, usually the fifth finger in Down syndrome.

cause-effect—(in reference to toys) the concept that something happens when the child activates the toy; e.g., a jack-in-the-box is a cause-effect toy.

clinodactly—a permanent curving inward of a finger, usually the fifth finger in Down syndrome.

dexterity—accurate and efficient hand movements for function.

digital-pronate grasp—a grasp used to hold a pencil or tool handle, in which the shaft or handle is stabilized in the palm, while the thumb, second, and third finger extend to the end; the second stage of grasp development.

distal—referring to the parts of the body that are furthest from the center of the body (e.g., the hands and feet are distal in the body). The opposite of **proximal.**

dominance—referring to the hand used for most activities; i.e., right-handed or left-handed.

extension—a movement of a joint, usually straightening it; e.g., elbow extension occurs when the elbow is straight. The opposite of **flexion.**

facilitate—to help something to happen.

flexion—a movement of a joint, usually bending it so that the two long bones come closer together. The opposite of **extension.**

forearm—the part of the arm between the elbow and the wrist.

hyperextension—straightening of the joint beyond the normal limits (sometimes referred to as being "double-jointed").

hypotonia—the condition in which muscles don't have the normal amount of tone, or contraction, so they appear loose and floppy. Also referred to as **low muscle tone.**

joint—the point where two or more bones meet, usually where movement occurs.

kinesthesia/kinesthetic—the sense of one's body in space; knowing where all one's body parts are in relation to each other.

laterality—refers to one side of the body or brain.

ligamentous laxity—loose ligaments around a joint, allowing it to move more than the normal amount.

low muscle tone—*See* hypotonia.

manipulation—the use of the hands to perform any function.

midline—the middle or center of the body in the vertical plane; e.g., the hands are in the midline when they come together in a prayer position.

muscle tone—the degree of contraction or firmness of muscles.

Neurodevelopmental Therapy (NDT)—therapy involving handling and positioning of the child to facilitate normal postural reactions and movement patterns.

opposition—the thumb and one fingertip coming together.

palmar digital grasp—*See* digital-pronate grasp.

palmar grasp—a grasp in which the utensil or pencil is held firmly in the palm by all the fingers and thumb; the first stage of grasp development.

peer—a child of the same age as a given child.

pincer grasp—the thumb and first finger come together to pick up small objects; inferior pincer refers to the pad of the thumb opposing the side or pad of the index finger; superior pincer refers to the tip of the thumb opposing the tip of the index finger.

prehension—the movement of grasping, or taking hold of something.

productive skills—activity done for a specific purpose; e.g., work and housework for adults; school for children.

pronation—(related to fine motor skills) the normal resting position of the forearms and hands (palms down); opposite of **supination.**

proprioception—the sense of position and movement from the sensors in our muscles, tendons, and joints.

proximal—the parts of the body closest to the center of the body; the opposite of **distal,** e.g., the shoulders are proximal, the hands are distal.

quadrupod grasp—a grasp used to hold a pencil or utensil, in which the shaft or handle rests between the thumb and three fingers; a variation of the tripod grasp.

reflex—an involuntary movement or action; e.g., a cough when something is stuck in one's throat is a reflex. Many early movements in babies are reflexes; e.g., the grasp reflex occurs when an object is placed in an infant's palm.

sensory/sensation—information available to use through our senses of sight, hearing, smell, taste, touch, kinesthesia, proprioception, and vestibular. Sensory activities use touch and movement to give sensory information.

sensory integration—the neurological process that organizes and integrates sensations from the body and the environment in order to make an adaptive response.

sensory processing—the neurological process of registration, orientation, modulation, interpretation, and integration of sensory information from the body and the environment in order to make an adaptive response.

stability—the ability to hold steady; stability of muscles forms a foundation and base upon which movement can occur.

storing—keeping small items tucked into the palm of the hand.

supination—(related to fine motor skills) rotating the wrist to turn the forearm and the palm up; opposite of **pronation.**

symmetrical—the two sides of the body are equal; positioned or moving in the same way.

transfer—to pass an object from one hand to the other.

transference—moving an object from the palm out to the fingers.

tripod grasp—a grasp used to hold an object, pencil, or handle, in which the thumb, second, and third fingers hold the object out of the palm. Static tripod refers to a pencil grasp in which the shaft rests between the pads of the thumb, second, and third fingers, where most of the movement comes from the wrist, elbow, and shoulder; dynamic tripod refers to a pencil grasp in which the shaft rests between the tips of the thumb, which is rounded, and the second and third fingers, where the movement comes from the small joints of the fingers and thumb.

vestibular system—the sensory system located in the inner ear that subconsciously informs us about movement and head position and helps us maintain an upright posture.

visual motor—refers to activities in which the eyes guide hand movement (e.g., printing, drawing).

voluntary movement—moving with intention; opposite of **reflex.**

Bibliography

Included in this bibliography are all books and articles I researched while writing this book. Some are cited in the text, as indicated by a number in parentheses. Others, such as those related to self-help skills, development, and handwriting programs, are included because they may be of interest to parents.

1. Anson, J. Greg (1992). "Neuromotor Control and Down Syndrome." *Approaches to the Study of Motor Control and Learning.* J.J. Summers (Editor), 387-411.

2. Baker, Bruce L. and Brightman, Alan J. *Steps to Independence: Teaching Everyday Skills to Children with Special Needs.* 4th edition. Baltimore, MD: Paul H. Brookes, 2003.

3. Benbow, Mary. *Neurokinesthetic Approach to Hand Function and Handwriting.* Corning, NY: Advanced Rehabilitation Institutes, 1994.

4. Blanche, Erna I., Botticelli, Tina M., and Hallway, Mary K. "The Use of Neurodevelopmental Treatment and Sensory Integration in the Assessment and Treatment of Children with Developmental Disorders: Down Syndrome." In: *Combining Neuro-Developmental Treatment and Sensory Integration Principles.* San Antonio, TX: Therapy Skill Builders, 1995.

5. Block, Martin E. (1991). "Motor Development in Children with Down Syndrome: A Review of the Literature." *Adapted Physical Activity Quarterly,* 8, 179-209.

6. Boehme, Regi. *Improving Upper Body Control.* San Diego: Singular Publishing Co., 1988.

7. Boehme, Regi. *The Hypotonic Child. Treatment for Postural Control, Endurance, Strength and Sensory Organization.* Therapy Skill Builders, 1990.

8. Burns, Yvonne and Gun, Pat, Editors. *Down Syndrome: Moving Through Life.* New York: Chapman & Hall, 1993.

9. Carr, Janet. *Down's Syndrome: Children Growing Up.* Cambridge: Cambridge University Press, 1995.

10. Cadoret, Genevieve and Beuter, Anne (1994). "Early Development of Reaching in Down Syndrome Infants." *Early Human Development,* 36, 157-173.

11. Capone, G. (2003). "Dual Diagnosis: Down Syndrome and Neurobehavioral Disorders in Children." National Down Syndrome Congress 2003 Annual Convention (audiotape of presentation), Philadelphia, PA.

12. Cohen, W., Nadel, L., and Madnick, M., Editors. *Visions for the 21st Century. Down Syndrome.* New York: John Wiley & Sons, 2002.

13. Cole, Kelly J., Abbs, James H., and Turner, Greg S. (1988). "Deficits in the Production of Grip Forces in Down Syndrome." *Developmental Medicine and Child Neurology,* 30, 752-758.

14. Connolly, B., Morgan, S., and Russell, F.F. (1984). "Evaluation of Children with Down Syndrome Who Participated in an Early Intervention Program: Second Follow-up Study." *Physical Therapy,* 64, 1515-9.

15. Cuskelly, M., Jobling, A., and Buckley, S., Editors. *Down Syndrome Across the Life Span.* London: Whurr Publishers, 2002.

16. Dunn Klein, Marsha. *Pre-dressing Skills.* San Antonio, TX: Therapy Skill Builders, 1999.

17. Dunn, W. *Sensory Profile: User's Manual.* San Antonio, TX: The Psychological Association, 1999.

18. Dyer, S., Gunn, P., Rauh, H., and Berry, P. (1990). "Motor Development in Down Syndrome Children: An Analysis of the Motor Scale of the Bayley Scales of Infant Development." *Motor Development, Adapted Physical Activity and Mental Retardation 30,* 7-20.

19. Edwards, Sandra J. and Lafreniere, Mary K. "Hand Function in the Down Syndrome Population." In: Martha Sasser, Editor, *Hand Function in the Child: Foundations for Remediation.* St. Louis: Mosby Year Book, 1995.

20. Erhardt, Rhoda P. *Developmental Prehension Assessment.* RAMSCO Publishing Company, 1982.

21. Freeman, Andrew R., MacKinnon, Joyce R., and Miller, Linda T. (2004). "Assistive Technology and Handwriting Problems: What Do Occupational Therapists Recommend?" *Canadian Journal of Occupational Therapy,* 3, vol. 71, 150-160.

22. Haley, Stephen M. (1986). "Postural Reactions in Infants with Down Syndrome: Relationship to Motor Milestone Development and Age." *Physical Therapy, 66 (1),* 17-22.

23. Haley, Stephen M. (1987). "Sequence of Development of Postural Reactions by Infants with Down Syndrome." *Developmental Medicine and Child Neurology, 29(5),* 674-679.

24. Hannaford, Carla. *Smart Moves: Why Learning Is Not All in Your Head.* Arlington, VA: Great Ocean Publishers, 1995.

25. Hanson, Marci J. *Teaching the Infant with Down Syndrome: A Guide for Parents and Professionals.* Austin, TX: Pro-Ed, 1987.

26. Harris, Susan R. "Physical Therapy and Infants with Down's Syndrome: The Effects of Early Intervention." *Rehabilitation Literature, 42, (11-12),* 1981.

27. Henderson, Sheila E. "Motor Skill Development." In: Lane, David and Stratford, Brian, Editors, *Current Approaches to Down's Syndrome.* New York: Praeger Special Studies, 1985.

28. Hohlstein, Rita R. "The Development of Prehension in Normal Infants." *American Journal of Occupational Therapy, 36, (3),* March 1982.

29. Hogg, J. and Moss, S.C. (1983). "Prehensile Development in Down's Syndrome and Non-handicapped Preschool Children." *British Journal of Developmental Psychology,* Volume 1, 189-204.

30. Janzen, Paul, Blackstein-Adler, Susie, and Antonius, Kim. *Cheap N Free Access Solutions for the Mac: Communication and Writing Aids.* Toronto: Bloorview McMillan Centre, 1997.

31. Jenkins, J.R., Fewell, R., and Harris, S.R. (1983). "Comparison of Sensory Integrative Therapy and Motor Programming." *American Journal of Mental Deficiency, 88(2), 221-4.*

32. Jobling, Anne (1999). "Attainment of Motor Proficiency in School-Aged Children with Down Syndrome." *Adapted Physical Activity Quarterly, 16,* 344-361.

33. Jobling, Anne & Virji-Babul, Naznin. *Down Syndrome: Play, Move and Grow.* Vancouver, BC: Down Syndrome Research Foundation, 2004.

34. Johnson Levine, Kristin. *Development of Pre-Academic Fine Motor Skills: A Visual Analysis.* San Antonio, TX: Therapy Skill Builders, 1994.

35. Lane, S.J., Miller, L.J. and Hanft, B.E. (2000). "Toward a Consensus in Terminology in Sensory Integration Theory and Practice: Part 2: Sensory Integration Patterns of Function." *Sensory Integration Special Interest Section Quarterly, 23.*

36. Lashno, Mary (1999). "Observations of Children with Down Syndrome and Autistic Spectrum Disorder." *Disability Solutions, 3,* issue 5-6.

37. Lashno, Mary (2003). Sensory Processing Disorder. National Down Syndrome Congress 2003 Annual Convention (audiotape of presentation), Philadelphia, PA.

38. Lauteslager, P.E.M., Vermeer, A., and Helders, P. J. M. (1998). "Disturbances in the Motor Behavior of Children with Down Syndrome: The Need for a Theoretical Framework." *Physiotherapy, 84 (1),* 5-13.

39. Law, M., Baptiste, S., Carwell, A., McColl M.A., Polotajko, H., and Pollack, N. *Canadian Occupational Performance Measures.* 2nd ed. Toronto: CAOT Publications ACE, 1994.

40. Lydic, J. S. and Steele, C. (1979). "Assessment of the Quality of Sitting and Gait Patterns in Children with Down Syndrome." *Physical Therapy, 59, (12),* 1489-1494.

41. Lydic, J.S., Windsor, M.M., Short, M.A., and Ellis, T.A. (1985). "Effects of Controlled Rotary Vestibular Stimulation on the Motor Performance of Infants with Down Syndrome." *Physical and Occupational Therapy in Pediatrics 5,* 93-118.

42. McGuire, Dennis. "The Groove," presented at the Medical Symposium: Adults with Down Syndrome. Understanding Their Complex Health Needs." Canadian Down Syndrome Society and Edmonton Down Syndrome Society, 2003.

43. Medlen, Joan, Editor. "Assistive Technology." *Disability Solutions, 3,* issue 2.

44. Meyers, Laura F. "Using Computers to Teach Children with Down Syndrome." In: Lynn Nadel, Editor, *The Psychobiology of Down Syndrome.* Cambridge, MA: MIT Press, 1988.

45. Miller, L. J. and Lane, S. J. (2000). "Toward a Consensus in Terminology in Sensory Integration Theory and Practice: Part 1: Taxonomy of Neurophysiological Processes. *Sensory Integration Special Interest Section Quarterly, 23 (1)* 1-4.

46. Murray-Slutsky, Carolyn and Paris, Betty. "Is it Behavior Or Is It Sensory?" STAR Services Inc. 2004.

47. Naganuma, Gay M. (1987). "Early Intervention for Infants with Down Syndrome: Efficacy Research." *Physical and Occupational Therapy in Pediatrics, 71,* 81-92.

48. Nommensen, A. and Frikkie, M. (1993). "Sensory Integration and Down's Syndrome." *British Journal of Occupational Therapy, 56 (12),* 451-454.

49. Oelwein, Patricia Logan. *Teaching Reading to Children with Down Syndrome: A Guide for Parents and Teachers.* Bethesda, MD: Woodbine House, 1995.

50. Olsen, Janice Z. *Handwriting without Tears.* Self-published, 1997. Available from 8802 Quiet Stream Court, Potomac, MD 20854. www.hwt.com

51. Perr, A., Petra, E., and Burwell, C. (2000). "An Investigation of the Use and Potential Use of Accessibility Options Built into Computer Operating Systems." *New York University Webpage,* NY University, Department of Occupational Therapy. http://education.nyu.edu

52. PREP Program. *Effective Teaching Strategies for Successful Inclusion: A Focus on Down Syndrome.* Calgary, Alberta: PREP Program, 1999.

53. Rast, M. and Harris, S. (1985). "Motor Control in Infants with Down Syndrome." *Developmental Medicine and Child Neurology, 27,* 675-685.

54. Reisman, J. E. and Hanschu, B. *Sensory Integration Inventory-Revised for Individuals with Developmental Disabilities: User's Guide.* Hugo, Minnesota: PDP Press, 1992.

55. Russell, D., Palisano, R., Walter, S., Rosenbaum, P., Gemus, M., Gowland, C., Galuppi, B., and Lane, M. (1998). "Evaluating Motor Function in Children with Down Syndrome: Validity of the GMFM." *Developmental Medicine and Child Neurology, 41,* 693-701.

56. Sahagian, Sandra D. *A Fine Motor Program for Down Syndrome Preschoolers: A Pilot Study;* unpublished thesis in partial fulfillment of Masters of Health Science, McMaster University, Hamilton, Ontario, 1985.

57. Selikowitz, Mark. *Down Syndrome: The Facts.* New York: Oxford Press, 1997.

58. *Sharon, Lois and Brams' Mother Goose.* Illustrated by Maryann Kovalski. Vancouver, British Columbia: Douglas & McIntyre, 1989.

59. Siegert, J.J., Cooney, W.P., and Dobyns, J.H. (1990). "Management of Simple Camptodactyly." *Journal of Hand Surgery* (British Volume) 15B: 181-189.

60. Smith, L., Von Tetzchner, S., and Michalsen, B. "The Emergence of Language Skills in Young Children with Down Syndrome." In: Lynn Nadel, Editor, *The Psychobiology of Down Syndrome.* Cambridge, MA: MIT Press, 1988.

61. Shumway-Cook, A. and Woollacott, M. (1985). "Dynamics of Postural Control in the Child with Down Syndrome." *Physical Therapy 33 (9),* 1315-1322.

62. Stock Kranowitz, Carol. *The Out-of-Sync Child.* New York: Skylight Press, 1998.

63. Thombs, Barry and Sugden, David (1991). "Manual Skills in Down Syndrome Children Ages 6 to 16 Years." *Adapted Physical Activity Quarterly, 8,* 242-254.

64. Uyanik, M., Bumin, G., and Kayihan, H. (2003). "Comparisons of Different Therapy Approaches in Children with Down Syndrome." *Pediatrics International 45,* 68-73.

65. Novak Hoffman, M., Lusardi Peterson, L., and Van Dyke, D.C. "Motor and Hand Function." In: Van Dyke, D.C., Lang, D.J., Heide, F., van Duyne, S., and Soucek, M.J., Editors. *Clinical Perspectives in the Management of Down Syndrome.* New York: Springer-Verlag, 1990.

66. Vermeer, A. and Davis, W.E., Editors. "Motor Development in Young Children with Down Syndrome." *Physical and Motor Development in Mental Retardation.* Basel: Karger, 1995.

67. Virji-Babul, N., Lloyd, J. E. V., and Van Gyn, G. (2003). "Performing Movement Sequences with Knowledge of Results under Different Visual Conditions in Adults with Down Syndrome." *Down Syndrome Research and Practice, 8(3),* 110-114.

68. Vulpe, Shirley German. *Vulpe Assessment Battery.* Toronto: National Institute on Mental Retardation, 1969.

69. Weeks, Daniel J., Chua, Romeo, and Elliot, Digby, Editors. *Perceptual-Motor Behavior in Down Syndrome.* Windsor, Ontario: Human Kinetics, 2000.

70. Williams, Mary Sue and Shellenberger, Sherry. *"How Does Your Engine Run?" A Leader's Guide to the Alert Program for Self-Regulation.* Albuquerque, NM: Therapy Works, 1996

71. Winders, Patricia C. *Gross Motor Skills in Children with Down Syndrome: A Guide for Parents and Professionals.* Bethesda, MD: Woodbine House, 1997.

72. Wishart, J. (2001). "Motivation and Learning Styles in Young Children with Down Syndrome." *Down Syndrome Research and Practice 7(2),* 47-51.

73. Yack, Ellen. Personal communication, 2004.

74. Yack, Ellen, Aquilla, Paula, and Sutton, Shirley. *Building Bridges through Sensory Integration: Therapy for Children with Autism and Other Pervasive Developmental Disorders.* Las Vegas, NV: Sensory Resources, 2002.

75. Zausmer, Elizabeth and Shea, Alice M. In: Siegfried M. Pueschel, Editor, *The Young Child with Down Syndrome.* New York: Human Sciences Press, 1984.

76. Zausmer, Elizabeth. "Fine Motor Skills and Play." In: Siegfried M. Pueschel, Editor. *A Parent's Guide to Down Syndrome: Toward a Brighter Future.* Baltimore: Paul H. Brookes, 1990.

Resources

Sources of Materials

The companies in this section offer adapted feeding utensils, pencil grips, special writing paper, computer adaptations, toys, and other items that may be useful in helping a child with Down syndrome with sensory processing and fine motor skill development.

ABLEDATA
8630 Fenton St., Ste. 930
Silver Spring, MD 20910
800-227-0216
test.abledata.com
    Information about assistive technology products and rehabilitation equipment.

Alert Program for Self-Regulation: How Does Your Engine Run?
Therapy Works
4901 Butte Place NW
Albuquerque, NM 87102
877-897-3478
www.alertprogram.com

Apple Accessibility
800-MY-APPLE
www.apple.com/accessibility
    Website provides information on accessibility technologies of Mac computers and other products.

ATC Learning
P.O. Box 43795
Birmingham, AL 35243
800-633-8623
205-968-0591 (fax)
www.atclearning.com
    Distributes *The Sensible Pencil,* a printing and handwriting program by Linda Becht.

Bridges Assistive Technologies
2121 Argentia Road, Suite 102
Mississauga, Ontario
L5N 2X4
Canada
800-353-1107
www.bridges-canada.com
info@bridges-canada.com
　　Provides assistive technology products and training in Canada.

Bumbo Babysitter Seat
c/o Benjamin Hill Consulting
P.O. Box 58861
Louisville, KY 40268
www.bumbo.ca (Canada)
　　Seating and positioning device for babies.

Different Roads to Learning
12 W, 18th St. , Ste. 3E
New York, NY 10011
212-604-9637; 800-853-1057
www.difflearn.com
　　Products include pencil grips, *The Sensible Pencil* by Linda Becht, stringing beads, lacing cards, a kit designed to help children learn to tie their shoes, and other items helpful for children with developmental delays.

Dragonfly Toys for Children with Special Needs
800-308-2208
www.dragonflytoys.com
　　"From toys to technology, for children with special needs." Offers toys and adaptive equipment suited for children with a variety of disabilities, as well as a toy search service and informational articles.

Flaghouse, Inc.
235 Yorkland Blvd., Ste. 300
North York, Ontario M2J 4Y8
Canada
800-265-6900
www.flaghouse.com
US: 601 Flaghouse Dr.
Hasbrouck Heights, NJ 07604-3116
201-288-7600
　　Adapted toys and equipment and Snoezelen equipment and resources.

Gymnic Balls
11770 Bernardo Plaza Ct.
San Diego, CA 92128
858-487-8641; 800-496-6427
www.gymnicballs.com
　　Offers ergonomic cushions such as the Movin' Sit and the Disc o' Sit.

Handwriting without Tears
8802 Quiet Stream Ct.
Potomac, MD 20854
www.hwtears.com
Handwriting without Tears printing and writing program workbooks, by Janice Z. Olsen.

Henry OT Services Ltd.
PO Box 145
Youngstown, AZ 85363
888-371-1204
www.henryot.com
Toolchest for sensory activities, also available in French, Spanish, and German, and other products for school-aged children.

IncrediBall Enterprises
Unit 111 – 20530 Langley Bypass
Langley, BC V3A 6K8
Canada
604-532-8191; 877-348-2255
www.incrediball.ca
Distributes the Movin' Sit cushion as well as other therapy products.

InfoGrip
1141 East Main St.
Ventura, CA 93001
800-397-0921
www.infogrip.com
Computer keyboard, mouse, and monitor adaptations.

IntelliTools, Inc.
1720 Corporate Circle
Petaluma, CA 94554
800-899-6687
www.intellitools.com
Offers the IntelliKeys keyboard and computer adaptations.

Don Johnston, Inc.
1000 N. Rand Rd., Bldg. 115
P.O. Box 639
Wauconda, IL 60084
800-999-4660
www.donjohnston.com
Intervention resources for reading and writing, including CoWriter and Write-OutLoud.

Kapable Kids
P.O. Box 250
Bohemia, NY 11716
800-356-1564
 Early feeding utensils; pencil grips and scissors; developmental toys.

Mayer-Johnson, Inc.
P.O. Box 1579
Solana Beach, CA 92075-7579
800-588-4548
www.mayer-johnson.com
 Software (including Boardmaker™), hardware, and books for persons with special needs.

Microsoft Accessibility
www.Microsoft.com/enable
 Information on accessibility features of Microsoft products and on assistive technology compatible with Microsoft Windows.

O.T. Ideas, Inc.
124 Morris Turnpike
Randolph, NJ 07869
877-768-4332
www.otideas.com
 Angled writing surfaces and other products.

The Pencil Grip, Inc.
P.O. Box 67096
Los Angeles, CA 90067
888-736-4747
www.thepencilgrip.com
 Distributes various pencil grips and other products.

Pocket Full of Therapy
P.O. Box 174
Morganville, NJ 07751
1-800-PFOT-124
www.pfot.com
 Products include raised-line paper, scissors, pencil grips; Touch Window (for computer monitor); typing and computer programs; fine motor activities.

Premier Integrations
800-775-7966 (Canada only)
www.schoolspecialty.ca/abilitations/products
 Sensory and developmental products for children with learning and sensory differences, including Movin' Sit cushion.

Sammons Preston Rolyan
755 Queensway East, Unit 27
Mississauga, Ontario L4Y 4C5
Canada
800-665-9200
www.sammonsprestonrolyan.ca
    In US:
4 Sammons Ct.
Bolingbrook, IL 60440-5071
www.sammonsprestonrolyan.com
    Resources include Fiskars scissors, loop scissors, self-opening scissors; Dycem (non-slip mats); Theraband; adapted cutlery and cups; various pencil grips; developmental toys and equipment.

Sensory Resources
2500 Chandler Ave., Ste. 3
Las Vegas, NV 89120
888-357-5867
www.SensoryResources.com
    Books, audio and video resources, and workshops on sensory processing.

Social Stories
The Gray Center for Social Learning and Understanding
4123 Embassy Dr. SE
Kentwood, MI 49546
616-954-9747
www.thegraycenter.org

Southpaw Enterprises
P.O. Box 1047
Dayton, OH 45401
800-228-1698 (in U.S.); 937-252-7676
www.Southpawenterprises.com
    Supplier of sensory integration equipment

Tash, Inc.
Unit 1-91 Station St.
Ajax, Ontario L1S 3H2
Canada
800-463-5685 (Canada); 800-463-5685 (U.S.)
www.tashinc.com
    Technical Aids & Systems for the Handicapped offers keyguards, keyboard adaptations, and switches.

TFH (USA Ltd.)
4537 Gibsonia Rd.
Gibsonia, PA 15044
412-444-6400
    A source of computer accessories and adapted toys.

Therapro
225 Arlington St.
Framingham, MA 01702-8723
1-800-257-5376
www.theraproducts.com

Therapy Skill Builders
555 Academic Court
San Antonio, TX 78204-2498
800-228-0752
    Products include: *Loops and Other Groups: A Kinesthetic Writing System,* by Mary Benbow; *Pre-Dressing Skills,* by Marsha Dunn Klein, and various books and other educational materials.

Variety Ability Systems Inc. (VASI)
2 Kelvin Ave. Unit 3
Toronto, Ontario M4C 5C8
Canada
416-698-1415
www.vasi.on.ca
    Adapted seating and other equipment, including the "Flip 2 Sit" seat.

Organizations

American Occupational Therapy Association
4720 Montgomery Lane
Bethesda, MD 20814
301-652-2682
www.aota.org

The Arc of the United States
500 E. Border St., Ste. 300
Arlington, TX 76010
817-261-6003
http://TheArcorg/welcome.htm

Association for Children with Down Syndrome
2616 Martin Ave.
Bellmore, NY 11710
516-221-4700
www.acds.org

Autism Society Canada
Box 22017
1670 Heron Rd.
Ottawa, ON K1V 0C2
613-789-8943
www.autismsocietycanada.ca

Autism Society of America
7910 Woodmont Ave., Ste. 300
Bethesda, MD 20814
800-3-autism (328-8476); 301-657-0881
www.autism-society.org

Canadian Association for Community Living
Kinsmen Building, York University
4700 Keele St.
Toronto, Ont. M3J 1P3
416-661-9611
http://indie/ca/cacl/index.htm

Canadian Association of Occupational Therapists
L'Association Canadienne Des Ergotherapeutes
CTTC, Suite 3400
1125 Colonel By Dr.
Ottawa, Ont. K1S 5R1
613-523-2268

Canadian Down Syndrome Society
811 14th St. NW
Calgary, Alberta T2N 2A4
403-270-8291;800-883-5608 (in Canada)
www.cdss.ca

National Down Syndrome Congress
1605 Chantilly Dr., Ste. 250
Atlanta, GA 30324
800-232-NDSC
www.ndsccenter.org

National Down Syndrome Society
666 Broadway
New York, NY 10012-2317
800-221-4602
www.ndss.org

TASH
29 W. Susquehanna Ave., Ste. 210
Baltimore, MD 21204
410-828-8274
www.tash.org
	Advocacy organization for people with disabilities.

Index

Accessibility options, computer, 136
Action songs, 93
Activity quilts, 36
Ambidexterity, 59
Apart/together activities, 61, 62
Arms
    early movements of, 33–45
    lifting, 34
    low tone of, 20, 42
    propping on, 36-38
    shifting weight on, 37
    short, 21, 42
Arts/crafts activities, 164–65
Atlanto-axial instability, 20, 164
Attention deficits, 11
Attention span, 7–8
Auditory memory, 8
Autism spectrum disorder (ASD), 182
Babies, early movement in, 33–45
Back lying, 34, 35, 36
Balloons, 51
Balls, 51–52, 61, 128
Banging toys, 60, 81–82
Bathing/showering, 85, 159. See also Water play
Beads, 63
Bed making, 163
Bedtime routine, 180
Bilateral coordination, 33, 57–65
    apart/together activities and, 61, 62
    banging toys and, 60
    board books and, 61
    bottle holding and, 60
    clapping games, 60–61
    daily living skills and, 105–06
    described, 2–3
    lacing activities and, 63
    paper and pencil activities and, 63–64
    positioning and, 60
    recreation activities and, 62
    salad spinner art and, 64
    self-help activities and, 62
    sensory activities and, 61
    toys and, 61, 63
    transferring and, 60
Blocks, 61, 62, 83, 90
Boardmaker™, 186

Body stability, 48–53, 59
Books
    adapting for easier page turning, 61
    fine motor skills and, 94–95
Booster seat, 40
Bottle, holding, 60
Bubble wands, 53
Building blocks, 2–3, 4, 29. See also Bilateral coordination;
        Sensation; Stability
Bumbo Babysitter seat, 39
Buttons, 151
Buttons and switches, 93
Callirobics, 133
Camptodactyly, 21, 91
Card games, 95
Cause-effect play, 58
Chairs, 127. See also Booster seat; Highchairs; Infant seat; Sitting
Chicoine, Brian, 186
Children's profiles
    Alexander, 96
    Amanda, 64
    Andy, 185
    Daniel, 74
    Danny, 170
    David, 55
    Diana, 184
    Emily, 88
    James, 190
    Mark, 134
    Michael, 160
    Sarah, 126
Circles, drawing, 120
Clapping games, 60–61
Classroom Language Skills for Children with Down Syndrome (Kumin), 129
Cleaning windows, 162
Climbing, 54
Clinical Perspectives in the Management of Down Syndrome, 111
Clinodactyly, 21, 91
Clothes/clothing. See Dressing
Clothespins, 91
Clothing
    choosing, 149
    sensitivity to, 175, 176, 178
Cognitive delays, 22–23
Collecting, 96
Coloring, 114, 122, 165

Community programs, involvement in, 163
Computers, 74, 135–39
Containers, 83–85
Crayons, 112
Creative/imaginary play, 164–65
Creeping, 42
Cross, drawing a, 121
Cues, visual/motor, 7, 132
Cupboards, emptying, 83
Cups, 156
Cursive writing, 133–34
Curved fifth finger, 21. *See also* Fingers
Cutting skills development, 106–10
    choice of scissors and paper, 108–09
    puppets and, 107
    ripping activities and, 108
    squeezing activities and, 107
    step by step, 109–10
Cutting/spreading (eating), 156
Daily living skills, 2, 4, 26, 27
        See also Dressing; Personal hygiene; Self-help skills
    bilateral coordination and, 105–06
    dexterity and, 105–06
    household tasks and, 161–63
    leisure activities and, 163–66
    sensation and, 105–06
    stability and, 105–06
Dehydration, 171, 188
Depression, 171
Dermatological differences, 69
Desks, 127
Developmental delay, 173–74
Developmental immaturity, 58, 59
Dexterity, 4, 25, 26, 27, 29
    action songs/finger rhymes and, 93–94
    books and, 94–95
    buttons and switches and, 93
    card games and, 95
    "collecting" in the hand, 96
    daily living skills and, 105–06
    defined, 77–78
    described, 3
    developmental patterns of, 99
    drawing at an easel and, 98
    dressing and, 96
    finger coordination and, 91–96
    finger feeding and, 88–89
    games and, 95
    "give me five" and, 97
    grasp and release and, 78–87
    household activities and, 95, 98
    musical instruments and, 99
    pinch (pincer grasp) and thumb control and, 88–91
    play and eating, 97
    play dough/plasticine and, 98
    pointing and, 92
    poking and, 92
    releasing into slots and, 89
    self-help activities and, 98
    self-help skills and, 147–48
    sensory activities and, 92
    sensory play and, 97
    spray bottles/squirt guns and, 96
    stacking activities and, 89, 90
    strengthening activities and, 90–91
    toys and, 90, 99, 101–04

wrist movement and, 97–99
Dictation to scribe, 134–35
Dislocation, of joints, 20
D'Nealian writing method, 133
Dominant hand, 57, 58
Doors, 49
Double jointed, 20
Down syndrome, children with
    attention span and, 7-8, 11
    auditory memory and, 8
    cognitive skills of, 22-23
    fingers of, 20, 21, 91
    hand dominance of, 59
    hands of, 21, 22
    healthcare guidelines for, 171
    hearing and, 172
    learning style of, 8
    ligament and joint laxity of, 20
    low muscle tone and, 19–20, 38, 69, 106, 112
    medical problems of, 22
    sensory processing issues and, 173-82
    short term memory and, 11
Down Syndrome Medical Interest Group, 171
Drawing, 98, 112, 120, 121, 122. *See also* Coloring
Dressing, 96, 148–54
    basic strategies of, 148–50
    common challenges of, 150–54
Drinking, 156
Dropping and throwing, 79
Dusting, 162
Dycem, 42
Early movements
    activity quilts and, 36
    back lying and, 34, 35, 36
    Bumbo Babysitter seat and, 39
    Flip 'n Sit seat and, 39
    hands and knees position and, 42–43
    infant seats and, 34, 35, 36, 39
    propping up on arms and, 36–38
    pulling to stand and standing and, 43–44
    reaching and pivoting and, 37–38
    rolling over and, 38
    side lying and, 34, 35, 36
    sitting and, 38–42
    stages of, 34–45
Easels, 98
Eating/drinking
    picky eaters and, 175, 176, 178
    with fingers, 88-89, 148, 154
    with utensils, 95, 156, 154–57
Educational program, fine motor goals and, 140–45
Emotional development, 164
Environment, adapting, 13–14
Expectations, realistic, 12, 149
Eye-hand coordination, 34, 59, 114
Fine motor activities, choosing, 12–14
Fine motor development, 20
Fine motor skills
    described, 1
    effects of Down syndrome on, 19–23
    effects of sensation on, 67-68
    house model of, 1–5
Fine motor skills, developmental sequence of
    birth to 2 years, 23–24
    early school age, 26
    middle childhood, 27

preschool, 25
teen years to adulthood, 28
Fingers
coordination of, 78, 91–96
differences in, 20, 21, 91
"Finger crayons," 112
Finger feeding, 88–89, 148, 154
Finger rhymes, 93
Flip 'n Sit seat, 39
Food, pickiness about, 175, 176, 178
"Frog-legged" position, 40
"Fun," 12, 13
Games, 95
Gardening, 74, 162
Gertie balls, 51
"Give me five," 97
Goals, 141–45
Grasp, types of
age range for acquiring, 111
inferior pincer, 79, 88
palmer, 78, 80, 85–86, 110, 111, 155
pincer, 88-91
pronated, 106
radial-digital grasp, 79, 87
raking grasp, 79, 80
reflexive grasp, 80
superior pincer grasp, 79, 86, 88
"thumb wrap," 112
tripod, 79, 87, 111, 112, 113, 155
Grasp and release, 77, 78–87
banging toys and, 81–82
developmental stages of, 81–87
dropping and, 82
pointing and, 86
puzzles and, 86–87
throwing and, 80–81
Grasping toys, 81
Groceries, putting away, 163
Grooming, 157–60
"Groove," the, 186
Gross motor skills, 1, 20
Gross Motor Skills in Children with Down Syndrome (Winders), 11, 33, 37
Gymnastics, 164
Hair care, 159–60
Hammering, 50, 55
Handedness, 57, 58, 59
Hand-over-hand assistance, 149
Hand play items, 217–18
Hands
characteristics of, 21–22
sensory awareness of, 70-74
skill development of, 1-5
stability of, 91
Handwriting without Tears (Olsen), 116, 117, 130, 131, 133
"Handy Basket," 101-04
Hardware options (computer), 136–38
Hearing, 172
Heart problems, 22
Highchairs, 41-42, 60
Household activities, 95, 98, 161-63
Household items for hand play, 217–18
House model of fine motor skills, 1–5
"How Does Your Engine Run?" (Williams and Shellenberger), 189
Hyperextension (ligamentous laxity), 20
Hypotonia (low muscle tone), 19–20, 38, 47, 69, 106, 112
Imitating, 128

IEP, 140-45
Inconsistency, accepting, 11
Infant development program, 15
Infant seat, 34, 35, 39, 60
Inferior pincer grasp, 79, 88
Jacket, putting on, 150–51
Joysticks, 137
Jumping rope, 53
Keyboard adaptations, 137–38
Keyboarding, 135, 139
Keyguards, 137–38
Knives, 95, 156
Kumin, Libby, 129
Lacing activities, 63
Laxity, ligament and joint, 20
Learning skills, steps in, 8–11
Left-handedness, 59
Leisure activities, 163–66
Lethargy, 171
Letters, forming, 129. See also Printing
Limbs, shorter, 21
Lines, printing on, 131
Low muscle tone. See Hypotonia
Magna Doodle, 130
Markers, 128
Massage, 71
Maturation, 173
McGuire, Dennis, 186
Meal preparation, helping with, 161–62
Medical conditions, 22, 171
Memory, 8, 11
Mental retardation. See Cognitive delays
Meyers, Laura, 135
Midline, 58, 59
Mnemonics, 129
Modeling, 149
Monkey bars, 55
Motivation, 11–14
Motor cues, 7
Motor planning difficulties, 182
Mouse, computer, 74, 136-37
Mouthing, 61, 69, 70-71
Movement, craving, 181
Multi-sensory approach, 8
Muscle tone, low, 19–20, 38, 47, 69, 106, 112
Musical instruments, 99
Music/dance, 93, 165–67
Myelination, 170
Name, printing, 10, 126
Neck, hyperextending, 36
Nervous system development, 69, 170–77
Neurokinesthetic Writing Program, 133
Obsessive-compulsive disorder, 174
Occupational therapists, 15–17, 113, 184, 190
Occupational therapy practice, 14
Olsen, Jan, 116, 117, 130, 131
Oral motor activities, 157, 183
Over-responsiveness, 175, 178, 179, 180, 184
Painting, 122
Palmer grasp, 78, 80, 85–86, 110, 111, 155
Paper, 109
Paper and pencil activities, 63–64
Paper and pencil, alternatives to, 130
Parents, role of in teaching, 17
Pencil
grasp, 110–14

grips, 132
pressure, 132
resistance to using, 113
Pegboards, 83, 84
Personal hygiene, 157–60
Physical characteristics, 19–23
Picture Communication Symbols©, 186
Picture processors, 138
Picture schedules, 186
Pinch (pincer grasp) and thumb control, 88–91
Pinch and thumb control, 78
Play
cause-effect, 58
wrist movement and, 97
Play dough/plasticine, 72, 98, 130
Pointing, 86, 92
Poking, 92
Positioning, 60, 126–28, 148
Posture, sitting, 126-27
Pouring, 50, 52
Preprinting skills, 110–24
bottom/middle and, 119
child's readiness for, 115
circle activities, 120
combining lines and, 121
concepts for, 115, 116
developmental chart for, 123-24
drawing, painting, and coloring and, 122
horizontal orientation and, 118
learning to print and, 114–24
left to right orientation and, 119
lines and circles and, 115
pencil grasp development and, 110–14
pencils, resistance and, 113
printing and coloring abilities progression and, 114–15
same/different, 118–19
scribbling, 117, 120
spatial attention and localization and, 116
start/stop concept and, 120
top and, 118
up/down, 116–17
vertical orientation and, 117
Pressure, craving, 181
Pre-walking stage, 48
Printing. See also Preprinting skills
alternatives to pencil and paper and, 130
child's own name, 11, 126
child's readiness for, 125–26
imitating and, 128
independently, 129–31
learning to print and, 126–32
on lines, 131
pencil pressure and, 132
positioning, 126–28
sequence, 128–31
tactile and visual cues and, 132
tracing and copying and, 128–29
underwriting and, 129
Pronated grasp, 106
Propping up on arms, 36–39
Proprioception, 3, 172
Pulling to stand, 43–44
Pupil Education Plan (PEP), 140
Puppets, 107
Pushing a swing, 53
Pushing/pulling open doors, 49

Pushing up, 42–43
Push toys, 48–49
Puzzles, 83, 86–87
Quilts, activity, 36
Radial-digital grasp, 79, 87
Raking, 52, 162
Raking grasp, 79, 80
Reaching and pivoting, 37–38
"Ready," being, 7–8
Reflexive grasp, 80
Release, 79–80, 89
Relevant, making it, 13
Repetition, 8
Ripping activities, 108
Rolling over, 38
Schellenberger, Sherry, 189
School desks, 127
School, sensory issues at, 178
School skills. See Cutting; IEP; Printing; Cursive writing
Scissors, 108-109. See also Cutting
Scribbling, 117, 120, 123. See also Coloring
Scribes, dictating to, 134–35
Seat, booster. See Booster seat
Seat, infant. See Infant seat
Self-esteem, 164
Self-help skills. See also Daily living skills
dexterity and, 147–48
dressing and, 148–54
eating/drinking and, 154–57
grooming, 157–60
Self-motivation, xii
Self-regulation/alertness, 188–90
Sensation, 33, 67–75
aversion to sensory play and, 70
awareness of, 68
daily living skills and, 105–06
described, 3
feeling games and, 71
finger painting and, 73
gardening and, 74
handling groceries and, 73–74
massage and, 71
mouthing and, 70–71
movement and, 68
purses/backpacks and, 73
pushing/pulling activities and, 73
rhymes/songs and, 71
sensory play and, 71–72
sensory processing and, 168
use of stickers and, 73
using a computer and, 74
water play and, 73
Sensory diet, 182-84
Sensory integration, 168
Sensory processing, 11, 167–91
adapting the environment to help with, 185–90
alertness/self-regulation and, 188–90
behavioral approaches and, 191
description, 167–69
developing of sensory skills and, 69–70
developmental delay and, 173–74
difficulties, 174–82
home heating system analogy and, 168
medical considerations and, 171
modulation and, 169–70
motor planning difficulties and, 182

nervous system development and, 170–77
over-responsiveness and, 175, 178, 179, 180
sensation and, 168
sensory diet and, 182, 184
sensory discrimination and, 68, 70
sensory impairment and, 171–72
sensory modulation and, 169–70, 175
sensory seeking and, 177, 181
transitions and, 186–88
under-responsiveness and, 176, 180
Sequencing, 149–50
Setting the table, 161
Shape sorters, 83, 84
Shoelaces, tying, 9-10, 152–53
Shoes, putting on, 154
Short-term memory deficits, 11
Shoulder stability, 52, 53–55, 107
Shoveling activities, 50, 162
Side lying, 34, 35, 36
Sign language, 25
Single simian crease, 21
Sitting, 38–42, 126-27
Skin, 69
Skipping rope, 53
Slant board, 127
Sleep apnea, 171, 188
Sleep problems, 180
Snoezelen, 190
Social interaction skills, 164
Software options, 138–39
Songs, action, 93
Sorting/folding laundry, 162
Sound, sensitivity to, 170, 176. *See also* Sensory processing
Spatial attention and localization, 116
Spoon/fork, using. *See* Eating
Sports, 164
Spray bottles, 96
Squeezing activities, 107
Squirt guns, 96
Stability, 33, 47–56, 62–64
    ball skills and, 51–52
    body, 48–53, 59
    bubble wands and, 53
    climbing and, 54
    consistent, 47
    daily living skills and, 105–06
    described, 2
    hammering and, 50
    poor body, 58
    pouring and, 50, 52
    pushing/pulling open doors and, 49
    push toys and, 48–49
    shoulder, 53–55, 107
    shoveling activities and, 50
    skipping rope and, 53
    streamers and, 52
    sweeping/vacuuming/raking and, 52
Stacking activities, 89, 90
Stairs, 54
Standing, 43–44
Stencils, 64
Stickers, 73, 116, 120, 165
Streamers, 52, 120
Strengthening activities, 90–91
Stress, 173–74
Subluxation, 20

Success, building on, 12–13
Superior pincer grasp, 79, 86, 88
Sweeping, 52, 162
Swimming, 164
Swings, 53, 55
Tactile defensiveness, 70. *See also* Sensory processing; Touch
Talking word processors, 138
Telephone use, 7, 164
Therapy balls, 128
Throwing, 80–81
Thumb tacks, 91
"Thumb wrap" grasp, 112
Thumbs
    double jointed, 20
    pointing with, 86
    tucking in palm, 85
Thyroid dysfunction, 171
Timing, 149
Toilet training, 158–59
Tooth brushing, 157–58
Touch
    aversion to, 69, 70, 178
    delayed reaction to, 172
    games involving, 71
Touch screen programs, 136
Toys, 45, 48–49, 61, 65, 75, 81, 90, 99, 100, 101–04, 146, 166, 192
Toys, tidying up, 161
Tracing/copying, 64, 128–29
Trackballs, 137
Trackpads, 137
Transferring, 57, 60, 78
Transitions, 176, 185, 186–88
Tripod grasp, 79, 87, 111, 112, 113, 155
Under-responsiveness, 176, 180
Underwriting, 129
Up/down, concept of, 116–17
Utensils
    adapted, 155
    eating with, 95, 156, 154–57
"Using Computers to Teach Children with Down Syndrome" (Meyers), 135
Vacuuming, 52, 162
Vestibular system, 3, 172
Vision, 22, 59, 172
Visual cues, 7
Visual learner, 8
Visual motor development, 4, 105
Visual motor worksheets, 195–216
Washing/drying dishes, 163
Water play, 73
Wilbarger, Patricia, 184
Wilbarger Protocol for Sensory Defensiveness, 184
Williams, Mary Sue, 189
Winders, Patricia, 11, 33, 37
Word prediction programs, 138–39
Word processing devices, 138
Workbooks, printing, 130
Worksheets
    stages of, 195–97
    visual motor, 198-216
Wrist movement, 78, 97–99
Writing/handwriting. *See* Cursive writing; Preprinting skills; Printing
Zaner-Bloser, 133
Zippers, 151–52

About the Author

Maryanne Bruni graduated from the University of Toronto with a Bachelor of Science degree in occupational therapy. She has worked in a variety of pediatric settings. For the past ten years, she has been the occupational therapist at an integrated preschool. She lives with her husband and three daughters in Toronto, Canada. Her youngest daughter has Down syndrome. The first edition of *Fine Motor Skills in Children with Down Syndrome* won a *Parent's Choice Award* in 1999.